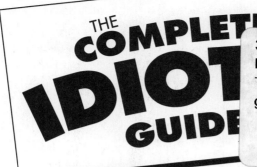

THE COMPLETE IDIOT'S GUIDE

Green Living

by Trish Riley

ALPHA
A member of Penguin Group (USA) Inc.

It is with great pleasure that I dedicate this book to my children, Rachel and Bud; to their future offspring; and to all children of the future—yours as well as mine. I have great hope that with the turning tide of public awareness, humanity will be able to ensure a happy, healthy future for those living on Earth. I am proud to help bring about that change through this book, and I thank you for joining the effort to preserve the Earth for all of our children.

ALPHA BOOKS

Published by the Penguin Group

Penguin Group (USA) Inc., 375 Hudson Street, New York, New York 10014, USA

Penguin Group (Canada), 90 Eglinton Avenue East, Suite 700, Toronto, Ontario M4P 2Y3, Canada (a division of Pearson Penguin Canada Inc.)

Penguin Books Ltd., 80 Strand, London WC2R 0RL, England

Penguin Ireland, 25 St. Stephen's Green, Dublin 2, Ireland (a division of Penguin Books Ltd.)

Penguin Group (Australia), 250 Camberwell Road, Camberwell, Victoria 3124, Australia (a division of Pearson Australia Group Pty. Ltd.)

Penguin Books India Pvt. Ltd., 11 Community Centre, Panchsheel Park, New Delhi—110 017, India

Penguin Group (NZ), 67 Apollo Drive, Rosedale, North Shore, Auckland 1311, New Zealand (a division of Pearson New Zealand Ltd.)

Penguin Books (South Africa) (Pty.) Ltd., 24 Sturdee Avenue, Rosebank, Johannesburg 2196, South Africa

Penguin Books Ltd., Registered Offices: 80 Strand, London WC2R 0RL, England

Copyright © 2007 by Trish Riley

International Standard Book Number: 978-159257-662-3
Library of Congress Catalog Card Number: 2007924616

09 08 07   8 7 6 5 4 3 2 1

Interpretation of the printing code: The rightmost number of the first series of numbers is the year of the book's printing; the rightmost number of the second series of numbers is the number of the book's printing. For example, a printing code of 07-1 shows that the first printing occurred in 2007.

Printed in the United States of America

Note: This publication contains the opinions and ideas of its author. It is intended to provide helpful and informative material on the subject matter covered. It is sold with the understanding that the author and publisher are not engaged in rendering professional services in the book. If the reader requires personal assistance or advice, a competent professional should be consulted.

The author and publisher specifically disclaim any responsibility for any liability, loss, or risk, personal or otherwise, which is incurred as a consequence, directly or indirectly, of the use and application of any of the contents of this book.

Most Alpha books are available at special quantity discounts for bulk purchases for sales promotions, premiums, fundraising, or educational use. Special books, or book excerpts, can also be created to fit specific needs.

For details, write: Special Markets, Alpha Books, 375 Hudson Street, New York, NY 10014.

Publisher: *Marie Butler-Knight*
Editorial Director: *Mike Sanders*
Managing Editor: *Billy Fields*
Acquisitions Editor: *Tom Stevens*
Development Editor: *Michael Thomas*
Production Editor: *Kayla Dugger*
Copy Editor: *Nancy Wagner*

Cartoonist: *Richard King*
Cover Designer: *Bill Thomas*
Book Designer: *Trina Wurst*
Indexer: *Heather McNeill*
Layout: *Ayanna Lacey*
Proofreaders: *Mary Hunt and Kathy Bidwell*

Contents at a Glance

Contents

Introduction

"In the end, we will conserve only what we love. We only love what we understand. We only understand what we are taught."

—Babia Dioum, Senegalese ecologist

While working on this book, I had the pleasure of speaking with Edgar Mitchell. An *Apollo 14* astronaut, Mitchell has a unique perspective—he's truly seen the big picture. Stunned by the beauty of the universe seen in 3D from the window of his spacecraft, Mitchell has been studying life on Earth—and in the universe—since taking his trip in 1971. He shared his interesting insight with me.

"In the twentieth century, we accelerated with the power of science and our technologies into a nonsustainable civilization. Our most immediate threat is what we're doing to ourselves because of our ignorance and unwillingness as nations and individuals to confront the environmental problems. To confront the excesses of our civilization, of nonrenewable resources and pollution, threats of garbage piling up and our oceans being polluted. The big problem is the fact that we in the western world are wed to our consumption patterns; that more is better and money is the only real value that can make you happy. It's simply not true. We have to change our thinking pattern and our approach to this if we are to survive.

"Our problem is learning simplicity. How many new automobiles do we need? How much is necessary to live a productive life? Money is not the source of our happiness. We know that happiness is an internal state—it is not brought about by material goods. Greed is a part of our problem—it is driving our economic system worldwide and it's just wrong. We have to go back and find our internal state of our heart and mind and central well-being; that is where the answers really lie. We need to learn to live in harmony with nature as opposed to conquest.

"The first thing is to become aware, to become educated to realize that all the talk of environmentalism is grounded in reality. The old solution was we can mess it up and God would clean it up, but I haven't seen God cleaning it up. We have to do it ourselves. We have to protect our environment and live in harmony with our environment.

"Our task must be to free ourselves by widening our circle of compassion to embrace all living creatures and the whole of nature and its beauty."

I think Mr. Mitchell has hit the heart of the problems that are causing global warming, and I think he is correct when he says that getting back to nature is key to overcoming the sure demise on the path we've set for ourselves.

We can do so much at home, at work, and everywhere to improve our outlook for a healthier future. It's just a matter of learning what we can do and how much of a difference we can make. In this book, I've offered a variety of starting points so you, the reader, can choose an area that matters most to you, something you know you can do to improve the green level of your work, your lawn, your home life, or your transportation plans that will make the world a better place for the children of the future.

But our kids aren't waiting for us to get the job started—college kids are helping their universities move into the future, and even a seven-year-old boy from California has gotten involved in trying to make his peers more aware of the situation. Two years ago, Ethan Matsuda wrote a book, *The North Pole Is Sinking*, to alert kids of the need to help save Santa from global warming.

Sometimes the kids are far wiser than we are when it comes to knowing what needs to be done and getting started on the right path. We need to let our kids know that we're dealing with the problems facing the earth and that they're safe in our care. This book is about helping all of us take those first steps toward a new, safer future, about breaking old habits and working together for the benefit of all. I hope this book helps make the difference we need to turn away from a global warming disaster and toward a healthier future. Cheers to you for looking this way!

What's in This Book

Here's a quick tour of the info we review:

In **Part 1, "Our Earth: The Big Picture,"** we review just the science behind global warming and learn what we can do to help prevent the worst effects from occurring.

In **Part 2, "Going Green at Home,"** we help you start making changes at home to save energy, save money, protect your health, and save the earth!

Part 3, "Green Living on the Road," covers travel. Whether traveling to work or around the world, you can reduce your footprint by minding your CO_2 p's and q's. Learn how to reduce your carbon emissions.

Part 4, "Green Living in Your Daily Life," is about your lawn, your home, your cosmetics, and your cleaning supplies. All contribute to global warming and an unhealthy environment for your family. Learn how to choose contaminant-free products to make your life more pleasant and better for you, your family, and the earth's future.

In **Part 5, "Going Green at Work,"** we look at business. Businesses understand that they won't survive if they don't adapt to a changing world. Enjoy seeing how many are changing their policies and practices for the better of all.

Part 6, "Living in the Emerald City," focuses on cities that are moving toward greener living and greener economies. Teaching children the importance of green living will help secure their future and so will your investments in green companies and projects.

Extras

For more information, we've provided these sidebars:

Going Green

Here you'll find tips to help you go green.

Green Speak

These sidebars feature quotes from experts.

Hazard

These sidebars contain warnings about things *not* to do.

def•i•ni•tion

To help with those mysterious words that come with the territory, we have these convenient boxes.

Green Gamut

These boxes contain news, facts, and statistics that might surprise you about the long-range effects of making the change to green living.

Acknowledgments

In spite of an amazingly short time frame, I've really enjoyed working on this book, and I certainly could not have completed the project without the help and understanding of several key people. I wish to thank my agent, Marilyn Allen, and Marcia Layton Taylor and David Kohn, who brought us together; Tom Stevens, acquisitions editor at Alpha Books, who enthusiastically brought ideas to me for this book and patiently worked with me when multiple events converged to complicate the process; my indispensable friends and colleagues Barb Freda, Patti Roth, Sandy Fruits, and Elbe Burke, who worked to help me research and complete the text as well as helped me move at the same time; Denise Robinette of the HealthyLiving Foundation and HealthyLiving Interiors, whose advise and talent were very helpful throughout the book; Elizabeth Guillette, who reviewed the scientific sections for accuracy; Jim Motavalli, editor of *E Magazine,* who agreed to provide a final review of my text; Janine Latus, whose personal and professional support has been invaluable; my daughter Rachel and son Bud, whose constant support has been sustaining; and Stella and Teddi, my sweet-hearts.

Special Thanks to the Technical Reviewer

The Complete Idiot's Guide to Green Living was reviewed by an expert who double-checked the accuracy of what you learn here, to help us ensure that this book gives you everything you need to know about green living. We extend special thanks to Jim Motavalli.

Jim Motavalli is the editor of the award-winning *E/The Environmental Magazine.* He is also a journalist and author of several books, including *Forward Drive: The Race to Build Clean Cars for the Future* (2000) and *Breaking Gridlock: Moving Toward Transportation That Works* (2002), both published by Sierra Club Books/Random House. He also edited *Green Living: The E Magazine Handbook for Living Lightly on the Earth* (published by the Plume division of Penguin), which was released for Earth Day 2005. His next book, *Naked in the Woods,* is about Joseph Knowles, who disrobed in 1913 to prove he could live off the land in rural Maine.

Trademarks

All terms mentioned in this book that are known to be or are suspected of being trademarks or service marks have been appropriately capitalized. Alpha Books and Penguin Group (USA) Inc. cannot attest to the accuracy of this information. Use of a term in this book should not be regarded as affecting the validity of any trademark or service mark.

Part 1

Our Earth: The Big Picture

Scientists are presenting piles of information about the rapidly changing temperatures of Earth and its effects on all of nature—which includes the earth, air, soil, water, plants, animals, and us. We review some of this emerging evidence about global warming to clarify our understanding of what's happening.

Then we take a quick tour of the many things we can do today to arrest the rush toward global meltdown. We can change the path we're on, but changing takes some knowledge and effort. The good news is that moving toward more sustainable energy and manufacturing policies will provide many healthful and happy benefits.

"Back in my day this was all ice. And summer? Didn't know the word!"

What Is Global Warming?

In This Chapter

◆ The causes for global warming

◆ The consequences if global warming continues

◆ Ways to stop global warming

Global warming is very much in the news today as we are being informed of its causes and effects on people and the planet on a daily basis. Moreover, the climate situation on Earth has become so dire that we all must do what we can to stop the increasing warming trend and avert potential disaster. This is what this book is about—making you aware of the role you play in this very important situation.

Al Gore's film, *An Inconvenient Truth*, released in 2006, helped bring to light the scientific evidence that our Earth is warming and that human activity is accelerating the process, laying to rest the subterfuge of controversies and questions posed by those benefiting from the industries largely responsible for the problem, coal and oil. The Intergovernmental Panel on Climate Change (IPCC), an international group of scientists convened by the United Nations to study global warming and its effects, finally produced incontrovertible scientific support that global warming is happening and is the result of excessive carbon dioxide in the atmosphere. The excess of CO_2 is caused by human burning of fossil fuels: coal and oil.

Yes, the Globe Is Warming

The term *global warming* defines the fact that the temperature of the earth is increasing at a much higher rate than it has done so in the past.

According to the 2007 reports released by the IPCC, more than 90 percent of scientists believe that global warming is causing the waters in the seas to be warmer. This in turn is causing an increase in extreme weather, such as heat waves, hurricanes, tornadoes, typhoons, wildfires, and droughts. As seas and land warm, more water is absorbed in cooling processes, leaving many areas dryer and contributing to drought.

Air and water current patterns are changing because of temperature changes, which affect temperatures worldwide. NASA and U.S. Geology scientists report an increase in earthquakes in Alaska already; Purdue and Massachusetts Institute of Technology scientists report that global warming causes increased hurricane activity and storm intensity. The warmer oceans are also causing the polar ice caps to begin melting, and huge chunks of glaciers are breaking off into the sea at unprecedented levels. As the ice melts, water levels will rise around the world. People living near the poles are seeing significant changes already.

def•i•ni•tion

Global warming describes a rapid increase in the temperature of Earth's surface, water, and atmosphere, which is causing changes in most natural systems (such as seasons and life cycles of plants and animals) with far-reaching effects.

Green Speak

"Scientists now predict the Arctic could be ice-free in the summer months by 2050, give or take 30 years. When it happens, it will be the first ice-free summer in a million years."

—"The Big Melt," by Margaret Munro, CanWest News Service, October 2006

The Ice Poles Are Melting

According to a World Wildife Foundation of Canada report released in October 2006, the North Pole is losing enough ice each year to cover Lake Superior. The permafrost (the land soil which is a blend of sand and ice) is melting so fast that whole chunks of land are washing into the sea. The Inuit people who live in this area use the frozen tundra as a place to store food supplies, so they're losing saved food resources as well as land, and the changing temperatures are affecting their hunting and fishing abilities.

Sea Level Is Rising

Already island nations are facing the challenges of rising water! The South Pacific island Tegua in Vanuatu's Torres islands chain has moved its 64 residents to an inland location because of rising seas. Also in the Pacific, residents of Papua New Guinea are the first peoples to be officially relocated from their homes as a result of *saltwater intrusion*. In addition to shrinking shore-lines, the salt water has covered springs that supply these people with fresh water. Living without fresh water is impossible, so residents collect rainwater and store it for use during the dry season, which is about half the year. Many homes have sloping roofs designed to channel water into tanks for storage. This is a simple, workable solu-tion to help capture diminishing supplies of fresh water.

def•i•ni•tion

Saltwater intrusion refers to the natural process whereby salt water encroaches on dried-up fresh water reservoirs and replaces the empty wells, aqui-fers, creeks, and so on with salt water.

Biological Clocks of Plants and Animals Are Changing

Also, changes in climate are causing seasons to shift and are affecting the biological clocks of flora and fauna. Polar bears have become a very visible creature suffering under conditions caused by warming air, land, and sea. The bears hunt for seals from icebergs floating in the sea; however, warmer waters and melting ice mean fewer platforms for hunting. So the bears have to swim farther distances in search of hunt-ing grounds and food. In the process, they lose considerable weight, approaching the point at which their bodies will not be able to reproduce. The combination of the lack of food for existing bears and decreased reproduction means yet another species faces extinction. The World Conservation Union reports a 17 percent decline in the polar bear population in the past decade and projects a 30 percent decline in the next 35 to 50 years.

Species Are Dying

The cover of *Newsweek*'s International Edition of October 16, 2006, shows a picture of a brilliant red, yellow, and black tree frog under the header, "Global Warming's First Victim." The story describes the loss of these colorful frogs from Costa Rica's pro-tected rain forest; they have not been found here since 1988, having been wiped out by a fungal disease that became a killer in the extreme heat.

Polar bears rely on diminishing glacial ice as hunting grounds.

Higher temperatures have given rise to parasites, diseases, and invasive bug infestations worldwide, overtaking whole species of native inhabitants, such as these bright tropical frogs. "We are seeing problems from pole to pole; we see them in the oceans and we see them on land," Lara Hansen, chief climate-change scientist at the World Wildlife Fund, told *Newsweek*. "There are very few systems that I can think of that are untouched by climate change."

Bug Infestations Are Increasing

Without cold weather to stall their reproductive cycles, mosquito and avian-borne diseases are spreading more rapidly. India is fighting an outbreak of tropical illnesses spread by mosquitoes, with more than a hundred dead from July to September in 2006. In Canada, beetle infestation, spurred by winters too warm to arrest the spread by freezing the insects, has destroyed millions of acres of pine trees. Since trees are the earth's principal means of processing carbon dioxide (CO_2) out of our atmosphere, the loss of forests also means we're losing our greatest natural defense against global warming.

And This Is Only the Beginning ...

All these changes and more are happening, and according to Ross Gelbspan, Pulitzer prize–winning editor, expert on global warming, and author of *Boiling Point: How Politicians, Big Oil and Coal, Journalists and Activists are Fueling the Climate Crisis—And What We Can Do to Avert Disaster* (Basic Books, 2004), we've only seen sea surface temperatures increase by 1 degree Fahrenheit. Canadian forestry scientists report an even higher increase in air temperature of 4 degrees Fahrenheit in their territory over the past century. Gelbspan says during this century we can anticipate an additional increase in water temperature of 4 to 10 degrees Fahrenheit, and the Union of Concerned Scientists projects an increase in air temperature of 6 to 14 degrees Fahrenheit by 2099 unless new emission control measures are enacted now.

CO_2 Is the Culprit

Most scientists agree that global warming is a fact; they also agree that the cause is the increase of CO_2 we've put into the atmosphere since the beginning of the industrial age 150 years ago. The IPCC reports, released in segments beginning in January 2007, confirmed that scientists are 90 percent certain that global warming is happening and that it is being caused by human activity, mostly by the burning of fossil fuels.

Energy Production and Auto Emissions

Ross Gelbspan states that each year humans put 6 billion tons of carbon into the atmosphere. Our factories, power supplies, home and auto fuels are all based on energy made from fossil fuels, and by burning coal and oil, we produce carbon emissions.

Today, according to a report by Co-Op America, a nonprofit organization of green businesses dedicated to promoting a socially just and environmentally sustainable society, U.S. power plants produce 40 percent of the nation's CO_2 emissions and 10 percent of worldwide emissions.

Big Money Doesn't Want to Let Go

As of September 2006, the Department of Energy reports that 154 new coal plants have been proposed for construction across the country and hundreds more are scheduled to be built in China and India. In a notable nod to environmental concerns,

def•i•ni•tion

Carbon sequestration is the as-yet unproven theory that carbon dioxide emissions can be captured and buried underground instead of being released into the atmosphere. Skeptics believe that the idea is a solution proposed by industry to try to keep coal-fired power plants in operation rather than encourage the development of clean renewable energies.

Texas energy company TXU cancelled plans to build eight plants, dropping the proposed total to 146 in the spring of 2007. If these plants are built, they will significantly increase carbon emissions and the effects of global warming. Although some technologies to reduce the CO_2 output from coal-fired power plants are underway, such as Integrated Gasification Combined Cycle (IGCC) and *carbon sequestration*, neither technology is sufficiently developed to be applied in these hundred-plus plants.

And the power companies will not wait for the efficiency technology to catch up with them because our current federal regulations and subsidy programs make it very easy and attractive to push forward with plant development plans now, before government regulations change in favor of cleaner, more expensive technology.

Even if the existing technologies were ready for large-scale implementation, they still don't address major issues related to coal: the mercury emissions which contaminate our waterways and sea life, affecting our fishing industries and health; and problems related to coal mining, called mountaintop removal, which devastates ecosystems and whole communities.

The federally supported enterprise FutureGen is proposing to implement an experimental sequestration project in California's central valley. The project, a joint effort by the U.S. Department of Energy and a consortium of coal and oil companies, will explore the feasibility of underground carbon storage. What if an earthquake opens the land where the CO_2 is supposedly stored?

The world's largest coal company, Peabody Energy, produces 10 percent of the energy used in the United States and digs 240 million tons of coal from the earth each year. Company revenues are more than $4.5 billion, and its CEO was paid between $6 million and $9 million in salary and stocks in 2006; and the average annual salary for miners is $45,000, according to the Virginia Mining Association. Peabody has proposed plans to build a new coal-fired power plant in Illinois that will emit 25,000 tons of toxic pollution each year.

Hotter Future Ahead

The IPCC report states that 11 of the last 12 years (1995–2006) have been among the 12 warmest years in recorded history. If we don't find a way to stop global warming, Gelbspan warns that our CO_2 emissions will double in this century, increasing the extreme temperatures and extreme weather to uninhabitable proportions.

Extreme weather causes other extremes as well. Governments impose martial law under national security measures to deal with disasters (as we've seen following Hurricanes Katrina and Andrew); food supplies diminish because of disrupted agricultural production, causing shortages that lead to desperate conditions, theft, and black market manipulation of resources. Jobs are lost; homes are lost; and the insurance industry is crippled by increasing claims. In 2005, the U.S. insurance industry lost $200 billion covering hurricanes and other disasters. These costs, which are all passed along to government and the public, pose a grave threat to our economy.

Clouding the Truth

The oil and coal industries represent the largest commercial enterprise in history, earning a trillion dollars per year. During the past few years of oil crisis and escalating gas prices, ExxonMobil, the world's largest oil company, earned 75 percent more in the third quarter of 2005 than it had the year before, posted the highest profits of any U.S. company ever for 2006 at $39.5 billion, and reported another 10 percent increase in the first quarter of 2007. The company's profits have soared while everyone has paid more at the pump and for just about everything else since transportation and power are essential for all business and commerce.

To protect this tremendous financial resource, representatives of this fossil fuel empire have been caught perpetuating false information about global warming, by using marketing, the media, and even scientists on the dole to spread misinformation designed to confuse the public about the relationship between burning fossil fuels and global warming. Gelbspan reports that in 1991, Western Fuels, a fossil fuel industry lobby group, launched a public relations campaign, recruiting three scientists who were among only a handful of global warming skeptics to vocally refute the prevailing climate science. The goal of the campaign, as stated in the firms' annual report, was to reposition global warming as theory rather than fact. *The New York Times* reported on April 26, 1998, that a group of oil industry companies, acting with the lobbying group the American Petroleum Institute in Washington, D.C., launched a multimillion-dollar campaign to confuse the public about environmental science on global warming to the effect that it was founded on false or unproven science. NASA scientist James Hansen made headlines in 2006 when he revealed that the federal government had attempted to suppress his studies indicating that global warming was underway.

The attempt to dupe the public is not unlike the treachery perpetuated by the tobacco industry for as long as it could get away with it. Tobacco companies have been called into court and penalized for criminally misleading the public, with an estimated 440,000 deaths each year as a result of tobacco-related illnesses.

The coal and oil industries' misinformation campaign has been quite effective—in America at least. Other industrialized countries have been more forthcoming with their citizens, choosing not to stall scientific solutions in an effort to prolong profiting from the sale of oil and coal. More than 160 nations—Australia and the United States being the only developed nations excluded—agreed to the Kyoto Protocol in 2000, an international treaty agreement to reduce carbon and other emissions to 5 percent or below their 1990 levels by 2012. Although U.S. President George W. Bush claimed while campaigning that he would ratify the agreement, he has refused to do so on the basis that it would hurt the American economy.

Unfortunately, American citizens began to question whether global warming was a fact or theory, setting the stage for a massive push of high-consumption activities. Suddenly huge sedans on truck chassis' (SUVs) became the car of choice for millions of Americans, gas hogs that sucked up more oil than any car in history and spewed more CO_2 and other pollutant emissions than ever before.

> **Green Gamut**
>
> The Sierra Club reports that from 1997 to 2000, Peabody spent about $400,000 each year lobbying congress to oppose emission regulations of the Clean Air Act.

At the same time, environmental regulations were relaxed for vehicle emission standards (many states halted testing altogether, as Florida did as soon as Jeb Bush took over the governorship), as well as high-polluting industries, including coal-fired power plants and other fossil-fuel processors. Government even mandated that the EPA close access to all files detailing scientific findings related to global warming. In August 2006, the Bush Administration implemented its "EPA FY 2007 Library Plan," which effectively shut down 26 EPA libraries across the country, boxing up 80,000 original documents that are not electronically available and thus ending public and staff access to EPA library collections. The move was written as a budget-cutting measure, but was implemented by the administration before the budget was even passed.

One evasive tactic that has been used is to suggest that the current increase in extreme weather and related disasters is all part of the biblical prediction of Armageddon. Theologians know that this is a distortion of biblical teachings. But even if people believed these biblical predictions were coming true, wouldn't they want to do something to help the situation?

Many Christians see the light. Bill Moyers reports that many evangelical groups are recognizing that taking care of God's green earth and protecting it from harm are in line with what God would want them to do. "God created this world. He commissioned us to take care of it, and that's that," Reverend Tri Robinson of Vineyard Boise Church, Iowa, told Moyers on his PBS television special, *Is God Green?* "We are called to environmental stewardship not because of Mother Earth, but because it belongs to Father God."

> **Green Speak**
>
> "I wonder if people realize that so much of the money they pay to their electric companies goes to hire lobbyists to fight against the public's interest."
>
> —Susan Glickman, consultant to the Natural Resources Defense Council

Another Downside of Coal

In addition to CO_2 emissions, coal-fired power plants spew mercury into the air. This heavy metal settles in water bodies, contaminating water and fish. Peabody Energy and other coal companies fight government regulation of mercury emissions, in spite of the fact that mercury is a known cause of autism and brain damage to developing fetuses and young children and, according to Sierra Club executive director Carl Pope, that one of every six women of childbearing age in the United States has unsafe levels of mercury in her blood.

The Public Interest Research Group (PIRG) reports that since 1948, the U.S. government has invested more than $111 billion in energy research and development; 60 percent went toward nuclear research and 23 percent went toward fossil fuels—coal and oil, spending just a fraction of that on renewable energies.

> **Going Green**
>
> Check with your congressmen and women about their voting records and campaign financial records. Find out who contributes to their campaign and whose interests they are representing.

PIRG says that the United States burns more than 900 million tons of coal each year, releasing 2 billion tons of CO_2 and 51 tons of mercury into our air and water. Production accidents spill 31,000 gallons of oil into U.S. waters each day.

What Can Be Done?

So what can we do to reverse these trends and chart a course for a greener future?

Subsidize Success

Adding to their massive commercial wealth, the coal and oil industries receive $200 billion in worldwide subsidies. Ross Gelbspan suggests what seems an obvious path to a solution to the global warming crisis: reinvest those public tax funds in 100 percent clean and efficient renewable energy resources. The often repeated rhetoric that says wind and solar energies are not viable resources to help meet current energy needs is simply false.

The problem is that power companies won't make any money if you produce your own energy with solar panels or a windmill. The reason they constantly repeat that these technologies are not the solution is because if you generate your own solar power with photovoltaic cells on your roof, the power companies won't earn any money from you! Most nations have discovered that an investment in clean, renewable energy pays off handsomely both environmentally and economically, and many power companies are actually poised to produce renewable energy.

Review the Facts

Gelbspan affirms that a consortium of scientists, experts, and industry representatives has determined that the technology to move to renewable energy is at hand and entirely doable. The only thing holding the big energy companies back from fully developing their renewable resources is the lack of governmental regulation or mandate to do so. One company might do the right thing, but another company might choose to follow the short-term economic route. It's an issue of competition. Without public insistence regulations won't be passed, but once passed, the transition to clean energy could be much quicker than we assume because the technology is already there.

> **Green Speak** _____
>
> "The science is unambiguous. In order to climate stabilize we need to reduce our emissions by 70%. Even if we all sat in the dark and rode bicycles we would not reach that goal. We need to change our fuel sources. We need laws that require utilities to only sell us renewable energy, laws that require carmakers to only sell us hybrid cars. More important than the emissions avoided by lifestyle changes, is the act of telling others about the issue."
>
> —Ross Gelbspan

Vote for Clean, Renewable Energy

Science has established that burning coal and oil are the major contributors to global warming and that if such activity continues unchecked, we will face intense temperature increases, intense weather, and rising sea levels that will flood coastal cities around the world, rendering them uninhabitable. Yet our government, the representative of the people, is doing everything possible to perpetuate these two industries rather than moving beyond them to the alternative renewable energy resources which have been proven to offer a safer, clean future.

The only way to change this direction is for businesses to take the lead and do the responsible thing for the future of our children. Even the coal and oil companies could and would do this if properly motivated. The public needs to speak out and let these companies, and our political representatives, know that we want and need a clean, healthy future. The voice of the people and market demand for renewable energy products will be the force that turns the tide on global warming.

The Least You Need to Know

- Earth's temperature is steadily rising.
- Global warming is caused by increasing emissions of carbon dioxide production from industry, energy production, and automobiles.
- As temperatures rise over the next century, many changes will take place—some dangerous for life on Earth.
- We can make changes today that will dramatically limit the future damages from global warming.
- We owe it to our children to reduce CO_2 emissions now.

Living in Harmony with the Earth

In This Chapter

- ◆ Defining green living
- ◆ Clean air
- ◆ Clean water
- ◆ Clean dirt

The toll of human civilization is becoming increasingly apparent on Earth; we've polluted our air, water, and soil to the point that its ability to sustain life comes into question. The damage we're doing could threaten life as we know it if the worst global warming projections occur. But now that we understand why these changes are happening, the first step in preventing that disaster is to recognize the importance of our natural systems.

Green Living Is All About Harmony

Protecting and respecting our Earth is very much like protecting and respecting our children and the people we love.

Consumer Culture Contributes to Global Warming

American consumers have grown up in a culture and economy that thrives on consumerism. Everywhere we go, we're confronted with persuasive propaganda to buy something new. Since television has become a mainstay in our homes, Americans watch an average of four hours per day, and in many homes the tube is on whether anyone is watching or not. With the exception of public broadcasting, every show is peppered with advertisements, each cleverly crafted to sell products. People go shopping in droves on weekends and holidays, buying up new colors, new styles, and new stuff they don't really need.

The Environmental Protection Agency (EPA) says that Americans discard 220 million tons of garbage each year. Old stuff is carelessly discarded at curbside; perfectly good furniture and all types of goods are shipped off to the dump every day, where they add to the more than 10,000 landfills across the country. Landfills are the largest producer of the greenhouse gas methane (although some dumps capture the gas and use it as fuel for operating the facility). In addition to producing so much trash, production of all these consumer goods creates industrial waste and byproducts that pollute our air and water as well as our land.

Working to Survive: Cost of Living Paid with Your Life

The traditional business model drives our consumer economy on the basis of "more is better." Each quarter businesses must demonstrate to shareholders that they've sold more or produced more goods and generated more income than the previous quarter. This approach to business puts constant, unending pressure on workers to run ever faster on their treadmills to try to keep up with escalating growth. Yet most workers don't benefit from increased sales; only shareholders and top-level management reap the financial rewards, while workers continue to earn the same hourly wage in spite of increasing workloads and demands.

In recent years, the rapid increase in gas prices has driven up the cost of pretty much everything else, from groceries to rent to healthcare and medications. Increasing market value has caused property taxes to skyrocket, and increasing disasters have more than doubled many insurance costs.

The cost of living for workers has not kept pace with salaries in our current economy. In most households both parents must work to make ends meet, and children are raised by low-paid strangers who can't begin to provide the nurturing and love that parents can give. We have less time to spend with our children and families, less time to relax, less time to pursue hobbies or indulge in creative projects that feed our hearts, souls, and minds. We're living to work and working to survive. Is this the life we want?

Going Green Can Be Good for Family Values

Perhaps, at this critical time in the world's history when we must make conscious changes to the way we power all of our activities, we should rethink other aspects of our lives as well. Perhaps we can create more than just a healthy environment for our children if we can think about how we approach life and put more focus on what's really important to us.

How much do we really need all that new stuff we hear about on TV and then rush out to buy on the weekend? How much money could we save if we didn't fall for sales pitches? How much time would that give back to us to use teaching our children the Golden Rule or working with them to build a hut in the yard for wild creatures? Remembering what's most important to us is the first step in making choices and changes that will lead us all to a better world. Think about what you really need and want—what you value most in your life—as you make decisions about your life and about going green.

Breaking the Chains ...

Living in harmony with the earth would come easier for us if we weren't so hard-wired with our consumer mentality. But our so-called "addiction" to oil—and consumerism—can't be that much harder to break than other addictions, such as smoking, drinking, or eating more than we need. It's all about changing our habits.

Our choices truly have the potential to change the very fabric of our lives. One consideration to help simplify our choices along the way is to think about the consequences of our actions and activities, not just for us and our neighbors, but for all living things.

Earth itself is a big living system, and all the living components work together to make the whole. The food chain you learned about in science class is a good example. From the single-celled paramecia to humans, the actions of one creature affect the others. We are an integrated system, but humans have separated themselves from the rest of the natural world in ways that harm both nature and people. We need to look at all living things with a newfound respect and remember that our survival depends on one another.

Another important thing we must remember to ask ourselves whenever we hear some new directive is who benefits from the message. Sometimes we may discover that the message that renewable energy isn't viable, for example, is coming from the power plant industry, and the reason they're saying it's not viable is because it doesn't help their bottom line. What's more important to you—their bottom line or yours? Be a discerning reader, viewer, and consumer to get to the truth of the situation.

Air Quality

Clean air is one of those basics that all life needs to survive.

How Air Quality Affects the Earth and Our Bodies

Burning fossil fuels emits mercury, which poisons our waterways and fish—two of our greatest natural resources. A Sierra Club report at www.CoolCitiesGuide.us states that coal-fired and other fossil fuel power plants are responsible for more than a third of the nation's emissions that cause global warming.

The British Journal of Obstetrics and Gynecology reports a correlation between pregnant mothers' exposure to low levels of air pollution and premature births. The American Lung Association State of the Air 2006 report says that air pollution from burning coal and oil results in dirty air for more than half the nation—more than 150 million Americans—and contributes to premature deaths. The National Center for Health Statistics says that 7 million children have asthma. Dirty air harms everyone.

Fossil Fuels and Their Contribution to Air Quality Problems

In October 2006, scientists on an EPA advisory panel objected to an EPA decision to keep air quality regulations at the same level they've been since 1997, stating that the level of soot particulate permitted annually was not sufficient to protect humans from significant adverse health effects. An internal EPA analysis indicates that with tighter regulation of soot in the air we could save several thousand lives per year. Interestingly, only 2 of the 22 members on the EPA advisory panel suggested keeping the regulations at the same standard, one a former General Motors employee and the other a former member of the Chemical Industry Institute of Toxicology. It would seem that their views carried more weight than the rest of the committee.

The EPA did reduce allowable levels of particulate matter emitted on a daily basis and so announced that they've established the strictest air-quality standard in history.

However, scientists warn that the overall effect will still result in thousands of deaths. The soot particles emitted from power plants, industrial factories, and vehicles can cause asthma attacks, lung disease, and heart attacks.

The American Lung Association has asked Congress to stop giving favors to corporate polluters. Please remember that your vote counts!

> **Green Speak** _____
>
> "EPA's political boss sacrificed the lives of 5 to 10,000 Americans each year, who will now die from air pollution related strokes and heart and lung disease."
>
> —John Walke, Natural Resources Defense Council

Water Quality

Water is another basic requirement for all life.

How Water Quality Affects the Earth and Our Bodies

Close your eyes and think about the last time water provided its signature refreshment to your body—when you drank pure, fresh mountain-stream water, perhaps, or when you dove into a cool, clear, spring-fed pool. Water inundates your body, seeping in through all your cells—we're 90 percent water and require a minimum eight glasses a day. Scientists now believe that we could avoid many diseases if we consumed more than that each day.

Many people in the world simply don't have access to clean, fresh water. Green Cross International, an organization founded by former Russian leader Mikhail Gorbachev that's dedicated to "developing a sustainable future by cultivating a sense of global interdependence and shared responsibility in humanity's relationship with nature," which includes resolving water issues, states that 1.2 billion people in the world do not have adequate potable water and another 2.4 billion lack proper sanitation. Engineering plans and industrial use have hijacked or contaminated their water supplies. This inadequate water supply is the cause of death for more than 5,500 children each day.

Threats to Water Quality

Industrial, agricultural, and what is known as nonpoint source pollution, as well as pharmaceutical contamination, wastewater issues, and degrading water pipes are all threats to water quality.

Industrial Contamination

Power plants and many factories consume millions of gallons of water each day to cool plant processes. Paper mills, chemical, industrial, and power plants flush rinse water laced with chemical effluent into rivers, streams, and the oceans in a process based on the faulty assumption that dilution will make the noxious elements disappear. They don't go away; they just spread further and further beyond our ability to recapture them, contaminating all the waterways and shore lands they come in contact with.

Agricultural Contamination

Farm runoff is a big polluter. Nitrogen from fertilizer gets into water as does sewage from livestock—both huge problems resulting in widespread contamination. E. coli contamination of spinach and lettuce crops downstream from livestock occurred in September 2006. Many illnesses and three deaths were attributed to affected leafy greens because cattle waste had contaminated the river water used to irrigate crops farther down the channel.

Green Gamut

Some 500 million tons of animal waste are produced at factory farms annually, and the waste is typically treated by pooling in lagoons, then being sprayed across land. Contaminants from the waste, which include pesticides, hormones, antibiotics, and bacteria, commonly run into streams and groundwater supplies. This process, called "agricultural storm water," is allowed under the Clean Water Act, clearly the result of industry lobbyists. The EPA says that livestock waste has polluted 35,000 miles of rivers and groundwater in 17 states. An informed citizenry can correct political injustices.

Red tide, an algal bloom occurring in the Gulf of Mexico, is thought to be caused by the nitrogen runoff from farms. For much of the year, red tide consumes the Gulf, killing fish and manatees and damaging the tourism trade that depends on beaches and fishing.

Florida's largest lake, Lake Okeechobee, is nearly dead, polluted by cattle waste from area beef ranches and dairies to the north and from sugar farms to the south. The lake is part of the Everglades water system that has been compromised by development and agriculture. The waste produced by the farms is nitrogen rich, and that nitrogen runs into the lake, fertilizing algae, which grows unchecked, sucking the oxygen from the water and making it impossible for fish or other plants to live. Once a popular and lucrative fishing destination, tournaments are being cancelled because of dwindling fish populations. The future of the entire South Florida region literally depends on resolving the water quality and quantity issues that continue to challenge scientists, the Army Corps of Engineers, water district management, agriculture and residential interests, and the Florida legislature.

Simple solutions are available for saving Okeechobee, yet none are implemented because of so many competing interests. They could shut down the farms, such as by ending the subsidies made to the sugar growers (as Hodding Carter III suggested in *Stolen Water*, Atria, 2004), but politicians are in the pocket of the sugar farmers thanks to generous campaign contributions. They could convert the cattle waste to energy, preventing it from contaminating the lake and producing a local energy resource at the same time. Florida's new governor Charlie Crist recently pledged to help create filtering ponds around the lake to help prevent pollution from entering the lake. This is a promising start.

The Army Corps of Engineers, which has taken responsibility for the inadequate dykes contributing to Katrina's floods, are shoring up the berm around Lake Okeechobee now, yet say they're concerned that their efforts might further damage the dike. These complications prevent the movement toward solutions. Locals hope that Lake Okeechobee doesn't become the next Katrina.

Nonpoint Source Pollution

Nonpoint source pollution, one of the biggest contributors to water pollution, is the runoff of water from land into waterways and groundwater supplies. Rains carry surface pollutants, such as fertilizers and pesticides on lawns or oil and other contaminants from streets and driveways, into the sewers and ultimately into lakes and streams.

Going Green

Protect groundwater by preventing polluted runoff from your yard: eliminate or reduce your use of lawn chemicals and block drains with filters to capture contaminants before they leave your property.

Pharmaceutical Contamination

Water everywhere is polluted with pharmaceutical drugs that have passed through the bodies of their prescription owners and back into the public domain through wastewater treatment plants.

Flushing unwanted drugs down the toilet seems to be a practice that should be stopped immediately since it causes some of this contamination, but most of the contamination occurs after human consumption of the drugs. Water treatment specialists told *On Earth* magazine in a Fall 2006 story that filtering processes are available but are too expensive to implement without assistance.

However, it seems better to find ways to prevent the contamination in the first place. Ask your doctor if there might be some other solution to medical conditions besides taking drugs; perhaps consider switching to composting toilets and filtration systems that process effluent at the source, rather than moving it around and compiling it into huge public repositories.

Scientists have noticed that the proportion of amphibians with female genitalia is increasing. Some males show signs of female hormones. The concern is that soon there will be only females—no males to help perpetuate these species. The situation of gender displacement in frogs is not insignificant. These small creatures are the proverbial canaries in the coal mine—as they go, so may we in due time, unless we find a way to clean the waters of these hormone disruptors and other contaminants.

Scientists have already detected a decline in male births proportionate to female births in industrialized countries over the past three decades, and there is also an increase in male birth defects, reproductive system disorders, testicular cancer, and low testosterone. These problems have been associated with hormone-disrupting chemical exposure through common pesticides and agricultural chemicals, plastics, and household products such as shampoo and soap as well as pharmaceutical contamination of waterways.

Wastewater

In some places, partially treated waste water is shunted into underground deep wells by an injection process. The theory is that the water will remain unchanged in the wells, and can be withdrawn for further treatment and use when needed. Unfortunately, these wells are leaking and their contents are contaminating groundwater supplies, lakes, rivers, and oceans. Yet the process continues to be offered as a viable solution for wastewater treatment. The process of digging into the stone aquifers—the natural underground water storage systems from where most public water supplies are drawn—fractures the limestone and other materials, causing cracks through which the water migrates out of their storage wells.

Many micro-viruses from such waste in water pass undetected through traditional filtering and treatment systems. For your home water supply, consider installing a reverse-osmosis water filtering system or a carbon-activated filter.

Degrading Water Pipes

Water systems throughout America are reaching the age at which the pipes they're constructed of need replacement. Metal pipes may rust or otherwise degrade, possibly leaching metals into the water supply as it makes its way from a water treatment plant to your home. Lead pipes leach lead into water supplies, and pipes made from poly-vinyl chloride (PVC), a material used in recent years, may leach toxic chemicals into your water supply as well.

Soil

Soil is essential to us because it provides nourishment for the foods we eat. If the soil is contaminated or lacks nutrients, it will affect the quality of food it produces.

How Soil Quality Affects the Earth and Our Bodies

Contaminated soil may poison our food supply with chemicals that can cause birth defects, degraded I.Q., and diseases.

Endocrinologist Candace Pert states that we now know that chemicals in our environment are a cause of many of our diseases, cancer in particular. Anthropologist Dr. Elizabeth Guillette has studied families exposed to agricultural chemicals over the past 30 years. She has documented developmental differences (including I.Q. deficiencies) and physical and mental development deficiencies among those exposed to agricultural chemicals and has replicated her studies in several communities in the United States, Mexico, and India.

Degradation of Soil from Agricultural Chemicals

The chemicals commonly used in farming and food production have lasting effects on the health of those who come into contact with them. Dr. Louis Guillette, Distinguished Professor of Zoology at the University of Florida, has found that amphibious life in Lake Apopka is showing signs of hormone disruption and gender disturbance, with males developing female genitalia. Other UF researchers in the area report an increased incidence of cancers and other diseases among farmers. To help protect their workers, they've created field sanitation systems to allow farm workers to wash the chemicals from their hands during the day while working in the fields.

The trend toward large manufacturing farms and away from small family farms has meant an increase in mechanized and chemicalized farming practices. Large factory farms raise fowl and livestock under conditions that some animal activists consider inhumane, and to use drugs to boost growth and production such as in dairy cows is common practice. Raising livestock is energy intensive and much more costly than raising grains and vegetables. John Robbins, author of *Diet for a New America—How Your Food Choices Affect Your Health, Happiness, and the Future of Life on Earth*, says that the cost of raising grain to feed cattle far outweighs the cost of raising grain to feed people. He suggests reducing our meat consumption and moving toward vegetarianism as a compassionate means of increasing food production to address malnutrition, particularly in developing countries.

Green Speak

"Not that long ago, people who ate food that was healthy, environmentally friendly, and caused no animals to suffer were considered health nuts, while those who ate food that caused disease, took a staggering toll on the resource base, and depended on immense animal suffering were considered normal. But all this is changing."

—John Robbins, author of *The Food Revolution and Diet for a New America*

Genetically modified foods are grains, such as soy, that have been altered to resist bug infestations—i.e., the pesticide is built into the food. It certainly sounds like something I'd rather avoid, but the huge factory farms love this development; it creates crops that are impervious to natural predators and are therefore cheaper to produce on massive scales. These large farms are big players in the political arena and wield great influence over laws and regulations governing farming. Therefore, to find that regulations favor these big corporate entities, while they may not be so attractive to small family farmers—or consumers—is not uncommon.

Degradation of Soil from Mining

Mountaintop mining is one of the most obvious instances of degradation of the earth for corporate gain. The practice of dredging coal from under the surfaces of our mountain majesties devastates whole communities. Not only does the mine require life-threatening work of locals, but stripping the land of its coal also entails a process that leaves waste and erosion behind. The lack of forest cover causes floods that routinely wipe out mining communities, and the coal slurry left in local lakes and streams ruins water supplies.

The Rainforest Action Network reports that we have already blown the tops off of 474 mountains in the Appalachians and polluted more than 1,200 miles of waterways with mining debris.

Green Speak

"Which mountain would God blow up? Which holler would God throw his waste into?"

—Judy Bond, a religious activist fighting the mining industry in West Virginia

Whole mountaintops are destroyed by systematic mining for coal throughout the Appalachian region.

Contamination of Soil from Nuclear Waste

Nuclear power also threatens landscape and soil resources with low-level contamination. No successful method of disposing of radioactive waste has been established. The United States has been planning to bury its radioactive waste inside Yucca Mountain for years, but plans have derailed in many ways as scientists are facing the fact that waste that will be radioactive for thousands of years can't be successfully contained in a way that is safe for current and future societies. We have no way of safely containing this material that will continue to pose grave danger to any who encounter it for thousands of years. To leave a radioactive mess behind for future societies to deal with is not responsible for us.

Furthermore, waste products and emissions at nuclear power plants have been found to be radioactive and have contaminated communities. For instance, a broken pipe at Hope Creek Plant in New Jersey allowed a steam leak that interfered with plant performance and safety in 2004. In another case, four workers died in an accident that occurred because corroded equipment caused a steam leak and malfunction at the Mihama plant in Japan in 2004. Also, the nuclear power plant at Indian Point in New York was shut down when a radioactive water leak was detected in October 2005. In March 2006, groundwater surrounding the Braidwood nuclear power plant in Braceville, Illinois, was found to be laced with tritium, caused by a leaking storage tank. Also in 2006, a lawsuit against a power plant in Florida was dismissed by a judge who refused to hear testimony suggesting a link between dozens of area childhood cancers to the leak of radioactive wastewater inadvertently poured down a plant sink that drained to a municipal dump until it was detected. Such incidents are routine in U.S. news, and we have only 103 nuclear power plants currently active in the nation—no new ones have been approved since the nuclear accident at Three Mile Island in 1979. There is a push to build up to 30 new nuclear plants while regulations are particularly favorable to the industry, but the track record of these plants does not support such an investment.

The U.S. government has issued incentives to build new nuclear power plants, with an application deadline of 2008. But is nuclear power a safe solution to our oil addiction? The Union of Concerned Scientists has issued a report stating that in the past 41 years of nuclear power plant operations, 51 plants have had to be shut down for one year or more because of functional problems. These plants have been found to leak low-level radiation into their surrounding communities, but often the level is not reported because it falls below the safety limit set by the Nuclear Regulatory Commission (NRC). Because many scientists feel that no level of radiation exposure is safe, they have urged the NRC to reevaluate those standards.

Hazard

Nearly 3 million Americans live within 10 miles of an operating nuclear power plant ... The potential danger from an accident is exposure to radiation (from the Federal Emergency Management Agency).

Preventing Problems vs. Fixing Problems

An international meeting of scientists, diplomats, statesmen, and women representing 32 countries conceived the Wingspread Statement, which has become known as the "Precautionary Principle." Recognizing the dangers to health and environment of introducing new products into commerce even before they have been tested for safety, the group developed this standard suggesting that products not be approved until they could be proven to be safe to consumers and society. A version of the Precautionary Principle was passed as law in Europe and should go into effect sometime in 2007.

This concept should be one of our first methods applied as we seek to find alternative sources of energy and more environmentally friendly ways of life for a healthier future for our children and theirs.

> **Green Gamut**
>
> "When an activity raises threats of harm to the environment or human health, precautionary measures should be taken even if some cause and effect relationships are not fully established scientifically."
>
> —1998 Wingspread Statement: The Precautionary Principle

The Least You Need to Know

- Going green gets us back to nature and supports our family values.
- Our Earth is under siege from current industrial and agricultural practices.
- The quality of the earth's natural resources affects our bodies and our health.
- Many of our energy-generating activities and other industries damage our natural resources.
- We can help protect our natural resources by preventing contamination of air, soil, and water.
- This is the framework of our task to begin living in harmony.

Chapter **3**

Sustainable Living

In This Chapter

◆ "Sustainability" and our future

◆ Some common unsustainable practices

◆ The difference between sustainable and unsustainable resources

◆ Sustainable approaches to building and energy

We hear a lot about sustainability in the context of green living and the changes we need to make to protect ourselves from the effects of global warming. What does it mean? In this chapter, we'll learn what is meant by sustainability, why it's important, and how we can apply the principle of sustainability in our lives for a healthier future.

What Is Sustainability?

Sustainability means that something can continue to be used as a resource without running out. A material is considered sustainable if it can be created or harvested and used without harming the environment, if it is *renewable* so its supplies will not be wholly depleted, and if its afterlife does not contribute to the waste stream. Biodegradable materials are best to use, and that inevitably means natural materials that have not been derived from petroleum products.

Our Earth was designed as a sustainable system. Each form of life has its own resources necessary to survive. People, for example, can survive by eating plants, drinking water, and breathing air. When we die, our bodies decompose into the earth, fertilizing the ground so that more sustaining plants can grow and provide a healthy resource for another generation of the species. (Of course, we've corrupted that cycle of sustainability by filling the veins of our dead bodies with plastics in an embalming process that prevents our flesh from decomposing, and we bury our dead in caskets impervious to disintegration.)

The common business model for the past 150 years has been that natural resources feed into the economy. Oil, coal, grains, and agricultural products, even water, are all used to create saleable products. But often, the process from raw material to finished product creates some unpleasant by-products—pollution—which go back to the environment. So the model has been to take from the environment and put back only waste.

We have reached the point where our environment can no longer continue to provide raw materials for our production of goods. We have created an unsustainable system, and now it is time for us to create systems that take less from the environment and give back to it or nourish it as we go along so that we can leave a healthy foundation for future generations.

Sustainable and Unsustainable Materials

Understanding whether materials and resources are sustainable or not is important when you're deciding which you want to use. Here are a few examples that give you an idea of what needs to be considered when determining sustainability.

Wood

All trees are critical to the earth's environmental cycle. Not only do they provide habitat and food for many species of wildlife, but trees also help counteract the effects of global warming by serving as a *sink* for increasing amounts of CO_2 released into the atmosphere.

Some types of wood are considered a sustainable resource because new supplies can be grown quickly without environmental damage or quality compromise.

Hardwoods, however, take decades to grow and simply can't be replaced as quickly as they have been taken away from the ecosystem.

Rainforests are filled with hardwoods that are endangered by development, timbering, and destruction by locals desperate to make a few dollars by selling charcoal made from burned forest wood.

Even bamboo, often touted as one of the more sustainable woods because of its fast-growing cycle and abundance, can pose environmental problems if it must be conveyed around the world before it's turned into flooring in your home. The *embodied energy* required to move materials raises the environmental costs considerably when transportation costs, fuel spent, and pollution created are taken into consideration.

def•i•ni•tion

A **sink** is something that absorbs greenhouse gases naturally, helping to maintain a healthy atmospheric balance on Earth. Forests serve as a natural sink for CO_2 because trees process the CO_2 into oxygen through photosynthesis; however, our diminishing forests mean less natural neutralization of atmospheric CO_2.

Embodied energy refers to the energy that goes into the manufacture and transportation of a commodity during its productive life.

Petroleum

Petroleum derives from fossil fuels, but those fuels are not sustainable for several reasons. Combustion of these products produces one of the most dangerous pollutants in the atmosphere, CO_2, the major contributor to global warming. Procurement of petroleum products is dangerous in that it can lead to war or be a factor in it, and mining for it is damaging to the earth and surrounding environment, such as with oil wells and coal mining.

Besides fuel, other products derived from petroleum, including nonbiodegradable plastics and carcinogenic synthetic chemicals, have lasting negative effects on the environment and are likely to hurt generations of species which follow us as well as those of us here now.

Fortunately for humankind, petroleum is nonsustainable; the supply is limited and it's eventually going to be exhausted—we've already used up about half of our available oil supplies. So whether we get chemical and coal companies to stop using fossil fuels or not, sooner or later they will be forced to find alternative solutions. The current problem is that we need to turn around on the path toward destruction by reducing our emissions of CO_2 by 70 percent within 10 years to avoid a catastrophic climate crisis, according to an accepted scientific analysis presented in a report from the Hadley Centre for Climate Prediction, a governmental agency of the United Kingdom (see Appendix B).

Energy production could be sustainable using renewable fuels such as sunlight and wind; they're consistently (though not constantly) available with supplies that are never depleted. Their use does not produce any pollutants or emissions nor any by-products that require mitigation.

Water

Water is not a sustainable resource because eventually it will all be used up or polluted and unusable, unless we can find a way to protect supplies from pollution and to more completely clean water after we've used it for various purposes.

Water was originally a sustainable resource, taken in by various life forms including plants, animals, and people, then excreted back to the soil as urinary waste, filtered through the ground, plants, soil, and sediments, before feeding back into the groundwater systems as fresh water.

Industries have corrupted this system by the huge overuse of water which then, partially treated, is dumped as wastewater directly back into our creeks and oceans. The unfiltered pollutants kill sea life and plants and migrate back into the groundwater and the public drinking supplies. Nearly all of our waterways today are contaminated with some level of pollutants. Our bodies are saturated with synthetic chemicals, some of which are known carcinogens and endocrine disrupters, which pose health risks including irreversible damage to developing brains and bodies.

Green Gamut

A landmark study conducted by the Environmental Working Group (EWG), called Body Burden, examined placental fluid of 10 infants, finding an average of 200 industrial chemicals in each sample, including 180 known carcinogens, 217 known as toxic to neurological and nervous systems, and 208 known to cause birth defects or abnormal development. What does this mean in terms of the child's health? No studies have been done so no one knows yet, but the rise of diseases and disorders in the twentieth century could be a huge clue.

Meat

Meat production is not sustainable because livestock use an excessive amount of resources, and factory farms produce massive quantities of crops that create an imbalance of natural resources, destroying the native systems of selection and evolution of species. Furthermore, if synthetic pesticides, herbicides, and fertilizers are used on crops, they pollute the ground, groundwater, and runoff water, affecting ecosystems far afield from application.

A Sustainable Economy

So we cannot wait until the wells run dry and the mountaintops have been removed before we begin converting to renewable energies and a sustainable economy. And we don't need to wait because the companies who provide our power and create the chemicals used in manufacturing, pharmaceutical, and other industries have already begun exploring more sustainable technologies in anticipation of this resource crisis.

Going Green

We need to let these companies know that we—consumers and buyers of their products—want sustainable products now. As they say, votes made with your pocketbook are the most effective.

Look Who's Leading the Way: Examples of Alternative-Powered Homes

Sustainable buildings are no longer just a dream for the future or the hippie pads of the past. Smart homeowners and corporations are implementing energy-efficient standards and sustainable practices in ever-increasing numbers. Let's take a peek at some of the innovators who have applied sustainable building principles to create their *ecohomes*.

President Bush's Crawford Ranch

Laura and George W. Bush have implemented many environmentally friendly practices at their 1,600-acre ranch in Crawford, Texas, where they plan to retire. They recycle rain runoff and wastewater for use in irrigating their lawn, which is planted with wildflowers and native grasses that are accustomed to Texas heat and periods of drought. They have a geothermal heating system that warms and cools the home using underground temperatures. The home is built of local limestone, minimizing the need for transporting building materials, and it's designed to capitalize on fresh breezes, reducing the use of air conditioning in summer.

def•i•ni•tion

Ecohome is a trendy catch term applied to sustainable design in home building.

Other Homes

Bill Hutchins and his wife Beth Knox spend an average of $250 to heat their Takoma Park, Maryland, home each winter. A corn-burning stove in the kitchen fills the two-story bungalow with heat, and biodiesel fuel produced by soy beans fuels a radiant floor heating system as well as the family cars. Their kids, one in high school and two in college, help collect corn in buckets from a neighborhood grain storage facility that serves several area homes, but that's about the only way their busy lives differ from their classmates' lives, with computers and homework taking center stage at home. Bill is an architect and designer who creates eco- and spiritually friendly homes and buildings worldwide with his company Helicon Works.

Ben Lynch and his wife power their Washington state home with wind, purchasing wind credits from Renewable Energy Choice, an organization that also provides power for Harvard and Duke Universities, the William Jefferson Clinton Presidential Library, and Yellowstone National Park. The company says that there is already enough wind energy produced in just three states to provide adequate electricity for our entire nation.

Bill Hutchins' Straw Bale Home. Architect Bill Hutchins used straw bale construction in his home in Takoma, Maryland.

(Photo by Angie Seckinger, Courtesy www.heliconworks.com)

Green Gamut

Wind credits are one way that those whose power supply comes from nonrenewable sources such as oil or gas can invest in wind energy instead. Many power companies provide customers the option of paying a few dollars extra per month to support wind or other renewable resources. The power company invests funds collected in research and development of wind or other renewable energy, so the buyer is helping to support the development of renewable energy.

Sloane and Roland Muench decided to convert their oceanfront home in the Florida Keys to solar when they retired there in 2003. John Nettles of Nettles Electric installed *photovoltaic cells* on their flat roof that collect enough energy even to run their air conditioning system, an unusual feat for the time. Muench, a retired physician from Washington, D.C., was raised in Germany, where solar power was much more prevalent.

He said that he and his wife hated watching the endless sunshine go to waste in their island home and that now they appreciate knowing that they're independent of the *grid*. Muench says they were amazed to discover that even the stars and moon generate a little electricity at night.

def•i•ni•tion

Photovoltaic cells are solar energy collectors that can be placed on rooftops and in yards. New technology even includes photovoltaic shingles and window film that make solar heat easier and more cost effective for homeowners.

The **grid** refers to the power supply network that connects homes and buildings to a municipal power source.

Roland Muench fully powers his home with solar energy.

(Trish Riley)

Green Homes and Condos to Buy or Rent

On Seabird Key you can vacation in a house, built from beautiful river-dredged cypress, that's completely off the grid, situated on its own private island. Photovoltaic cells on the roof provide power (with backup generators); a cistern collects water; and all systems are designed to conserve natural resources. The home, built by Deborah and Jim Davidson as the perfect tropical getaway, rents by the week with boats and water toys and even music piped out to the private beach.

Complex in Colorado

At Solar Village in Longmont, Colorado, you can buy a condominium in a new urban community called Prospect Newtown. The wind and sun power Solar Village homes, built with nontoxic sustainable materials such as solid wood cabinets and granite countertops, were laid out in a design to encourage pedestrian traffic and reduce the need for vehicles.

You can rent this solar-powered ecohome on Seabird Key.

(Trish Riley)

New Green Subdivisions: Ecohomes En Masse

It appears to be just another ubiquitous suburban development, spreading over once pristine acreage that somebody probably fought about in the earliest years of the plan. Nearly 1,000 houses, each a shade of Palm Beach peach, sit in various configurations. Some are stacked like cracker boxes; some have slices of green between them; others are surrounded by grand expanses of mature trees and natural-looking wetlands. A lake sits amidst the new construction, giving the place that Florida stamp of appeal. From above, Evergrene no doubt looks just like all the other puzzlelike pieces of urban sprawl, eating into the wilderness faster than anyone can stop it.

But this community is at least slightly different, even if that's not obvious at first glance: a few of these homes have incorporated some planet-saving options. A dozen homebuyers, to be exact, of the 985 homes in the community elected to invest in energy-saving upgrades such as high-efficiency air conditioning systems, low-flow showers and toilets, and ultra-effective blown-in insulation. (See Chapter 5 for more on these and other home-based energy-saving ideas.)

WCI, a mainstream production builder, is a publicly traded firm that has more than 50 new communities for sale and has built homes and high-rises for more than 160,000 people over its 60-year history. WCI's first green model home, called Geni G in the Evergrene Community in Palm Beach Gardens, Florida, gave potential buyers the chance to see what carpet made from soda bottles—and not formaldehyde—looks and smells like. The yard, certified as native by the Florida Yards and Neighborhoods program, features plants whose flowers attract butterflies and fragrant herbs instead of thirsty, pesticide-, fertilizer-, and herbicide-dependent turf. Sidewalks and driveways are made with pavers spaced slightly apart to allow water to drain back into the soil and aquifer instead of sewers (water that washes oil-stained driveways is a major source of water pollution). A rain barrel catches rainwater to irrigate the yard, and a composting bin is nestled in the bushes to recycle vegetable and plant trimmings—there's no garbage disposal in the kitchen, also a source of water pollution.

The list goes on to include $75,000 worth of ecofriendly upgrades that buyers may choose if they're willing to pay for them, from dual-flush toilets and low-flow shower heads to ceiling fans, improved insulation, and paint that doesn't emit volatile organic compounds.

The 364-acre community of nearly 1,000 homes, priced from $200,000 to more than $1 million, sold out ahead of schedule in $2^1/_2$ years. Buyers have been drawn to innovations related to indoor air quality, like low VOC paints and formaldehyde-free floorings, which are more conducive to a healthy family environment; and to things that make a home more energy efficient, like ceiling fans, improved insulation, and Energy Star appliances (read more about Energy Star in Chapter 5).

In many cases ecoinnovations are visually indistinguishable from traditional choices. Nontoxic paints come in all the trendy colors; air filters and insulation are hidden from view; energy and water-saving appliances are sleek and modern and just as reliable as less-efficient models. Bamboo floorings are sexier than many kinds of traditional wood, and carpets made from recycled soda bottles are bright, durable, soft, and cushy just like traditional fibers.

The community also has an Audubon certification, which means it's designed to protect wildlife habitats. Evergrene includes a 36-acre lake, and many old oak and mahogany trees on the property were moved to the perimeter of the development rather than razed in the development process.

The builder has moved on to begin developing similar environmentally friendly communities in the northeast states of New York and New Jersey.

Mainstreaming the Sustainable Model

WCI has taken the learning curve element out of the transaction in a subsequent community, making some green features standard. In addition, WCI has created a Green DVD that's available free to anyone interested in ecofriendly homes.

Rebates and tax incentives help make green innovations easier to implement for homeowners. Some states offer rebates for solar water heaters and photovoltaic cells, and there are "green" mortgages that can be extended to help cover environmental construction.

The U.S. Green Building Council's Leadership in Energy and Environmental Design (LEED) program applies points for each ecosensitive feature, based on how much energy a building consumes, what impact it makes on the local environment, how well it conserves natural resources, and whether it provides educational information to buyers and residents (this one turns out to be one of the more challenging requirements).

The U.S. Green Building Council reports that there are about 5,000 LEED-registered projects nationwide and in 12 other countries, and the National Association of Home Builders says its members reported building more than 61,000 green homes from 1990–2004, calling the green revolution a quiet one, yet one of the most significant new developments in the housing industry. According to the Virginia Sustainable Building Network, new homes are twice as efficient as they were in 1970, yet residential buildings account for about 20 percent of national energy use. Paul McRandle, home building specialist for the Green Guide, an ecofriendly e-newsletter, notes that subsidy programs encourage people to buy energy-efficient appliances, but although appliances are more efficient, manufacturers are making them larger, reducing the benefit. McRandle points out that according to the Worldwatch Institute's State of the World 2004, per capita electricity use has doubled in the last 30 years in all states except California.

Green Living: The E Magazine Handbook for Living Lightly on the Earth, a book written by editors of *E Magazine*, reminds readers that California's energy crisis in 2001 spurred consumers to begin buying energy-saving items. The state invested $730 million in an advertising campaign to help educate its residents.

Green building projects may still be anomalies, but they are popping up across the country, with ecofriendly condos in New York City, housing communities in Minnesota, and in cites from Maine to California.

Rampant growth and development driven by financial gain are often blamed for eco-waste and environmental damage. In a wry twist, maybe following the money will lead us to a healthier planet this time.

The Least You Need to Know

- Sustainable materials and practices help preserve the environment for future generations.
- Water was originally a sustainable resource but is becoming increasingly polluted and unusable.
- Some wood is sustainable, but hardwoods are an example of woods that can be considered unsustainable.
- Energy production could be sustainable using renewable fuels, such as sunlight and wind.
- Meat production is not sustainable because livestock use a relatively excessive amount of resources.

Chapter 4

Changing Our Energy Habits for a Healthier Future

In This Chapter

- ◆ Breaking bad energy habits and learning better ones
- ◆ Energy alternatives for different situations
- ◆ Self-contained power systems versus those that hook into municipal supplies

We've heard that our measures to conserve energy and to switch to more fuel-efficient lifestyles might help this global warming situation, but people sometimes think that their own individual efforts to make changes won't be enough to avert the potential disasters associated with global warming.

But actually our efforts will be the very thing that makes the difference. As consumers, we set the pace of all markets. When we let our business leaders and government leaders know that we're only interested in buying sustainable products, that's what they'll give us. We can definitely trigger the change. In fact, chances are good that until we insist that companies and regulations support a healthier future, we're not going to get it.

Changing our energy habits begins at home. And that doesn't mean we have to go back to the Stone Age or give up the modern conveniences and comforts we've come to rely on.

Changing Our Habits

Let's take a look at how to switch to cleaner lives with more sustainable systems. Today's energy needs are met with a mix of mostly nonrenewable resources. Coal, oil, natural gas, and nuclear power dominate the landscape, with just 10 percent coming from hydropower and 6 percent from the sun and wind.

> **Green Speak**
>
> "Hope for the earth lies not with leaders but in your own heart and soul. If you decide to save the earth, it will be saved. Each person can be as powerful as the most powerful person who ever lived—and that is you, if you love this planet."
> —Helen Caldicott, *The Newman's Own Organics Guide to a Good Life* (Villard Books, 2003)

The Worldwatch Institute and Center for American Progress report that renewable energy resources are used to provide 6 percent of energy in the United States (as of late 2006), but they project a rapid increase in future years, thanks to improving technologies that are bringing costs into competitive range with fossil fuels, coupled with the environmental, security, and economic costs of using fossil fuels.

Most states offer incentives to homeowners who choose to use renewable energy, and several have passed renewable energy laws and regulations to support the development of renewable resources and limit production of greenhouse gases.

> **Green Gamut**
>
> Remember, power companies don't earn anything from you if you're producing your own electricity with solar panels on your roof. And they spend big bucks to influence government officials, who in turn appoint them to public service commissions, which make the decisions about power resources available to citizens. The power industry has become one of the biggest businesses in the nation. Like all businesses, it has a profit orientation.

Nuclear power plants may produce power without oil, but they also produce radio-active waste products—an unresolved issue.

As of late 2006, California, a proven leader when it comes to new technologies and ideas, generates 31 percent of its electricity from *renewables*. In September 2006, Governor Arnold Schwarzenegger passed landmark legislation to reduce the state's carbon emissions by 25 percent by 2020 and by another 80 percent by 2050. These regulatory measures are seen by environmental activist Ross Gelbspan as a critical step toward enabling power companies and fuel suppliers to improve their renewable technologies.

def•i•ni•tion

Renewables refers to renewable energy resources such as solar, wind, geothermal, hydro, and biofuel power.

From an economic standpoint, renewables are also promising. The Worldwatch report says that renewables create more jobs than fossil fuels for every dollar spent on energy production. We'll take a look at the types of new job opportunities in Chapter 21.

Steven Strong, president of Solar Designs Associates, Inc., has been designing and installing solar power systems for more than 25 years at such prestigious addresses as the White House, the Pentagon, and U.S. Embassies around the world, as well as in private homes, apartment buildings, and hotels. "I like to offer an alternative," he says, "one based on nuclear fusion—93 million miles away. Renewables are ready. They are proven, reliable, and off-the-shelf. We have the tools and the technology to begin the transition to the post-petroleum era. We need only the political will to use them."

Solar Power: Options, Cost Comparisons

For an average American home, going fully solar today may cost from $30,000 to $50,000. It's a high price to pay, but state and federal incentives may reduce the initial cost by as much as 30 to 70 percent. If you're putting the effort into a new home, you may be eligible for an Energy Efficient Mortgage, which increases your mortgage amount by translating energy savings achieved with efficiency improvisations into income. The equipment prevents tons of pollution and once it has paid for itself, it usually has years to run before repairs or replacement becomes necessary.

Solar cells collect sunlight and convert it into electricity using DC power inverters that change the energy to AC power for household use.

(Courtesy Kilowatt Ours)

> ### Green Speak
>
> "The solar resources of just seven southwest states could provide 10 times the current electric generating capacity."
> —Worldwatch Institute and Center for American Progress

Interestingly, in the 1940s, solar water heaters were on every rooftop in Miami, but those were displaced when oil became "cheap" after World War II. Florida Power and Light does not use solar energy as part of its power generation, in spite of the fact that the sun shines daily in the Sunshine State. Other companies are leading the way with solar technology, however, including British Petroleum (BP) Solar, which utilizes solar power to run some of its fossil fuel stations across the United States.

Wind Power: Costs Less Than Oil

Renewable Choice Energy, a company that promotes alternative fuel resources, says three U.S. states already produce enough wind energy to provide adequate electricity for the entire nation. Whole Foods Market, which became the largest company in the nation to offset 100 percent of its electricity usage with wind power in 2006, purchases its wind credits from Renewable Choice Energy.

The American Wind Energy Association says that the cost of producing wind energy has dropped by 80 percent over the past 20 years, thanks to improved technology and increasing demand. Electricity from wind can now be generated for as little as 5¢ per kilowatt hour, a rate competitive with energy produced from fossil fuels.

> **Green Speak**
>
> "We imagined a world that makes children the standard for safety. What about designs that 'loved all the children, of all species, for all time?'"
>
> —Bill McDonough and Michael Braungart, *Cradle to Cradle: Remaking the Way We Make Things* (North Point Press, 2002)

Texas has the most wind turbines in the nation, and Florida Power and Light is the largest owner of wind energy in the nation. Interestingly, FPL does not offer wind energy as an alternative to its Florida customers, except for those willing to pay a premium. Although wind power is much more widely developed in European countries, the United States may be catching up. In 2005, we installed more wind turbines than any other country.

Opponents of wind energy complain that wind turbines will disrupt their views, and groups have formed specifically to oppose wind turbines on mountain ridge lines. In some cases the wind turbines could generate more power if placed along mountain ridge lines, but the units seem sleek rather than unsightly, and certainly are more attractive than nuclear cooling towers or smokestacks from coal-fired power plants.

Another oft-voiced concern is that wind turbines may kill birds. In some isolated incidents birds have hit turbines, but in most studies, the number of bird casualties did not compare significantly to other hazards facing the wild bird population. The Audubon Society estimates that 25,000 birds die from wind turbine collisions annually but compares that to more than 800 million bird deaths from windows, wind shields, buildings, and power lines. The Audubon Society is working with the American Wind Energy Association to develop wind resources safely to protect birds and wildlife.

Windmills produce emission-free energy.

(Courtesy American Wind Energy Association)

Coal-fired power plants emit CO_2 and particulate soot, which damages lung tissue and can cause death from respiratory illnesses and lung cancer.

(Trish Riley)

Hydropower: Water Works Hard Already

In use for decades, hydropower is the most used renewable energy resource in the United States today. Across the country, dams have been built to capture the energy from the flow of the nation's powerful rivers.

Unfortunately, dams do pose environmental problems for a number of reasons. When a dam and reservoir reduce water flow for electricity production, farming communities, wildlife, and terrain downstream suffer a reduction in water supply. Also, working against the forces of nature has proven dangerous time and again. When dams break, the communities that have established themselves in the dry areas where water once flowed are frequently flooded, as the water tends to go back to its original course. The floods in New Orleans when the dam around Lake Pontchartrain burst during Hurricane Katrina is a good example; another is when a dike around Lake Okeechobee burst, drowning thousands of people during the Labor Day Hurricane of 1929. So while hydropower provides a clean, renewable energy source, future development of more hydropower resources is not practical or advisable because of potential side effects of building dams.

Geothermal Power: How Does It Work?

Geothermal energy, like the system used at the Bush Ranch in Crawford, Texas, utilizes a heat pump to convey fluid—usually something like antifreeze—underground, where natural earth temperatures are between 50 and 60 degrees in both winter and summer. The fluid captures the warmth and carries it back to the house, where the heat pump draws the warmth from the water and uses it to heat the house. In summer, the underground temperature is cooler than summer weather, and the fluid carries the warmth from the house out to the ground, bringing the cooler temperature into the home.

def•i•ni•tion

Geothermal simply means "heat from the ground."

Installing a geothermal pump system can be expensive, but they save considerable money on energy costs, keeping building temperatures moderate in both winter and summer so that other sources of heating and cooling need be used only minimally. If it's good enough for the president …

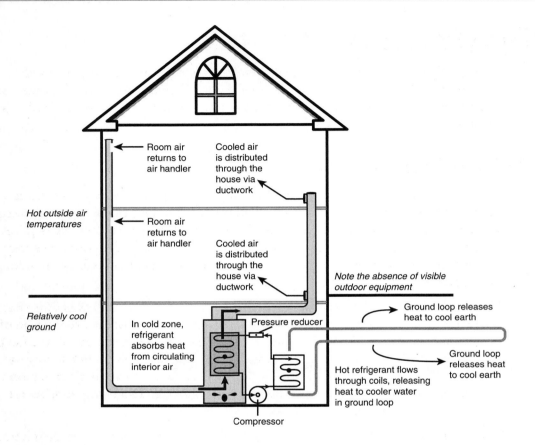

Diagram showing a geothermal system.

Biofuel Power

Biofuels made from corn, soybeans, plant material, wood, and other natural matter are emerging as possible fuel sources for the future. Already some biofuels are being used to power auto engines as well as homes with oil heating systems.

Wood stoves have evolved into super-efficient options for space heating, and newer stoves burn dried corn kernels and pellets made from natural bio waste such as sawdust, wood chips, plant stalks, corn, and other grains. Pellets burn at very high temperatures, and pellet stoves produce high heat very efficiently. The downside of using a home stove for heat is that you must constantly maintain the stove and the fire and keep a supply of fuel, whether wood, corn, or pellets. Burning these materials produces emissions, including CO_2, which contribute to global warming.

Living Off the Grid

"The grid" refers to the infrastructure created to convey power through cities and regions from the main power supplies, usually power plants. Most people's homes are tied to the grid, receiving power from a main power station, usually a coal-fired power plant, natural gas plant, or nuclear power plant.

The Cost of Living on the Grid

Although power supply began as a public utility, most such utilities are now run as for-profit enterprises rather than co-ops that simply split operational expenses among members. Maintaining profit margins for hungry investor shareholders causes prices to rise, and maintaining regulatory controls for least expense to the power company means that a considerable amount of operating funds are spent on lobbyists to influence governmental regulators.

Weaknesses in the existing grid system have been exposed when the system has shut down under duress. During the blackout of 2003 in the northeast, an overdemand of supply caused a power outage affecting 10 million people in Canada and 40 million in the United States. It was the largest blackout in North American history, lasting for two days throughout most of the region. During disasters, such as hurricanes, power outages can last for weeks because infrastructure systems of above-ground wires are vulnerable to destruction from storms.

Many homeowners who've incorporated alternative energy resources into their home systems are pleased to be independent of the grid, an aging infrastructure that may run aground at any time. They are no longer dependent on municipal power supplies or systems to maintain power resources in their own homes and businesses. Solar and wind systems are both well suited to powering individual systems.

Larry Sherwood of the Interstate Renewable Energy Council estimates that between 35,000 and 70,000 homes in the United States live off the grid and use solar power as their sole energy resource.

Net-Metering: Giving Back to the Grid

Sherwood also states that the number of off-grid homes is growing, but even more popular are self-sufficient homes that are connected so they can feed their excess power into the public or municipal system. This concept is known as net-metering, an innovation that 14,000 or more homes are practicing.

John Hammerstrom and Diane Marshall built the first net-metering home in the Florida Keys that connects to the pubic utility. When they proposed net-metering to the Florida Keys Co-Op, the utility needed to learn about the idea before they could approve it, but eventually a workable agreement was forged, and a few others have followed.

Most states require fair payback systems so that if a home is producing more energy than it needs, it trades it back to the public utility at a one-for-one rate against its electricity use from the utility. In several states no such regulations exist, and the utility buys homeowner's power at a wholesale rate, then charges retail rates when the home needs to access public utility resources. This is called dual-metering.

Growing pains are not uncommon when new procedures like net-metering come on the scene, but as the kinks get worked out, some innovations turn out to be win-win for all.

The Least You Need to Know

- Changing habits and systems is easier when we understand the importance and value of making the switch.

- Solar, wind, water, geothermal, and biofuel power are better energy solutions than the traditional choices of coal, oil, gas, and nuclear power.

- We can take charge of our own power needs and become independent of municipal networks.

- Net-metering is the practice of a home generating its own power and sharing it with the community.

- Some states require municipal power companies to compensate customers for power at the retail rate, while others pay only wholesale rates.

Part 2

Going Green at Home

Let's take a close look at the many things we can do to change our energy usage patterns to become more efficient so we'll produce less of the greenhouse gases that cause global warming. Whether you're buying a new home or renovating an existing one, you can do much to make it more ecofriendly.

We can also learn to conserve water more effectively and to reduce our contribution to the landfills—simple techniques and reformed habits all begin with the knowledge about what we need to do and why.

"You'd save a lot of water if you'd let me clean those."

Chapter 5

Saving Energy at Home

In This Chapter

- ◆ Environmentally friendly building materials
- ◆ Ways to conserve energy at home
- ◆ Achieving greater energy efficiency in new and old homes
- ◆ Factors for the best location for your home

Whether it's time for you to build a new home or renovate an existing one, you can do many things to create a more energy-efficient and healthy home environment. The changes you make can go a long way toward improving indoor air quality as well as conserving your home energy bill.

In this chapter, you find ideas on how to make your home more energy-efficient. Whether you've been there for years or are building a new home, you can make energy improvements in many areas of your home.

Roofing Choices for Energy Efficiency

Roofs seem to be a singularly overlooked element that can make a significant difference in a home's efficiency. Why do roofers always offer dark-colored shingles? Pulling that solar heat into the home might be a good solution for really cold climates, but for most homes, light colors are a better choice because they reflect heat, making it that much easier to cool the interior of a home during warm months.

Going Green _____

I like the way Jersey Devil architect Jim Adamson put it when I interviewed him for the *Miami Herald:* "We use honest materials." He meant real wood instead of pressed or composite wood—no artificial ingredients added. Look for natural materials that don't have to travel long, energy-intensive, and expensive distances to get to your building site.

Reflective finishes can be applied to some roofing surfaces to reduce roof and interior temperatures. For example, white acrylic or aluminum-based silver paint can be applied to asphalt roofs to increase reflectivity of solar radiation, reducing the roof temperature by as much as 15 degrees Fahrenheit. Reducing the temperature of a black asphalt roof helps protect the asphalt from deterioration and also reduces the need to cool the building, thus saving energy and reducing carbon emissions related to the structure. Reflective roof coatings are available at home and building supply stores and cost about the same as household paint, although because reflective paints are thicker than household paints, it takes more reflective paint to cover the same size area.

def•i•ni•tion _____

A **radiant foil barrier** is a thin metallic material much like aluminum foil that can be applied under the roof to block up to 90 percent of radiant heat from entering or leaving the interior. It can make a significant difference in energy usage.

If you apply a *radiant foil barrier* under the roof, it will direct the sun's hottest rays away from the home, considerably increasing efficiency. The same technology helps keep heat in the home during winter months. Radiant foil barrier material costs about 10¢ per square foot before installation; it's an inexpensive fix that makes a big difference in your energy bill.

Using the foil requires a vent to carry the deflected heat away from the home. Ridge vents along the top roofline with screened vents under the roof overhang work well with or without the barrier to move breezes up through the roof area and keep hot air from stalling over the house. These vents cost an additional $3 to $4 per foot, plus installation.

A metal roof reflects heat and lasts many years longer than shingles. If you're collecting water as it runs off the roof, metal is a better choice to use because the water won't pick up asphalt from shingles on its way to the collection gutters.

> **Green Gamut**
>
> A metal roof can last twice as long as an asphalt shingle roof.

Tile and slate are also durable natural materials and a good choice for roofing (if they don't have to travel around the world to reach your home).

One of the most exciting new technologies available as a roofing option is solar shingles. Photovoltaic (PV) cells look like roof shingles but can be used instead to provide roofing protection and collect solar energy at the same time. The PV cells collect the solar heat and send it to a DC inverter, which converts into AC power, electricity that is compatible with household usage needs. The great news is that you may be able to put on a solar roof for nearly the same cost as a conventional roof thanks to local, state, and federal incentives and tax credits. Be sure to consider this option when making decisions about this important investment.

Windows, Doors, and Awnings

If you have the opportunity to design your home, keep in mind that windows and doors are essential to provide adequate ventilation and daylight. The larger the openings, the more breeze and light you can capture. Locate windows so they will be in the path of both breezes and sunlight, and place them strategically to carry the breeze through the home.

Passive solar warmth and light are great in winter, but when summer sun brings in too much heat, you want to be able to prevent those solar rays from heating up your home. Using awnings or shade trees to protect your windows from sun is a relatively simple and cost-effective way to reduce your energy usage. Select awnings that you can raise or lower to either invite or discourage the sunlight's entry into your home. Sturdy awnings made of metal can double as hurricane shutters or wind shields to protect windows in climates with intense weather. You can also buy wooden or canvas awnings or build an arbor to support plants that vine to shade the window.

def•i•ni•tion

Passive solar refers to capitalizing on the warmth of the sun's rays without further devices. Allowing sunlight to stream through windows and fall on materials such as concrete, which holds the sun's warmth for long periods of time, is a good way to reduce the need for additional heat sources, cutting expense and energy use.

Going Green _____

The federal government offers tax credits of up to $2,000 for energy efficiency measures taken in new home construction, such as efficient windows, doors, appliances, insulation, and so on. Check with the IRS or your accountant to take advantage of these tax benefits.

Double-pane windows help insulate your home. Both in winter and in summer, it's essential that windows be tightly sealed to protect against heat and cooling loss.

You can protect your home from the sun's rays with tinted windows or film—but remember that will also block warmth in winter.

Opening doors and windows whenever possible to allow the breeze to refresh your home is key to maintaining healthy indoor air quality. Using ceiling fans to move the air through the home helps to keep your family feeling cooler; you can keep the thermostat set a few degrees higher and avoid using air conditioning. Although all fans help with circulation, the Hampton Bay Gossamer Wind fan increases efficiency, saving an average of $20 per year, and improves circulation, creating a more comfortable home. The fans are available at Home Depot stores or online at www.fsec.ucf.edu.

Wind and Light "Thermal Chimneys"

Another design feature that lends light and air to a home is an interior "chimney" that carries heat from the kitchen upward to escape through roof vents. This central channel to the roof can also include skylights to carry light down into living areas of the home. In some homes the stairwell can serve as a thermal chimney with the addition of windows or vents and a fan near the ceiling; the principle is similar to an attic fan, which carries warm air upward and out of the home.

Jack Parker, an environmental studies professor at Florida International University, incorporated many green design principles into his own Miami home. His wife Janat showed me the thermal chimney he created over the kitchen stove and oven. A fan pulls the heat up the sunlit tunnel to the roof, where it's vented out through a high window. "This works so well that you can never smell my holiday dinners through the house—a little too well, I guess," she laughed.

This thermal wind chimney carries warm air up and out of the home quickly and efficiently.

(Trish Riley)

Add Insulation

Insulation helps prevent the flow of heat into or out of the home. With several types of insulation available, you'll want to choose a type that is appropriate for the climate where you live. You can learn more about finding appropriate R-value (or heat Resistance) from the U.S. Department of Energy at www.eere.energy.gov/consumer/your_home/insulation_airsealing/index.cfm/mytopic=11320?. Increase the insulation value of your home to R-30 for temperate climates or as high as R-38 in colder climates, especially in the ceiling and attic to protect from heat loss. New environmentally friendly foam insulation can be professionally blown into hard-to-reach walls and attics. Also many insulation products are made from recycled materials such as paper, fabric, even Styrofoam, a synthetic material that's destined to rest without rotting in landfills for centuries.

An old building technique has been revived by some adventurous homeowners that provides incredible insular value—straw bale building. Bill Hutchins of Helicon Works built a straw-walled addition to his Washington, D.C., bungalow.

Architect Bill Hutchins used an age-old technology to insulate his home—bales of straw under a stucco finish.

(Photo by Angie Seckinger, courtesy www.heliconworks.com)

An efficient heating, ventilating, and air conditioning system (HVAC) can reduce energy costs by 25 percent. Always keep filters clean and air ducts properly sealed for best performance. The Energy Star office also recommends a programmable thermostat, which they say can save about $100 per year.

Going Green

In dry climates, a swamp cooler provides cooling as well as adds moisture to the air. A fan blows air past a container with wet paper, wood chips, or other material, carrying moisture into the atmosphere, which cools the air by as much as 20 degrees Fahrenheit. The swamp coolers use a quarter less electricity than a conventional air conditioner and are much less expensive to buy.

Adjust the Thermostat

Another good way to conserve energy is simply to adjust your regular thermostat. You can reduce your energy usage by 5 to 15 percent by raising the thermostat temperature to about 78 degrees Fahrenheit in summer and lowering it to 68 degrees Fahrenheit in winter. If you do this at least during times when you're sleeping or not at home, you can extend the time when your heating and cooling system is not in use. Replacing older thermostats with a programmable model can reduce energy use, too.

Compact Fluorescent Lightbulbs

Compact fluorescent lightbulbs (CFLs) can dramatically reduce your electricity use, and you can make this quick, simple change in an afternoon without the help of a contractor or professional. While the bulbs are more expensive to buy than conventional lightbulbs at $1.50 to $3 per bulb, their long-term cost is less because they last many years longer—even without considering the reduction in your energy bill. The best benefit from this change will be realized when millions of people make the switch—so let's just do it! Begin by replacing the bulbs that are on the longest each day, such as the dusk to dawn outdoor lights. But remember that light pollution is another cause of concern, and if you don't need to leave lights on for safety or other reasons, you can save energy and reduce light pollution by flipping the switch to "off" when not in use.

CFLs can make a big difference to the environment and our pocketbooks because they use about 70 percent less energy than standard bulbs. Imagine—if every U.S. household would swap five of its most-used incandescent lightbulbs for compact fluorescent bulbs, annual energy costs would be cut by $6.5 billion, saving each family about $60 per year. In terms of greenhouse gas emissions, this would be like taking 8 million cars off the road, according to the United States EPA Energy Star Program.

When they first came on the market, CFLs weren't readily accepted because their glow was more green than yellow and rather unflattering, but these super-efficient bulbs have come a long way since their introduction. Today you can find full-spectrum CFLs that produce ambient light—and even if it's not quite the same as we're used to, the difference is negligible compared to the cost and energy savings you can achieve. This is a great way to make an instant reduction in your personal energy consumption and a huge impact on the CO_2 contributing to global warming.

Although early versions of the super-efficient bulbs were spiral-shaped, today you can find CFLs in many shapes and sizes, indistinguishable from incandescent bulbs. Because these bulbs have proven to be so beneficial, Energy Star has challenged all Americans to switch at least one bulb to a CFL to reduce greenhouse gas emissions by 450 pounds per bulb.

Choose compact fluorescent lightbulbs for energy and dollar savings!

(Courtesy U.S. Energy Star Program)

Energy Star Appliances

Household appliances are much more energy-efficient today than in the past. When selecting appliances for your new or existing home, try to select the most energy-efficient equipment available. Energy Star–rated appliances include documents stating the energy usage and cost you can expect; use these to calculate your savings, and take that into consideration against cost when making your final decisions. If the electronic appliance you're considering buying has the Energy Star logo, you know it's passed the energy efficiency standards of the U.S. EPA Energy Star Program, the current benchmark for efficiency in the United States.

An Energy Star–rated washing machine uses about half the water and electricity as standard models. Clothes dryers haven't become much more efficient, but you can reduce your dryer time by using a clothesline for some items, such as towels and linens that take a long time—and a lot of energy—to dry.

An Energy Star dishwasher can reduce energy by 25 percent and also uses less water than conventional models. Be sure to fill your dishwasher before running it, and don't use the prerinse or the heat-dry cycles.

Refrigerators with an Energy Star rating can cut electricity use by 15 to 40 percent. However, side-by-side models are less efficient than those with the freezer above or below the refrigerator. When locating your refrigerator, allow room for air to circulate around the condenser coils in back; don't place it near a heat source or hot appliance; check that door seals are secure; and set temperatures to 35–38 degrees Fahrenheit and 0 degrees Fahrenheit for the freezer.

Some consumers prefer gas appliances, and in cases where the gas is readily available, use of gas can be more economical and more efficient than electricity. Gas is plentiful in the United States; however, accessing natural gas supplies does require some mining, which can be invasive in some areas. Evaluate your local situation to determine whether gas or electric appliances will provide the best cost and energy savings to you.

Water Heater Choices

Solar water heaters are highly recommended as an immediate way to reduce energy costs. Although the solar system will cost more than a conventional water heater at purchase time, after a few years of energy savings, the solar heater will have paid for itself, giving you cost-free hot water for years to come.

New tankless water heaters don't expend energy to keep water hot when it's not in use. The system is a network of water pipes that keep water circulating through the house at all times and heats water instantly when you turn on the tap. This system eliminates the very inefficient process of keeping 40 gallons of water hot night and day in case it's needed, which consumes about 20 percent of your energy bill. These systems are more expensive than conventional water heaters, but will reduce energy costs by 10 to 30 percent over time. You can find these alongside conventional water heaters at national hardware stores, ranging in price from $200 for under-the-sink models to $600 to $1,000 and up for whole-house units.

Although the conventional water heater is cheaper, it loses about half the energy it expends to keep water warm. With the simple application of wrapping a thermal or insulated blanket around your water heater and pipes, you can minimize the heat and energy loss and increase the benefit, too. This is especially effective in colder climates. Be sure to locate your water heater in a heated space of the home, rather than in an unheated garage, where it will have to work harder to keep water warm.

Simple Fix: Unplug

Many small appliances, such as computers and stereos, have instant-on features that cause them to constantly use electricity. Many people assume that it's harmful to

Green Speak

"If half the nation's households replaced their regular TVs with Energy Star–qualified models, it would be like shutting down a power plant."

—Maria Vargas, U.S. EPA Energy Star Program

power off their computer every day, but in fact, it's good to give the machine the chance to untangle its memory storage and refresh for a new day. Plus, you're cutting your energy usage considerably if you power down at night instead of leaving the machine on. Most small appliances have sleep modes that use very little energy when engaged. But for a dramatic drop in energy usage, you must unplug some items, including cell phone chargers and all other chargers, when not in use.

Site Selection

You should take advantage of many things when deciding on the best location for your new home and in choosing the best way to position the house on your property. Before buying a lot, check with the Environmental Protection Agency and local environmental regulation agency to ensure that the property has clean air, water, and soil. Ask neighbors or check with area environmental groups to find out about potential problems or environmental issues, such as nearby chemical plants, landfills, or power plants, that may affect your property and quality of life in the future.

Hazard

When moving to a new area, check with local environmental groups to find out about any environmental issues that may affect your new home. Check that water, air, and soil quality has not been compromised.

When I moved to Florida, I bought a house before I realized that I was living in what should have been Everglades—developers had dredged and ditched nearly half of the Glades, creating an environmental strain on water supplies, wildlife, and the Florida Bay. My neighborhood was part of the problem.

Hitesh Mehta, a landscape architect who specializes in creating ecolodges, points out that sustainable site planning can lesson a building's environmental impact. His suggestions for siting ecolodges, detailed in his book *International Ecolodge Guidelines* (The International Ecotourism Society, 2002), can also be applied to home building. He suggests the following:

◆ Select a site that offers natural areas, and place your home in such a way as to minimize disturbance to the natural landscape.

◆ Check about accessible infrastructure for electricity, water, sewage, telephone service, and transportation needs.

- Find out if the site is appropriate for solar or other renewable energy resources.

- Determine if you can keep trees and foliage intact to shade and naturally cool the dwelling.

- Consider future development in the area, which might affect the site.

- Determine if the location is pedestrian- and bike-friendly so you can reduce your need for a vehicle.

It's wise to build in peace with your environment.

(Hitesh Mehta)

When developing plans for an ecolodge, Mehta not only considers placement of the building but also reviews the site's cultural history. Often locating his ecolodge projects in other countries, he likes to have sites evaluated by metaphysicians, such as feng shui masters, who assess the energy flow of the site and help to locate the building harmoniously. Finally, Mehta suggests taking time to sit quietly on the site and become familiar with the place through your senses—how does this location look, feel, sound, smell, and taste? Choose a place that feels right for you.

> **Green Speak** _____
>
> "You can have harmonious lodges in natural places. They don't have to be ugly. They don't need to pollute the environment. They need to be at peace with it."
>
> —Hitesh Mehta, landscape architect

Trees, Glorious Trees!

For the past 30 or 40 years, it's been unfortunately popular for developers to plow down all vegetation on a building site before beginning construction. Trees and native plants were seen as obstructions to the earth movers and materials needed to commence the project. All those carbon dioxide processors laid asunder …

But today we know better. Trees are valued for their role in absorbing carbon in the air and also for their tremendous cooling abilities. Temperatures in the shade can be 10 degrees cooler than in full sun, and 10 degrees can make a big difference when it comes to cooling your home. Trees also play an important role in helping to convert atmospheric CO_2 to oxygen, which helps reduce the buildup of greenhouse gases. Leave existing trees onsite, and build so that your home can take advantage of their natural shade on the roof to cut cooling costs. And although it may take a few years to realize the benefits of new shade trees, strategic planting of native trees to help shade and cool your home will offer a pleasant payoff in the future.

Trees add a wonderful ambience to your neighborhood and also help carry breezes, which can cool interiors when allowed to flow through the house. The architectural team Jersey Devil, famous for pioneering the design/build concept by which architects follow through with the construction of their conceptions, is known for positioning warm climate homes on stilts, raising living quarters off the steamy earth and up into the treetops to catch the cool breezes. Anchored by Steve Badanes, John Ringel, and Jim Adamson with a revolving cast of interested participants, the architects often pull little Airstream trailers onto the building sites and live on the property during construction—saying it allows them to get a feel for the place and informs their work.

Green Speak

"The key to reducing dependence on external resources is not to increase the supply but to decrease the demand."

—John Hammerstrom, builder of the first net-meter home in the Florida Keys

By reducing your energy usage at home, you can help reduce the emissions from power plants, which will help slow global warming. As more and more people make their homes more energy-efficient, the benefit multiplies. We can make a difference—and it begins at home with each and every one of us.

The Least You Need to Know

◆ Select the best materials for your home construction and interior decorating to save energy and create a healthier home for your family.

◆ There are many ways to reduce your home's energy consumption, whether building a new house or renovating an older one.

◆ Some innovative ideas for green homeowners include photovoltaic roof shingles, thermal chimneys, and compact fluorescent lightbulbs.

◆ Going green at home does not necessarily cost more than less environmentally friendly and energy-efficient options.

◆ Choosing the best location for your home can help protect your family from environmental hazards and make the most of natural resources, such as wind and sun.

◆ Landscaping can play a role in your home's energy efficiency as well as enhance the beauty of your home.

Chapter 6

Saving Water at Home

In This Chapter

- ◆ Our rapidly dwindling water resources
- ◆ Threats to existing water supplies
- ◆ Becoming aware of water conservation
- ◆ Measures you can take to save water in your home
- ◆ Reducing water usage outside your home

In our society today, we want many things we don't really need, but one thing that our very lives depend on is water. About 70 percent of the earth's surface is water, and our bodies are 90 percent water. Doctors advise us to drink eight or more glasses of the fresh stuff each day.

In this chapter, we'll take a look at how our water supply is currently being threatened by pollution and careless usage, and what we can do to begin protecting our water resources more effectively.

The Importance of Fresh Water

Lack of fresh water and proper sanitation is the most pressing public health issue in the world, said by the United Nations to kill 5 million people per year. Many diseases are linked to an inadequate supply of clean water washing through our systems, carrying nutrients in and toxins out of our bodies.

Our supply of fresh water is limited. Even the melting ice caps won't be able to help us. Although some of this melting fresh water will evaporate and be filtered into rain, replenishing our supplies on land, much of it drops into the salty seas. Scientists have postulated that frozen meteors of ice pelt the earth from space, but that hasn't proven to be a reliable or substantial resource for fresh water, either.

The big problem is that we treat our water resources with very little respect. We dump huge amounts of waste into rivers, streams, and the oceans and expect the water to carry away the crud just as it washes wastes out of our bodies. But when it comes to the rivers and oceans, there is no "away." We are dumping sewage, slurry, and all manner of other wastes into our finite water supply.

The world's coral reefs are diminishing rapidly, and the death is caused by nutrient pollution (runoff from farms and sewage), bleaching, and by rising sea temperatures caused by global warming. So you're thinking, good thing you had the chance to see the coral during that snorkeling or diving vacation a few years ago, right? So what's the big deal if we lose the reefs? The answer is: we just don't know. But we do know that the seas make up 70 percent of the earth's surface, and so far, we haven't found any aspect of nature that exists without significance—every single piece of the earth's natural ecosystems is interdependent, and when one piece goes missing, problems occur down the line. Furthermore, according to marine scientists at the Harbor Branch Oceanographic Institution, we have discovered 20,000 plants in the sea, including some with anti-cancer and other disease-fighting qualities. Our reckless destruction of the seas is likely to have far-reaching and very damaging effects for all living things.

Hazard

Contaminated water can cause problems far and wide. In 2006, an outbreak of E. coli associated with fresh spinach occurred in states across the country, with 199 illnesses and 3 associated deaths reported, according to the federal Centers for Disease Control. The outbreak was traced to contaminated water used to irrigate crops. Spinach was shipped around the nation—spreading E. coli contamination and subsequent illness from coast to coast.

Even when water has been processed at water treatment plants, growing evidence suggests that microbial contamination persists because filtration is not sufficient to remove these microscopic viruses and bacteria. Further contamination occurs in the pipelines as the water leaves the treatment plant and makes its way to your home. Some pipe materials, like lead (which is no longer in use in the United States, but old pipes could be lead) leach toxic substances into the water. PVC, another popular piping material, is presenting recently recognized dangers of chemicals leaching into water supplies. The water infrastructure across the country—our plumbing systems for conveying water into our cities, homes, and buildings—is reaching an advanced age, and these crumbling systems will need to be replaced on a large scale in the near future.

Going Green

Aging water pipes are causing sinkholes around the nation, according to a *Los Angeles Times* article, "The Looming Sinkhole Crisis" by Thomas Rooney. "When pipes break, two things happen: water or sewage gets out, and water or dirt gets in. Havoc results when dirt enters a broken pipe and is whisked away, as though on a magic carpet ride. Soon, even if only by a spoonful a day, the dirt disappears from above the pipe and below the sidewalk—or below the road, park, building, etc."

You may wish to consider installing water filtering systems in your home to eliminate such contaminants as the chemicals used in water treatment, those leached into the water during transmission, and microbial viruses and bacteria too small to be caught in traditional treatment filters. Experts suggest activated charcoal filters to remove organic compounds, and reverse osmosis filters to purify water. I know a pair of scientists who use both—the charcoal as an all-house filter, then the water is passed through the reverse osmosis system for drinking and cooking. And they start with "pure" treated city water!

Ensuring that your own tap water is fresh, pure, and safe can save you buckets of money because you won't need to buy bottled water and you'll be preventing tons of plastic trash from piling up in the landfills.

Next step—can we find a way to filter our used water as it leaves our homes and businesses (similar to the way septic systems work) to reduce the demand on municipal water treatment systems? I have seen systems like this in place at ecolodges and in demonstration projects, where filtering marshes are created specifically to process wastewater on site. Probably not an urban solution, but some sort of onsite filtering, such as with composting toilets, could go a long way toward protecting our water supplies.

Conserving Water at Home

Saving water at home is a crucial step in protecting existing resources. Adding in all the water that goes into everything we do, from growing the plants we eat to washing our cars, the average American consumes 1,600 gallons of water each day, adding up to a total usage of 3,600 billion gallons per day in the United States, according to *Natural Home* magazine. But you can do some things to cut down on water usage, like installing water and waste saving appliances as well—low-flow showers and toilets can help protect our water supplies.

Don't Let the Water Run Unnecessarily

First, cut down on water use at home by turning the faucet off! Never run water when it's not needed. For example, don't run the water when you brush your teeth: you can save 4 gallons per minute, which equals 200 gallons per week for a family of 4.

Going Green

When purchasing a new dishwasher or clothes washer, choose a water-saver model. Waiting to run these machines until you have a full load can save as much as 1,000 gallons a month.

Instead of rinsing fruits and vegetables, clean them in a bowl of water. Whenever possible, save water for secondary uses, such as watering indoor or outdoor plants. Don't rinse dishes before putting them into the dishwasher; just scrape off food and load them (and don't run the dishwasher until it's full).

Instead of using the garbage disposal to send food waste into the water stream, try composting your kitchen scraps and turning it back into rich soil for your garden. This will save water and prevent the need for filtering and treatment down the line.

When possible, turn off the shower while you soap up or lather your hair; then turn it on to rinse. If you can limit your shower to 5 minutes, you'll save an average of 1,000 gallons of water per month.

Install Low-Flow Showerheads and Toilets

Save 20 percent or more of your water by switching to inexpensive low-flow showerheads. They make up for lost water by aerating the flow so that you won't notice a loss in pressure and the water savings is significant.

Most new toilets now conserve water better than older models. Thanks to a mandate with the Clean Water Act of 1972, toilets went from using as much as 7 gallons of water to flush waste away to today's rule of no more than 1.6 gallons. Although a few design hiccups occurred along the way—some people had to flush twice to get the job done, wasting even more water!—today's low-flush toilets are reliable and effective.

But why do we have to pollute our fresh water just to carry off our daily waste, anyway? There are several models of waterless urinals and toilets on the market, and they are gaining in popularity. Flush-free waterless urinals use a urine-repellant liquid that helps move the urine into the piping system and also creates a vapor seal that keeps urine or sewer fumes from rising up through the pipes. They save as much as 3 gallons of water per use. Clivus Multrum has been creating composting toilets for more than 30 years. They've become popular in remote locations, such as parks, but the newest model—which uses just 3 ounces of water—is also suitable for in-home use. Users claim they are odorless, and they pull usable composted fertilizer out of the base of the commode (usually located on the floor below, such as in the basement).

Waterless urinals are even easier to maintain and are also increasingly popular in public facilities. This technology holds great promise for protecting our future water supply, and if you can find a way to use it in your home—if we can help this idea catch on in a large way—we will be protecting huge quantities of fresh water from contamination (although the level of water contamination from human waste pales in comparison to that of animal waste from factory farms, where 500 million tons are produced annually).

Going Green

Learn more about the Clean Water Act of 1972 at www.cleanwateraction.org and urge your congressional representatives to vote to increase our water protections.

Green Gamut

The EPA says that the Clean Water Act of 1972 has resulted in keeping 900 million pounds of sewer waste plus 1 billion pounds of toxic chemicals out of the water supply each year, yet thousands of miles of our waterways continue to be polluted. The Sierra Club declares we still allow 7 billion pounds of toxic chemicals to be dumped into our waterways annually and that 40 percent are unsafe for fishing or swimming.

Saving Water Outdoors

American lawns soak up a staggering 10,000 gallons of water each, every summer—one third to one half of a household's annual water consumption. We also dump 100 million pounds of pesticides and fertilizers on our lawns, which contribute to greenhouse gases, contaminate water supplies, and degrade soil and lawn quality.

However, we can modify our landscaping practices in several ways to save water, protect fresh water supplies, and reduce CO_2 emissions.

Lawn Care Options

Lawn mowers use 300 million gallons of gas each year and are notorious unregulated polluters, often emitting many times more greenhouse gases than a car.

Consider buying a new-fangled but old-fashioned push mower that runs on human power instead of electricity, giving you a great workout and producing zero emissions in the process. New models on this old standard are reputed to be much easier to use than the old ones. You can find them at www.yardiac.com, priced at $100 to $400.

And don't mow your lawn too short—it will use more water and allow more weeds to grow.

Landscaping Options

Choose plants with low water needs for year-round landscape color and save up to 550 gallons each year. Native plants—those that are indigenous to your area—are a better choice for your lawn because they're acclimated to your area's waterfall levels and drought seasons and have natural resistance to pests in the region. They need less water, fertilizer, and pesticides.

Xeriscaping is a landscaping technique that replaces turf with drought-tolerant plants and plans out garden plots to capitalize on water availability. For example, it locates thirsty plants in lower areas where water might puddle and groups plants with similar needs together.

Add lawn waste, such as clippings and grass trimmings, to the compost pile, and then use compost to enrich soil and conserve moisture when planting new trees and flowers. Use mulch and compost liberally around plants.

Wear baseball cleats or special spiked garden shoes while walking around your lawn to aerate soil.

Irrigation Options

Irrigate from a free local water source, if available, such as a backyard lake or pond. The water you use for your yard will simply flow back into the pond, another reason to keep poisons to a minimum on your lawn.

Ask your plumber or builder whether it's feasible to run *gray water* outside to be reused in lawn irrigation. Check with your local government to make sure this is allowed.

Water your lawn in the morning and when the wind is minimal to ensure that the water finds its way to your plants rather than to evaporation.

def•i•ni•tion

Gray water is water from your laundry, shower, and kitchen sink—it's been used and is no longer drinkable, but it can still be used to water the lawn or rinse the car.

Other Ideas

There are many other little things you can do to use your water resource more effectively.

- ◆ Instead of hosing off patios, sidewalks, and driveways, use a broom—you'll save as much as 80 gallons.

- ◆ Wash your car on the lawn so the runoff will go back into the ground. It will be naturally filtered before finding its way back to the groundwater supply, instead of carrying driveway dirt and oil into the sewage system.

- ◆ Instead of paving your driveway with asphalt, choose gravel or tile pavers that you can set an inch or two apart to allow rain water to wash down into the ground instead of running off into the sewers.

- ◆ Capture rainwater with a rain barrel placed under your gutter spout, and use the water to irrigate your plants.

- ◆ If you want to go all out, build a cistern to collect rainwater for all or most of your household use. These operate with simple filtering systems and can eliminate your need for public water altogether.

Encourage birds and wildlife to visit your yard by creating habitat hideaways with bushes and trees and positioning feeders and freshwater bowls or birdbaths around the yard. Call your local agricultural extension agent to find out which flowers you can plant to attract birds and butterflies to add to the ambience your family can enjoy.

It's important that we begin thinking about water a little bit differently than we may have in the past. When we recognize that water is a precious fluid of limited supply, it's easier to remember to treat our supplies with respect and to make the most of each drop rather than shunting it on out to waste. Every drop of water is truly the elixir of life.

The Least You Need to Know

- We can't live without fresh, clean water, and thousands of people die each year for lack of it.

- Turn off the tap when you're not using the water.

- Save 20 percent or more of your water by switching to inexpensive low-flow showerheads.

- Whenever possible, allow rainwater or water from your hose or sprinkler to run back into the ground instead of across driveways or roads and into sewer systems.

- Try cutting back on lawn irrigation by planting native plants, which are best suited to your climate moisture levels.

- Be careful not to contaminate water supplies with household chemicals, pesticides, or other poisons that may run into streams or water sewer systems.

Chapter 7

Reusing, Reducing, and Recycling Waste

In This Chapter

- Prevention as the first line of defense in waste management
- Breaking away from our consumer mentality
- Preserving vast quantities of natural resources and limiting greenhouse gases
- The importance of using natural materials

In this chapter, we'll consider ways that we can help cut back on the huge piles of garbage piling up in landfills around the world. Quite often, the goods put out as trash still have considerable usable life left, either as they are, like used furniture, or when broken down into components, such as used electronic equipment. Not only can we extend the useful lives of our resources this way, we can also protect the environment—chemicals frequently leach away from landfills, contaminating the air, soil, and groundwater nearby.

Managing Waste

When it comes to dealing with the waste we produce on a daily basis, we have three plans of attack: reuse, reduce, and recycle.

Reuse

Reusing items for as long as possible before discarding them is always best. When the time comes to get rid of something, first consider whether you can extend the life of the item by selling it or donating it to a service, such as Goodwill, the Salvation Army, or similar local organizations in your area. Another option is to list it online at www. freecycle.com to find a new owner.

Reduce

Reducing waste is an important step toward preserving natural resources, conserving energy, and protecting our land and water from contamination.

When you buy things, think about waste and choose items with the least disposable packaging materials. Avoid plastics whenever possible because they don't biodegrade. They also produce toxic by-products in production as well as in recycling processes. Select items wrapped in paper and cardboard or—the best choice—not wrapped at all, whenever you can.

Recycle

Recycling helps keep natural resources in use instead of in the landfills. If your town doesn't offer a recycling program, ask your representatives to implement recycling for your community. The U.S. EPA reports that in 2005, recycling and composting kept 79 million tons of material out of landfills and incinerators, about 32 percent of U.S. solid waste. This effort was successful thanks to curbside recycling and community drop-off stations. Let's take a look at some of the ways different types of materials can continue to be valuable in subsequent incarnations.

Glass

One of the nation's biggest trash companies, Waste Management, says they recycle more than 1 million tons of glass each year, with 80 percent of that going back into new glass bottles. Yet that's only 20 to 25 percent of the glass we use; the rest goes to the landfills.

That is a great deal of waste, especially since glass is one of the easiest materials to recycle. The reuse program we used to have, which allowed consumers to return bottles to the grocer for deposit refunds, was effective. However, this practice was essentially abandoned with the advent of one-use individual containers, such as aluminum cans and plastic bottles, so the recycling progress was diminished. Now some municipalities are lobbying to reinstitute bottle deposits to encourage reuse as a way of keeping so much valuable material from reaching the end of its functional life by hitting the landfill.

The nation's biggest campaign to clean up litter, Keep America Beautiful, was organized by packaging companies and soft-drink trade associations which lobby against bottle deposit legislation in favor of litter taxes. This saves the corporations the work and money associated with processing recycled containers, and keeps production of new containers high along with litter and garbage levels.

We can toss glass bottles of all colors into our recycling bins, and the glass will be sorted electronically by color, then used accordingly. Recycling glass saves 40 to 50 percent more energy than recycling plastic or aluminum. Recycling also saves as much as 70 percent in raw materials as creating new glass, which means less emissions and greenhouse gases are produced in the process and less glass goes to waste in the landfills. Glass containers can move from the recycling bin back to the supermarket shelf in just a month.

Always rinse all glass bottles and food containers before placing them in recycling bins. You can also recycle broken glass, ceramics, window glass, and lightbulbs, but separate these from food and beverage containers, including glass bottles.

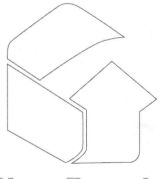

Look for this logo indicating recycled glass products that can be recycled again and again.

(Courtesy Glass Packaging Institute)

Glass Recycles

Paper

The paper industry, with more than 500 mills around the country, is the third largest energy user in the nation and the biggest consumer of wood, according to Treecycle Recycled Paper Co. The average American uses 700 pounds of paper each year; our nation uses 100 million tons of paper each year. It takes 20 trees to make 1 ton of virgin paper.

Wood pulp is used to make most paper today, although paper can also be made from many other sources of fiber including fabric and other, more sustainable plants, such as *hemp* and *kenaf*.

def•i•ni•tion

Hemp and **kenaf**, both fast-growing and easily cultivated fibrous plants, are excellent resources for paper and fabric making.

According to the Environmental Defense Fund, half of the world's tropical forests have been destroyed over the past half-century, and the United States has less than 10 percent of its natural forests still intact. More than 50 percent of the world's living species of flora and fauna reside in the remaining native forests on Earth. Now we know that our forests help offset the carbon emissions we produce by soaking up the carbon dioxide through photosynthesis and producing fresh oxygen to help sustain life on Earth. So destroying our forests contributes to global warming in two ways—with the energy emissions created in the process of logging wood and paper milling and by the loss of the carbon sink provided by the trees.

Green Speak

"If the current rate of deforestation continues, the world's rain forests will vanish within 100 years—causing unknown effects on global climate and eliminating the majority of plant and animal species on the planet."
—NASA Report

While paper and timber companies proclaim they plant as many new trees as they cut down, tree farms do not begin to replace native forests, which provide habitat to so many species.

Turning trees into pulp for paper is a toxic business, and the toxic chemicals are rinsed back out to municipal sewers, streams, and rivers. Dioxin-contaminated rivers, like the Pigeon River in Tennessee, suffer fish loss and gender-bending—the few fish species left in the polluted, black water show signs of hormone disruption, such as males with eggs but lacking some male characteristics. European consumers have made it clear to paper manufacturers that they'd rather have unbleached, chlorine-free paper than toxic streams, and the paper industry complies. Many mills have separate facilities to create TCF—Totally Chlorine Free—paper for export to Europe and bleached paper for the uninformed U.S. market, which mistakenly equates "white" with "clean" when it comes to toilet paper, diapers, paper towels, and other disposable paper products—all of which would work just as well in toxic-free, unbleached form.

More than 40 percent of the garbage in landfills is a paper product, although TAPPI, a pulp and paper industry organization, says more paper is recovered for recycling than is sent to landfills.

> **Green Gamut**
>
> Super-polluter plants are often found in rural areas where people are desperate for jobs and where the polluting aspects of the industry don't get much attention or cause the alarm that might arise in a better educated or more highly populated community.

Recycling paper saves 70 percent more energy and uses 55 percent less water than creating new paper. It also reduces water pollution by 35 percent and air pollution by 74 percent. The EPA reports that 70 percent of the 24 million newspapers published in our country each year is recycled, and about half of all paper is recycled. Waste Management reports that they recycle 2.5 million tons of the stuff.

However, the increasing demand for paper and wood products and resultant production is outpacing recycling success. While recycling paper is an essential step in the paper trail, it is not a solution to the major problems posed by continuing deforestation and global warming.

However, we can take action to help create a market for recycled paper:

- Buy recycled paper products made with post-consumer waste. Choose unbleached or chlorine-free whenever possible. Look for PCW (post-consumer waste) or TCF (totally chlorine free) on the label.

- Recycle newspapers to save trees from being cut down; the process reduces the amount of energy needed to produce more paper by about half and reduces air pollution emissions. Read more newspapers online, and don't print out things you can more easily and effectively read and store in your computer.

- Use washable rather than paper plates, cups, or napkins.

- Choose tree-free paper products, such as those made from hemp and kenaf. Try this directory of tree-free paper suppliers: www.rainforestweb.org/Rainforest_Protection/Wood_Alternatives/Tree-Free_Paper/.

Plastics

Plastic, created with petroleum, has become a very popular material in many products since petroleum became more readily available after World War II. Although we use about 32 billion pounds of plastic each year, unfortunately, we only recycle about 2 percent of it.

Cheaply created in the laboratory, plastics are so popular because they're very durable. The downside of that has become painfully apparent in recent years. Plastics don't biodegrade—they never go away. Although they do break down into smaller particles over the course of hundreds of years, the process releases toxic gases, and the plastic is still there.

Plastic waste is piling up everywhere: in dumps, rivers, and roadsides. The *Los Angeles Times* reports that a pile of trash the size of Texas floats in the Pacific Ocean, and trash, most of it plastic, covers the nearby beaches of Midway Atoll in Hawaii. More than 200,000 of the 500,000 young birds born on Midway Atoll, an important breeding roost for the albatross, die from eating plastic, according to a *Los Angeles Times* special report, "Altered Oceans."

Plastic trash is filling our waterways and littering our land.

(Courtesy Container Recycling Institute)

Marine scientists estimate that 80 percent of the trash in the oceans is plastic, outnumbering the most basic fish food—zoe plankton—by 6 to 1. Plastic litter in the oceans kills more than 100,000 marine creatures each year, and when the creature dies, the plastic in its digestive system makes its way back into circulation to kill something else.

Then we have those ubiquitous plastic bags. More than 200,000 of these hit the landfills every hour; that's 500 trillion per year, according to Planet Ark. The United States uses 100 billion per year—that's 552 per family—and usually each bag is used for just half an hour or so to carry goods home from the store. The bag might find a second use, such as receptacle for pet poop, but most are discarded. Haven't you noticed them blowing in the wind, caught in fence rows and trees everywhere?

And when the grocery bag boy asks you, "Paper or plastic?" remember that paper isn't necessarily the natural option, either. The American Forest and Paper Association reports that Americans used 10 billion paper grocery bags in 1999, requiring 14 million trees.

Bring Your Own Bag

In Ireland, the plastic bag issue is being successfully addressed. In 2002, a tax was levied on the bags, reducing consumption of them by 90 percent and generating millions of dollars for environmental programs. The nation used 1 billion fewer bags in its first year, saving 184,755,614 gallons of oil in the process, according to www. ReusableBags.com.

Similar bag tax bills have been introduced in cities and states in the United States; and many stores have taken the lead by charging customers for disposable plastic bags, encouraging them to bring their own or buy reusables onsite instead. These measures could go a long way toward bag waste reduction in our communities.

The EPA says that 34 percent of all plastic bottles are recycled. Recycling saves about half the energy used to make a new plastic bottle and conserves petroleum. We can extend the functional life of plastic through recycling into many different products, including other containers and even durable planks to replace wood in outdoor building projects, such as walkways and benches in parks.

> **Green Gamut**
>
> Thirty million water bottles are disposed of each day in the United States. Only 15 percent are recycled because we carry them on the go and toss them in trash cans for lack of public recycling receptacles (*E Magazine,* Sept/Oct. 2003).

Which Plastics Are Recyclable?

There are many different kinds of plastic, each made with a different blend of chemicals, some of which are toxic. (See Part 4 to learn more about phthalates and other toxics in plastic and PVC.) Some of the chemicals can't mix with others, and if the wrong kinds of plastics are blended together, the result can be a ruined and contaminated batch of melted material that cannot be recycled.

Follow manufacturer recommendations for recycling. Find a symbol on the package to guide you. The familiar triangle of chasing arrows is used to indicate recyclable or recycled goods, with a designating number in the center. If the number is 1, 2, or 3, the item is recyclable in your municipal recycling bin. Items labeled with 4, 5, 6, or 7 should not be recycled with other plastics, although there may be separate opportunities to recycle those items. Check with your local recycling facility for the specific rules for recycling plastic in your community.

What Can We Do?

We can do some things to reduce plastic use and reuse what we have:

Ask your grocery store if it accepts used shopping bags, Styrofoam trays, and egg cartons for recycling; many do. Always recycle any plastic hazardous waste containers with other hazardous wastes and not mixed with other items.

Use cloth instead of paper napkins and towels. Use washable cups and plates instead of paper or Styrofoam.

Take your own reusable bag(s) when shopping so you don't have to use disposable bags from the store.

Replace plastics with reusables and biodegradables. Chemical companies know petroleum resources are dwindling and so are already at work developing "green" chemicals that are much friendlier to the environment. A new biodegradable plastic has been developed using corn and soy products. Biota water is packaged in these bottles, which biodegrade in commercial composters in just a few months.

Fill your own reusable bottle at home instead of buying individual-size water bottles.

Aluminum and Other Metals

Aluminum production requires hydropower, meaning dams and mining, both of which damage habitats, destroy natural resources, burn energy, and produce carbon dioxide and acid rain. Recycling aluminum prevents much of that damage from being repeated and saves more than 90 percent of the energy used to make new aluminum.

A report published by the Worldwatch Institute states that Americans consume the contents of 100 billion cans per year, about half of global consumption. In 2004, we only recycled 40 percent of these cans, which means that 810,000 tons of aluminum were landfilled, the equivalent of pouring the gross product from 5 aluminum processing plants right back into the ground. If we had recycled that aluminum instead, it would have saved 16 billion kilowatt hours—enough to power 2 million homes in Europe. Recycling one can saves enough energy to power a computer for 10 hours!

However, aluminum isn't just used in cans. It is a major component of automobiles and building materials, and it's all recyclable. Steel and iron are also common natural metals used in building, and both are recyclable. The steel industry says it remelt 18.2 billion cans in 2003.

Choose glass or metal for containers or as material for other applications over plastic because both are produced from natural resources without the addition of toxic chemicals and without producing such toxics in manufacture or breakdown. Always recycle glass and metal containers and other items, either curbside or at municipal facilities, where you may be able to receive compensation for metals you collect and return for recycling.

Hazardous Wastes

Hazardous wastes include paints, thinners, any flammable liquids, used motor oil and oil filters, insecticides and pesticides, toxic cleaning chemicals such as oven and drain cleaners and spot removers, fluorescent lightbulbs, batteries, pool cleaning chemicals, tires, and propane tanks.

You cannot include these hazardous wastes with your municipal garbage, but most cities offer drop-off collection sites for hazardous material disposal. Avoid buying toxic items (check for warning labels) whenever possible and dispose of hazardous wastes properly—check with your municipal waste department for special instructions or drop-off locations for hazardous wastes.

Use rechargeable batteries so you never have to throw them away. Batteries contain mercury, so do not toss them into the trash, but reserve them for hazardous waste disposal.

Electronic Wastes

Electronics represent one of the most visible signs of our modern consumeristic society. Technology moves forward at such a fast pace that our computers, cell phones, televisions, and other small appliances can become obsolete within a few years, and sometimes it's just too tempting to pass up the latest in gadgetry, speed, and services. If we've got the disposable income, we buy more disposable electronics. We've been well trained. The EPA says we're tossing phones at a rate of 130 million per year and computers at 250 million over 5 years.

Computer monitors and televisions often contain lead, and other electronics may contain mercury and many other toxic metals, *brominated flame retardants*, and plastics that can migrate into groundwater and air if not properly disposed.

def•i•ni•tion

Brominated flame retardants are used in many materials including sleepwear and mattresses. But research has found that some flame retardants are carcinogenic and others are endocrine disrupters. These chemicals migrate from the clothing and furniture they're applied to and leach into water from landfills and into the air through incineration, spreading their contamination into the food chain.

As tempting as it is to stay on the cutting edge of technology by constantly updating our equipment, we as consumers might want to take a breath before buying each new gadget. Ask yourself if you really need that new cell phone, or if your old one works well enough to keep for another year. Or extend its life by donating it to a charity that reprograms the phones and provides them to those in need of emergency communication devices. Go over the same thoughts before buying new computers, televisions, video players, and home phone systems. Before sending these items to the trash, consider whether you might know someone who can still get some good out of your discards.

If you're buying a new computer, consider donating your old one. Service projects such as www.Recycles.org provide a national networking exchange system to help those with electronics to donate find those in need.

It's important to realize that even if you have deleted files from your computer, they are still lurking in the system and can be retrieved until the disc has been properly cleaned. See Appendix B for a list of many data-cleaning programs provided by the EPA.

Zero Waste Stream

The "Zero Waste" principle is a movement to eliminate waste and, at the same time, modify standard practices to reduce waste generation. The Zero Waste International Alliance has formed to provide resources and encouragement around the world. The idea is to move our waste processes toward patterns such as the sustainable cycles in nature. The goal is to eventually ban materials that can't biodegrade or stay within the sustainable cycle from production. So try to restrict your purchases to recyclable or recycled materials to help reduce your waste stream down to zero. Reducing our use of fossil fuels, thus energy, is a big part of reducing our toxic wastes, too. For more info, visit www.zerowaste.org.

New Zealand has set a national goal to be waste-free by 2015, with 70 percent of the local communities committed to the program thus far.

Converting Waste to Fuel

The practice of burning waste products was virtually abandoned years ago for good reason—burning trash releases all manner of toxic gases, CO_2, and other greenhouse gases into the atmosphere where they cannot be contained and their damage cannot be controlled. We know now that some of these gases contribute to global warming. So why are some companies proposing new initiatives to burn garbage and calling it an energy generator?

And yet, we obviously can't keep piling garbage up in landfills.

The bottom line is that some garbage should not be burned, such as plastics, which emit so many different chemicals, and paper, which could be put to better use through recycling. But some waste, such as livestock waste, can actually be used as a power source.

Some dairy and livestock farms have begun processing their waste onsite using anaerobic (oxygen-free) digesters, where gases from the degrading waste are captured and redirected as fuel, called biomethane, for use on the farm, and to the community, as in the case of the Central Vermont Public Service, CVPS. Several farms across the state—each with 500 or more cows—process the animal waste through *anaerobic digesters* to produce between 1.2 and

def•i•ni•tion

Anaerobic digesters are pits or bins where animal waste is "cooked" at a temperature of about 100 degrees Fahrenheit for 3 weeks, which converts it to methane, and the gas is then forced out through pipes to be used for energy. The dry material left behind is said to be largely odorless, and is used as animal bedding and to replace sawdust.

3.5 million kilowatt hours each year. This is one of those win/win solutions to a huge waste problem.

Methane gas is also produced in landfills as all of the many materials break down. This gas can be captured and used to fuel the landfill operation itself, which is done in many landfills today. This practice serves a dual purpose—it prevents the greenhouse gas methane from entering the atmosphere and contributing to global warming problems, and it provides energy for the landfill, saving energy and other natural resources.

The Least You Need to Know

- When in need of something new, consider looking for the item at a resale shop if a recycled product will work for you.

- When making buying decisions, look for items with minimal disposable packaging.

- When disposing of an item, consider whether it might have use for someone else or another purpose before discarding it in the trash.

- Recycle as much of your waste as possible.

- There is a movement to reduce our waste stream to zero by developing fully sustainable cycles of resource use.

- Waste from landfill and from livestock farms can be processed to capture greenhouse gases and to use them as energy.

Part 3

Green Living on the Road

Transportation is one of the biggest contributors to global warming gases, and we can reduce the impact that our travel habits have on our future in many ways. You can modify your own car and change your driving habits; you can upgrade to a fuel-efficient vehicle; and you can take more advantage of mass transit opportunities if they're available to you.

Traveling far from home provides more opportunities to begin saving energy and cutting down on your greenhouse gas emissions. You might consider ecofriendly hotels and select a method to offset your travel miles with carbon exchanges—trade your miles for a few days' investment in wind or solar power, for example.

"Your new tandem hot rod is just soooo groovy."

Chapter 8

Green Driving

In This Chapter

- ◆ The evolution of fuel efficiency
- ◆ Driving and maintenance tips for efficiency
- ◆ A review of alternative fuels
- ◆ Future fuel possibilities

In this chapter, we'll look at ways to stretch our fuel consumption, from increasing the efficiency of our vehicles to finding ways to cut down on our individual driving patterns. We'll also take a look at alternative fuels of today and in the future.

The Price of Oil Consumption

The United States uses more oil than any other country, and two thirds of that oil goes right into our gas tanks. As the Union of Concerned Scientists points out in a 2005 report, every gallon of gasoline burned expels 24 pounds of polluting greenhouse gases. And our vehicles produce more than 20 percent of the greenhouse gases produced in the United States.

Going Green _____

According to HybridCars.com, if we would increase our fuel efficiency by just 5 miles per gallon, we could reduce U.S. oil consumption by 1.5 million barrels per day. This would reduce carbon dioxide emissions by 55 million metric tons per day.

The Corporate Average Fuel Economy (CAFE), a government standard established in 1975, resulted in a quick reduction of fuel use and emissions, saving $92 billion in 2000, reducing oil consumption by 60 billion gallons of gas, and preventing 720 million tons of greenhouse gases from contaminating the air. And although the technology exists to reduce our auto emissions considerably, without enforcement, those standards have been allowed to drop, so that our fuel efficiency has decreased over the past 25 years and our government and automakers resist attempts at regulation.

Today, the United States spends $200,000 per minute on foreign oil. Yet the technology exists to increase our fuel efficiency 40 to 80 percent using *hybrids* and *fuel cells*.

It's easy to imagine oil and auto executives laughing all the way to the bank about the gas-guzzling station wagons and sedans they perched on truck chassis and sold at huge profit margins for $30,000 and more to masses of American consumers. Their partners in government share the toast.

The Environmental News Service carried a story on a report from Environmental Defense stating that the United States owns 30 percent of the world's autos and contributes 45 percent of automobile exhaust carbon dioxide. ExxonMobil earned a record-breaking $39.5 billion in profit in 2006—the largest annual profit of any U.S. company, ever. And the United States, under the administration of George W. Bush, refuses to sign the Kyoto Protocol, a worldwide mandate to reduce greenhouse gas emissions.

def•i•ni•tion _____

Hybrid cars are specially made to run on both gasoline and electricity, getting more miles to the gallon and conserving fuel. **Fuel cell** technology is hydrogen-based alternative fuel that is promising in development but is not yet commercially available.

Coupled with sky-rocketing gas pump prices, Americans are suddenly recognizing that global warming is a serious concern, and citizens are taking an interest in doing what they can to reduce fuel costs and their contribution to global warming.

The Other Price of Oil Consumption

In late 2006, I had the opportunity to fly into southern California at night. From a great distance I could see a strange, orange cloud—it looked like tasty cotton candy.

But as the plane flew closer, this cloud was not nearly as delectable. It was the perpetual cloud of smog that hangs over the Los Angeles basin, lit from below by city lights. Angelinos live in the most polluted city in the nation, although you can find a brownish-yellow haze on the horizons of many cities today. The good news is that California air quality has improved over the past few decades as the state has developed some of the toughest emission laws in the world to try to overcome the pollution problem.

According to the American Lung Association, 4 million Californians have lung disease, which air pollution can cause and aggravate and which can be fatal. In 1990, the organization worked with the state to promote legislation to move 2 percent of the state's vehicles toward zero-emissions within 8 years. General Motors had introduced electric cars, 90 percent cleaner than their gas-powered predecessors, so the goal did not seem unreasonable. But promotion and development of the cars halted, stymied by the fact that the cars could travel only 100 miles or less before needing a charge, which takes hours. Several automakers sued the state, claiming that the proposed legislation to reduce auto emissions was illegal, something that only the federal government could enact. The U.S. government, under President George W. Bush, stepped in to support the auto makers.

Finally in 2006, a dozen states took the Environmental Protection Agency and the federal government to the Supreme Court, insisting that Clean Air standards be enforced. A lawyer representing the government argued that complying with Clean Air regulation could have a negative effect on the economy because 85 percent of the U.S. economy is dependent on industries and activities that emit greenhouse gases. Yikes! We have a lot of work to do, and it clearly begins at the philosophical stage.

The Power of Consumer Demand

Japanese carmakers Toyota and Honda have surged ahead in the field of uber-efficient vehicles, and their hybrid models far outpace the increasingly inefficient American cars in sales. Suddenly, Detroit auto manufacturers are stepping forward with announcements that they, too, can develop more efficient vehicles. All it took was consumer demand—an excellent demonstration of our power.

Automobile fuel economy provides us with a perfect example of industry following the

Hazard

One downside of hybrid vehicles that many consumers complain about is that they don't have the fast pick-up that some drivers like.

money. Many large companies have demonstrated again and again that when a profit is at stake, they will go to great lengths to protect that potential revenue stream.

So let's see what we can do to move ourselves and the world in the right direction. Informed car owners and buyers can make wise choices to increase fuel efficiency—simple steps drivers can take to make the most of each gallon of gas they put into the tank.

Squeezing Every Drop from Each Gallon of Gas

When you're in the market for a car, choose the most efficient vehicle you can. Check online and among friends for fuel efficiency reports—the EPA ratings posted on the cars at dealerships and online are often unrealistically optimistic. Study comparisons of hybrid and other alternative vehicles at www.greenercars.org, www.hybridcenter.org, or www.fueleconomy.gov.

Don't buy a bigger car than you need—the heavier it is, the more fuel it takes to move it around.

You can cut fuel usage before you even get into the car. Check the trunk and remove anything you don't really need. Weight adds burden to the engine; like piling more packs on a mule, more horsepower is needed to pull the load, and that takes more fuel. So unload anything you don't need. Simplifying is a great process for the spirit as well.

Going Green

Different engines have different octane requirements. Be sure to check your engine manual and use a fuel of the recommended grade.

Don't pile things on top of the car or on a rack if you don't have to; remove bike racks when not in use.

Maintain your car according to manufacturer's recommendations. Have you had the engine tune-up performed as needed? Following your automaker's guidelines for maintenance and proper fluids, especially the correct grade of motor oil, will improve your mileage by an estimated 2 percent. And for the best mileage, select the lowest octane gasoline recommended for your car.

Engine problems, such as a broken oxygen sensor, can reduce fuel efficiency by as much as 40 percent. If your "check engine" light comes on, see your mechanic right away. If your air filter is clogged, a new one can net you another 10 percent in efficiency.

Are the tires inflated to the proper levels suggested for your car? Check the label pasted inside the driver's door for tire inflation recommendation per square inch (PSI). Use the highest suggested inflation value to get the most efficiency—tires can make up to a 3 percent difference in fuel efficiency.

You may have been advised to drive without air conditioning because air conditioning uses additional fuel, but that doesn't mean open the windows. Open windows cause more "drag" on the aerodynamic projection of the vehicle, slowing you down more than you save in fuel economy by not using the air conditioning. If you can be comfortable with the windows up and the vehicle airflow vents open without the air conditioning turned on, that's the most efficient mode of car travel. Tint your windows to keep the car more comfortable in warm weather.

Have you noticed how some drivers tend to blast on the gas and rush ahead in traffic? It's an inconsiderate way to deal with this communal aspect of city living, and the result is often flaring tempers; sometimes even accidents occur as a result of drivers cutting in and out of traffic lanes. Ask anyone over 40—things were much different when people were considerate of one another instead of pushing to get ahead of everyone else all the time.

Instead of jumping on the gas and hitting the brake as you move through traffic, use a more measured approach. Surging forward and making quick stops burns excess gas and raises your and other drivers' blood pressure at the same time. Who needs it? Going with the flow can save you up to 30 percent on mileage on the highway and about 5 percent on city streets.

Staying within the speed limit helps save gas, too. For every 5 miles per hour over 60, you're burning about an extra quarter's worth of gas. When driving on the highway, use your highest gear, overdrive or cruise control, to get the best mileage.

Don't leave the car running when you're not moving. Running the car while sitting in line or waiting for someone just burns gas for no reason, polluting the air and costing you money. Knock off the engine whenever you're sitting for more than a minute, unless you're in traffic. It's easy to turn it back on.

One thing that makes hybrid cars especially more efficient is that they shut down automatically when the car is stopped for brief periods at stoplights.

Carpooling, Biking, Walking, and Combining Trips

Of course, reducing our use of fossil fuel–powered vehicles is a no-brainer in the equation of becoming more environmentally friendly. Let's look at how we can reduce this use.

Carpooling

Carpooling is a great way to reduce the number of drivers in the highway lanes during rush hour, as well as the amount of toxic emissions rising above each urban city, creating that barely discernible yet undeniable haze on the horizon. Check with your coworkers and neighbors to find people heading in the same direction as you morning and night so you can take advantage of the high-occupancy lanes on the highway and get home sooner each day.

If your driving needs are limited, consider joining one of the membership-based car share programs, Flexcar or Zipcar. Both have cars—many super-efficient hybrids—parked around urban metro areas for members to use as needed, by appointment. Depending on how often you use the cars, rates run about $8–$10 per hour with gas, insurance, and maintenance included. Both companies continue to add cities to their networks. Check Appendix B for contact info to determine whether cars are available where you live or in cities you plan to visit.

Biking and Walking

Can you bike or walk instead of driving now and then? If your need to travel is all about visiting a local market or neighbor, consider using your feet or your bike. And enjoy the benefit of a little exercise at the same time.

According to the International Bike Fund, 40 percent of trips are within 2 miles of home. If you choose to bike instead of drive, you will reduce water pollution, because bikes don't drip petroleum fluids. You will also reduce air and noise pollution since bikes don't emit toxic fumes and are much quieter than cars. Another advantage of riding a bike is that you'll be able to reach your destination without tangling in traffic, plus you'll burn calories and give your cardiovascular system a workout! For more info on the benefits of biking, visit www.ibike.org.

Combining Trips

Instead of dashing out to the store when you need a single item, create a list and make the trips less frequently if possible. You're not one of those low-exercise, high-risk individuals in the studies, are you?

Alternative Fuels to Cut Costs and Cut Carbon Emissions

In the past few years, as oil quantities dwindle and gas prices skyrocket, several fuel alternatives have come on the scene. Many of these innovative solutions have been around for decades but never became the mainstream because oil was readily available and automakers developed technology around the commodity. A sort of partnership developed between oil companies and auto companies, and they worked in tandem to push competition aside. As the companies grew in size and power, it was easy to generate the support of government through incentives to use their products and subsidies to produce them.

Today, as we reach the end of the age of oil, both automakers and government are taking another look at alternatives along with us.

Ethanol: Savior or Smoke and Mirrors?

When the U.S. public suddenly became interested in renewable fuels and global warming, triggered by the release of former vice president Al Gore's film, *An Inconvenient Truth*, ethanol garnered a lot of attention. Made with corn in the United States, ethanol has been popular with farmers in the corn belt for years because it created a market for their product.

Although the idea of developing ethanol received a great deal of support from government, there are some problems with it at this point. For one thing, if we use all our corn supply to produce ethanol—leaving none for human or animal food—we would only have enough to make 1.5 million barrels per day of ethanol, a very limited supply compared to our daily oil consumption of 21 million barrels per day. Furthermore, converting corn and soybeans into fuel is a very energy-intensive process, which actually burns nearly as much or more energy than the resulting ethanol fuel would provide. Unless production is powered by renewable energy, such as wind or solar, its benefit is negated.

Nonetheless, ethanol is currently available as an alternative fuel at many stations across the country, especially in the Midwestern farm states. Ethanol costs about the same as gasoline at the pump, and blends of up to 10 percent (E-10) can be used in all vehicles made since the 1970s without modification. Higher blends such as E-85 (85 percent ethanol and 15 percent petroleum gasoline) require special engines, which I discuss in Chapter 9.

Brazil has been a leader in developing ethanol using sugar cane instead of corn, which creates a fuel that has more energy than corn-based ethanol and is more efficient. Seventy percent of Brazilian vehicles have flex-fuel engines that can run on gasoline, ethanol, or a blend of the two. Most pumps provide both choices of fuel in Brazil, and the nation has a nearly independent fuel supply, according to *The New York Times* (April 10, 2006).

Further development of ethanol processes in the United States could yield a more viable product. Scientists are studying the possibility of making ethanol fuel from waste plant material, such as corn stalks and other chaff left in the fields after harvesting. Called *cellulosic* ethanol, this would leave current harvests intact and help dispose of material that otherwise has no recognized value. While these studies are promising, they are still in development and not providing any alternative fuel solutions at this time.

The Union of Concerned Scientists (UCS) regards ethanol as a useful fuel to begin moving us toward alternatives, but does not see corn ethanol as a promising answer to our emerging fuel needs of the future.

The UCS suggests that rather than only investing heavily in corn ethanol development, we diversify our focus on developing cellulosic ethanol along with other *biofuels* and renewable energy alternatives as well as efficiency and conservation efforts, utilizing ethanol while we reinforce those options with research and development. As in other areas in need of change, such as our power supply, the solution is more likely to be found by developing several resources that can work compatibly together, rather than expecting to find a single "silver bullet" answer to all of our clean energy and clean fuel needs.

def•i•ni•tion

Cellulosic refers to the source material, specifically to plant matter such as wood chips, stalks, grasses, and leaves rather than grains that are also food.

Biofuels or biomass fuels refer to fuels derived from sustainable biodegradable resources including wood, plant material, and grains, such as soy, which is converted to oil and used as biodiesel oil.

Biodiesel: "Fryer Fuel"

Biodiesel is also an emerging fuel resource that can be developed and supported by our nation's farms. Biodiesel is an oil, usually made from vegetables, soybeans, or canola. Used oil works fine in diesel engines that are adapted to use it, as long as it is filtered before going into the engine. Refined biodiesel oil that has been prefiltered is usually a better solution for the health of your engine. As a matter of fact, the diesel engine was originally designed to run on peanut oil, but that fuel was displaced by petroleum-based gas when the diesel engine was taken up by automakers.

Individuals who are mechanically knowledgeable can modify auto and truck engines relatively simply at a cost of a few hundred dollars. I've met several people who have personally made the changes to their engines and who collect free used fryer oil from fast-food restaurants (nicknamed "greasel") to power their vehicles.

Liz Donnelly and David Silver adapted the engine of their camper truck and drive around the country demonstrating the biodiesel technology to anyone interested in learning about it. They also help people make the changes to their own vehicle engines.

Liz Donnelly and David Silver demonstrate their home-brewed greasel engine.

(Trish Riley)

Willie Nelson, who travels the nation year-round with his band in a big diesel bus, has teamed with a fuel station in his home state of Texas to provide biodiesel fuel to truckers passing through. Nelson and his partner are helping to spread the biodiesel stations around the country, creating a network for large diesel trucks to gas up *au naturel.*

Biodiesel can be made from 100 percent vegetable oil to be petroleum free (called B100), or it can be blended with conventional diesel to reduce petroleum use and CO_2 emissions. When it burns, biodiesel still produces carbon dioxide, so it does not relieve us of greenhouse gases, but it can be produced without producing gases, which means it's more environmentally friendly than straight petroleum.

Fryer oil will thicken in cold temperatures, so it may need additives or a heating unit in the engine to prevent solidification. Partial biodiesel, called B20 because it's 20 percent biodiesel, remains fluid because of the petroleum in the mix. The downside of B20 is that it offers little reduction in foreign oil dependence or greenhouse gas emissions, and diesel emits 10 to 20 times more toxic particulate emissions than conventional gasoline.

I recently toured a small business in Vermont where biodiesel is processed and sold to farmers for farm vehicles and equipment. The owner, Scott Gordon, is a former chemistry professor who co-founded the biodiesel manufacturing and distribution business with a former student whose ideas showed promise. Gordon says his driving motivation was to create a truly sustainable business, and that appeals to his customers. The business, Green Technologies, collects used grease from restaurants for a small disposal fee and then filters and processes it through several vats until it becomes biodiesel.

Biodiesel can cost about the same as diesel gasoline and up to twice as much. Gordon says that he sees even more potential for biodiesel as a home heating fuel than as engine fuel.

Green Speak

"We live in a sustainable world. The problem is, there aren't many green tools."
—Scott Gordon, founder and CEO, Green Technologies, LLC

Like ethanol, biodiesel is not likely to provide a single-point solution for our automotive fuel needs. But combined with ethanol and other measures, such as fuel economy, efficiency, and conservation, it can help to reduce our dependence on fossil fuels and our emissions of the greenhouse gases that cause global warming.

Check out Appendix B to find biodiesel distributors around the country and more information on switching your diesel vehicle to biodiesel.

Natural Gas: CNG

Although most current U.S. supplies of natural gas are from within the states, an increase in demand could create a dependence on foreign supplies of the fuel. While vehicles and other power generators that run on natural gas do emit 75 percent less toxic and greenhouse gases than petroleum-based diesel fuels, natural gas still is a nonrenewable, nonsustainable fuel that requires drilling for extraction.

However, among passenger vehicles, the Honda Civic GX, which runs on compressed natural gas (CNG), is one of the cleanest cars available in terms of emissions, matched only by zero-emission electric cars. Natural gas is cleaner than diesel, but our future supplies are limited, making this a good temporary solution addressing the problem of greenhouse gas emissions.

The bottom line in terms of vehicle efficiency is fuel economy, by which we can make great strides in curbing our dependence on foreign fossil fuels and our greenhouse gas emissions, while the alternative fuels available to us today make small steps in the right direction. As with all other changes on the horizon toward a clean energy future, public demand is the most effective tool in setting the stage for a healthy, renewable energy future.

The Least You Need to Know

- Maintaining your car properly can reduce your gas consumption.
- There are several alternative fuels in development today, including cellulosic ethanol and biodiesel.
- There are more promising fuel possibilities on the horizon, such as hydrogen fuel cell vehicles.
- Ethanol made from corn is not very energy efficient and will drain our food supply of corn, but other sources are currently being studied.
- Biodiesel fuel can be produced from a number of domestically produced crops and can be available relatively soon, although it is not emission-free so still contributes to global warming.

Chapter 9

Hybrids and Other Green Options

In This Chapter

◆ Reducing oil consumption through greater fuel economy and efficiency

◆ A look at hybrids

◆ Biodiesel and flex fuel vehicles

◆ Hydrogen fuel cell cars: not ready yet, but …

The health of the world depends on reducing our output of carbon dioxide, a large portion of which comes from automobiles used in the United States. Technology exists today to reduce that by half or more and perhaps to zero in the future. Consumers are catching on quickly, and carmakers are jumping to their tune; nearly every major auto manufacturer has an innovative, high-efficiency vehicle on the market today and something even better in the works. This single area can make a tremendous impact on our CO_2 emission problem, the main cause of global warming.

In this chapter, we'll look at some of the options available for more efficient vehicles today and in the near future.

Hybrids

Hybrids are cars that run with two drive trains, both gasoline and electric. The batteries are recharged by the gasoline engine while in operation. The gasoline engine runs the car and the electric motor supplements the power.

Japanese automakers Toyota and Honda took the lead in developing hybrid cars in the past few years, while domestic automakers put their money on gas-guzzling sport utility vehicles. However, as gas prices soared and scientists insisted we take seriously the threat of global warming, hybrids have surged ahead in popularity. Honda was first to introduce a hybrid to the U.S. market in 1999. But Toyota's Prius, which was the first gas/electric hybrid to become commercially available in 1997 (in Japan), has become the top-selling hybrid car in the United States and the world in 2006. For the first time in history, Toyota out-ranked General Motors as the leading car maker in the first quarter of 2007.

> **Green Gamut**
>
> "About a third of CO_2 produced in the United States comes from transportation, and 90 percent of that travel is by automobile."
>
> —*An Inconvenient Truth* by Al Gore (Rodale, 2006)

Hybrid cars (but not hybrid SUVs) use about half as much gas as conventional cars and produce half or less toxic emissions. Hybrids cost an average of $4,000 more than comparable conventional cars but will save about 20 percent more than that in reduced fuel costs over the car's lifetime. The Union of Concerned Scientists (UCS) advises that adopting hybrid technology available today will enable us to increase fuel economy to 40 miles per gallon (mpg) or better immediately, reducing the continuing CO_2 emissions from automobiles while hydrogen fuel cell technology is further developed—the best solution currently on the horizon to our automobile energy needs.

Our federal and state governments offer tax incentives and credits to buyers of efficient hybrid vehicles, ranging from $250 to as much as $3,400 for buyers of the most efficient Toyota Prius. The credit, set to run from January 2006 to December 2010, was set for reduction after 60,000 new vehicles were sold. For Toyota, that happened in just six months' time. Hopefully new credit and incentive programs will be instituted in response to the increasing market demand for these vehicles. In comparison, the Internal Revenue Service offered credits of up to $100,000 to business buyers of SUVs, the least efficient vehicle on the road. Encouraging fuel economy and efficiency makes much more sense.

New vehicle models are constantly in development as automakers strive to meet consumer demand for more fuel efficient and environmentally friendly vehicles. The auto industry anticipates growth of hybrid sales from 251,000 in 2006 to 800,000 in 2012. Another study by The Freedonia Group of Cleveland, Ohio, estimates that demand for hybrids will reach almost 8 million by 2020. Here's a sampling of a few on the road today.

> **Green Gamut**
>
> "In 2015, we would cut our national oil use by 2.3 million barrels per day—nearly as much as we currently import from the Persian Gulf—if we increased fuel economy to 40 mpg over the next decade."
>
> —Hybrid Center, Union of Concerned Scientists

Toyota Prius

Toyota Prius, the first hybrid introduced (in Japan), remains the most popular and the most efficient hybrid vehicle on the road today with economy as high as 60 mpg on the highway. The Prius is commended for its ability to run on electricity during high-speed highway travel. The Prius continues in popularity even after outrunning its $3,150 tax credit. Priced from $22,000 to $23,000, the Prius provides superior fuel economy at 50 to 60 mpg. Prius has no conventional engine, but compared to the conventional Toyota Corolla, the Prius takes just two years to earn back its higher price in reduced fuel usage.

Toyota Camry Hybrid

The Toyota Camry Hybrid combines the larger mid-size four-door sedan style with efficient hybrid technology to produce a vehicle that nets about 30 to 40 mpg, with a faster acceleration rate than the hybrid Prius—one of the biggest complaints about the efficient little cars is their slow pick-up. The Camry Hybrid costs about $25,000.

Honda Insight, Civic, and Civic GX

Honda created a super-efficient hybrid with the Insight, the first hybrid introduced to the American market in 1999. However, the tiny two-seater caught the attention of only a limited audience and was quickly surpassed by the more standard economy-style Prius.

The Honda Civic soon followed suit with a hybrid model that was comparable to the Prius, but with a lower mpg and sluggish driving performance, according to reports. In 2006, Honda introduced an improved and highly touted Civic Hybrid destined to give Toyota a run for its money, although still not quite as efficient as the Prius. The Hybrid Civic cost $23,000 in 2006 and clocks about 50 mpg when highway and city mileage are combined.

Honda Insight.

(Trish Riley)

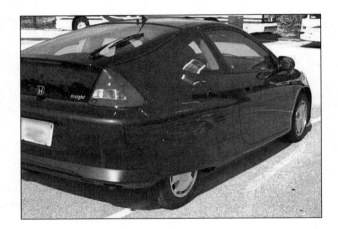

The Honda Civic GX is a unique car that runs on Compressed Natural Gas (CNG), a plentiful resource in the states, although it does require mining, which can be destructive. Available as a fleet vehicle since 1998, the GX is now available commercially in California and New York. There are 750 CNG fuel stations across the country, many exclusively used by municipal fleet vehicles, but Honda also sells a home-fueling appliance kit so owners can charge their car with natural gas overnight. The car will travel about 200 miles on a tank, producing near 0 emissions. According to Honda, the CNG internal combustion engine is the cleanest available.

Nissan Altima Hybrid 2007

Nissan introduced the first hybrid vehicle made in the USA, the Altima Hybrid 2007. Produced in Tennessee, it is another low-emission, high mileage gas/electric vehicle, with the added advantage of more conventional interior than many other hybrids, which can be a little space-age looking and somewhat spartan. The Nissan hybrids aren't on every dealer's lot, but the vehicles are becoming increasingly available.

Hybrid SUVs

The Ford Escape Hybrid, the first hybrid SUV, was introduced in 2005 and has found a comfortable niche as a public transport vehicle, outfitting taxi fleets in San Francisco and New York City. Miami expects to have 1,000 city hybrids by 2012.

Ford reports that a city-use Escape Hybrid saves 1,666 gallons of gas and prevents the emission of 32,000 pounds of CO_2 over 100,000 miles. Compared to the Ford Escape conventional engine (nonhybrid), this hybrid takes just two to three years to pay for the cost over the conventional model—the least payback time of any hybrids with a matching conventional model. The 2007 Escape Hybrid costs around $25,000 and gets about 34 mpg in combined driving.

> **Green Gamut**
>
> Because hybrid vehicles utilize their electric engine features for in-city driving, their use as taxis and public vehicles capitalizes on the fuel efficiency, using less gasoline and producing less CO_2.

In 2007, the Toyota Highlander is also available in a hybrid, listed from $30,000 to $34,000. It's classified by California as a Super Ultra Low Emission Vehicle (SULEV) that gets 27 to 32 mpg.

Lexus brought the first luxury hybrid SUV to market in 2006 with the Lexus RX 400h, a SULEV that costs $11,000 more than its nonhybrid counterpart. With 28 to 33 mpg, the Lexus hybrid costs $38,000 to $40,000.

Mercury offers a Mariner Hybrid in 2007, costing about $27,000. General Motors offers hybrids of the Sierra and Chevrolet Silverado trucks.

Plug-In Hybrids

In 2006, GM announced its intention to revive an improved version of the electric vehicle technology it introduced in the 1990s with new plug-in hybrid cars set to come off the racks in 2008. Californians who welcomed the EV (electric vehicle) in the '90s have questioned its demise, and some have suggested that the nonpolluting, oil-free car was killed because it didn't support the oil industry.

> **Green Gamut**
>
> *Who Killed the Electric Car?* is an independently produced documentary of the corporate and government influences at play in the quick demise of this small vehicle. But some contend that the electric car flopped simply because its range was limited to about 100 miles before it needed a lengthy recharge.

GM has announced a goal for its Saturn Vue SUV plug-in hybrid to achieve record-breaking 70 mpg in 2009—a promising development that will be great to see in the future.

Going Green

If you're mechanically inclined and have about $10,000 to invest, you can convert your small, lightweight, gas-powered vehicle to an electric, although it is said to be a difficult job best left to experts. *EV World: The World of Electric, Hybrid, Fuel Cell, and Alternative World Vehicles* provides a conversion kit and instructions for the self-motivated: www.evworld.com/evguide.cfm?section=evguide&evtype= conversion.

These are just a few of the emerging options for hybrids; some are more efficient and economic than others, but all are moving in a direction desired by consumers and beneficial for our future energy and air quality.

Green Speak

"Switching the U.S. fleet over to hybrids that more than double fuel economy could cut our global warming pollution as much as 275 million metric tons of carbon equivalent emissions by 2025."
—Union of Concerned Scientists

Biodiesel and Clean Diesel Vehicles

Since gasoline prices in Europe have been higher than in the states, highly fuel-efficient diesel vehicles have developed greater popularity there.

But a disadvantage of diesel has been high emissions of cancer-causing particulate matter and sulfur, which causes acid rain as well as contributes to the greenhouse effect. In 2007, the U.S. EPA instituted new low-sulfur diesel fuel regulations, initiating a new generation of clean diesel and renewed interest in diesel vehicles in the United States. BMW and Mercedes Benz introduced top models of passenger diesel vehicles, both of which can also run on B5 and B20 blends of biodiesel made from grains and grasses, which does not emit any sulfur, and petroleum diesel. An average 30 percent higher fuel economy, lower emissions, higher mileage, and less gasoline usage are all benefits of these new diesel options.

I had the pleasure of driving a Mercedes E320 Bluetec, a total luxury sedan that runs on "clean" diesel. Driver and passengers could easily detect its comfort, style, and performance level in keeping with its $550,000 price tag. In terms of economy, it is rated at 26 to 37 mpg, so it still has a way to go to meet the emerging need to double fuel economy and eliminate emissions, but it does provide a luxurious opportunity to move a step above less efficient ultra-comfort cars.

Volkswagen has been incorporating diesel into its fleet for years, so is well-positioned at the forefront of the clean diesel movement. The 2006 Jetta is competitive with hybrids with 36 to 41 mpg, but emissions are probably still more noxious than hybrid electric vehicles.

Flex Fuel Vehicles

Flex fuel vehicles (FFVs) are aptly named because they have flexible fuel requirements that enable them to use straight gasoline or a blend of up to 85 percent ethanol, 15 percent gas, called E85. They've been produced and in production for several years, and many makes and models of cars are FFVs. Check your car by reading the label inside the fuel hatch door, or check online at www.e85fuel.com. As long as your car is made to accommodate ethanol, it will perform just fine, except that mileage will be reduced by 20 to 30 percent because ethanol does not have as much energy content as gasoline.

Hydrogen Fuel Cell Vehicles

Hydrogen fuel cell vehicles are not yet available on a mass scale, but most auto manufacturing experts seem to think that these will be the best long-term solution to our automotive needs.

Hydrogen is the most abundant element in the world. Hydrogen fuel cell vehicles emit only water—zero greenhouse gases. One problem with fuel cells, though, is that electricity is required to produce the hydrogen by splitting it away from other molecules. This is an energy intensive process, but future technology with renewable energy supplies are promising.

Scientists at EVermont, a hydrogen research facility in Burlington, Vermont, have built a hydrogen fueling station, powered by a nearby windmill, that serves one hydrogen-burning vehicle, a converted Toyota Prius used by the local public works department.

Green Speak

"It's time to get serious. The vision for a hydrogen future is crucial. Civilization has transitioned from one primary energy source to another over thousands of years ... and in all likelihood, it will be hydrogen's time in the years ahead. In the interim, it's equally crucial to commercialize all logical alternative fuels, optimize the use of conventional fuels, and conserve through improved efficiencies to address energy and environmental needs in the short- and mid-term. To do less is to short change our future."
—Ron Cogan, editor and publisher of *Green Car Journal* (Fall 2006)

When I visited the site, engineer Harold Garabedian provided a tour of the station and explained a bit about the car. He and his colleagues are working to determine whether hydrogen fuel cell vehicles could be a good alternative for public vehicles in the cold climate of Vermont. Because the car emits water, this could conceivably create a puddle that could freeze in cold weather and pose a potential road hazard, but he felt that was an unlikely scenario.

Hazard

Some people remember the Hindenburg when they think of hydrogen fuel—the gigantic hydrogen-filled zeppelin airship exploded in flames in 1937. But hydrogen was not to blame for the fire, according to investigators, and hydrogen fuel cell vehicles are considered safe because hydrogen is no more flammable than gasoline and is not self-combustible, although gasoline is.

The station they've built has the capacity to serve up to six fuel cell vehicles, but at this time only their modified version is available. Garabedian said the station and vehicle cost between $2 and $3 million, emphasizing that they are far from ready for commercial production. "The car is ready," he said, but the infrastructure must be developed. There are only a few dozen hydrogen fuel stations in the country.

Garabedian thinks hydrogen cars are safer than conventional gasoline vehicles and that hydrogen is a totally clean energy. "I think we're moving incrementally to a cleaner and safer place."

Daimler Chrysler has been a world leader in the development of hydrogen fuel cell technology, with more than 100 test vehicles around the world. The company expects fuel cells to increase in popularity over the next decade and projects improvements that will make the vehicles less expensive.

General Motors plans to release the world's largest test market of fuel cell vehicles in the fall of 2007, putting 100 of its Chevrolet Equinox fuel cell SUVs on the road in major cities of California, New York, and Washington, D.C. Based on the results of this test run, the company projects commercial release of the vehicles in 2010.

This modified Toyota Prius runs on hydrogen.

(Trish Riley)

Honda has introduced a fuel cell concept car, the FCX, which it says will lead their way into production vehicles in 2008. The company is moving forward aggressively to trump the competition in the development of increasingly efficient fuel cell technology, achieving efficiency levels that are twice those of hybrids and three times those of gasoline-powered cars. The company says these concept cars give an idea of what their commercially available FCX vehicles will be like when they are ready for marketing, in "a couple of years." Honda has presented a small, compact sports coupe that provides a nice view of the sleek, sportier hybrids of the future.

As you can see, while automakers are rushing to satisfy consumer demand for more efficient, cleaner automobiles, we are just at the forefront of the movement to cleaner cars, and the technology is improving rapidly. Without a doubt, consumers should consider buying a vehicle that gets at least 40 mpg, with the lowest possible emissions, for their next vehicle purchase.

The Least You Need to Know

- Traditional gas-powered internal combustion engines consume massive quantities of oil and produce massive quantities of greenhouse gases.

- We can dramatically reduce our oil consumption and CO_2 emissions by doubling fuel economy.

- The hybrid vehicle market is becoming increasingly competitive with more options and better prices.

◆ Biodiesel is a fuel created from vegetable oil that can be used in specially converted vehicles to save gas, but it still produces some emissions.

◆ Hydrogen fuel cell cars are the most likely solution for the future.

Chapter 10

Transportation Beyond Home Base

In This Chapter

- ◆ The good and bad aspects of carbon exchanges on the environment
- ◆ Ways to cut back on your CO_2 emissions without avoiding travel
- ◆ Ecologically responsible choices for traveling
- ◆ Ecologically sound vacation choices

Any time you use power, you produce greenhouse gases—when you power your home or your business; drive your car; or take the bus, train, or plane. Now you can ease your conscience a bit if you can't avoid using greenhouse gas–emitting services when traveling beyond home base. In this chapter, we'll learn how to balance out our emission output to a net-zero basis so we don't make global warming even worse while we're trying to find workable means of producing energy that's emission free. It's not the solution to our global warming problem, but it's a step in the right direction.

Carbon Neutral Exchanges

The Chicago Climate Exchange was formed in response to international governmental agreements to allow industries and businesses to buy credits to offset their industrial pollution. Six greenhouse gases—carbon dioxide, methane, perfluorocarbons, hydrofluorocarbons, nitrous oxide, and sulfur hexafluoride—could be mitigated through purchases on the Chicago Board of Trade.

The program began in the 1990s when it became necessary to remove lead from gasoline because its toxic effects on human health were recognized, and then was used again to try to reduce the amount of sulfur dioxide emissions because of acid rain damage. One company that produced a high level of one of the gases, for example, could buy credits from another company that produced something that mitigates the gas.

Critics considered the SO_2 program successful because the emissions were reduced ahead of regulatory requirements and at less than anticipated cost. Today more than $2 billion changes hands annually in the SO_2 exchange. The model has grown beyond big business as a way to help individuals support environmental progress in other areas as well. Carbon off-setting has become all the rage as a way to take our trips and eat cake, too.

Good or Bad?

Let's get clear about something right off: trading a long-distance trip for credits with a wind farm does not make the carbon dioxide and other emissions produced during the trip go away. Carbon off-setting, or the use of *green tags*, is based on the idea that you can trade a few smokes for an infusion of oxygen, but it's not really that simple or that clean.

Some offset services say they'll plant X number of trees for every mile you travel, at a rate of $X, which you pay them to make yourself feel better about doing what you want to do. But how many trees can they plant? How many years will it take those trees to mature so they can produce more oxygen and soak up more CO_2? What happens in the meantime? What if those trees are subsequently mowed under in favor of a parking lot? It can surely happen.

def•i•ni•tion

A **green tag**, or carbon offset, is money you pay to offset your energy usage.

Other services take your "green tag" and invest it in renewable technology, such as wind or solar power. All this investment is good, of course, but does it make a difference in the long run? Each of these programs requires administrative fees—is that the best use of your offset dollars? Only in as much as it helps move us toward a better understanding of our environmental challenges and energy issues, raises awareness, and helps set the stage for truly effective changes to come will this idea make a difference.

So yes, buy offsets, but don't quit there. They'll help buy time and fund research, but real changes in our energy structure are coming, so be prepared.

This is consumerism's retail therapy at its height ... addressing global warming.

Green Speak

"Most of the carbon credits being sold to industrialized countries come from polluting projects that do nothing to wean the world off fossil fuels, such as schemes that burn methane from coal mines or waste dumps. The bulk of fossil fuels must be left in the ground if climate chaos is to be avoided."

—*Carbon Trading: A Critical Conversation on Climate Change, Privatisation and Power*, published by the Dag Hammarskjold Foundation

Carbon Exchange Opportunities

If you want to purchase carbon offsets, you can use online carbon calculators to determine your carbon emissions. Then select the best plan from which to purchase your carbon offsets.

But first, consider whether the company selling the green tags is a for-profit or nonprofit (your nonprofit purchase is tax deductible), and look into how exactly they make the investment. Do they contribute to renewable energy, plant trees, or fund research? Another important consideration you'll want to ask about is would the project be happening without the funds from the offset arrangement? You want to add value to the project, not just displace funds for another purpose. Find the combination you feel will make the most of your investment dollars.

Some carbon exchange opportunities include the following.

RECs

Renewable Energy Credits (RECs) provide an easy way to participate in the mitigation program. Pay a little extra on your utility bill to buy wind or other renewable energy, which the power company will then add to the power resources on the grid serving your area. Not all companies offer the option, but if it's available to you, it will help encourage a market for renewable energy.

RECs for consumers evolved from much larger scale business trading of greenhouse gases as discussed above. The practice continues to be controversial because of the wide profit margin that does not go toward mitigating greenhouse gases and related problems.

NativeEnergy.com

*Native*Energy.com is a for-profit venture owned by Native American tribes, most of which are nonprofit. One of the most popular offset ventures, *Native*Energy sells RECs and offsets for new project construction or support for those already in action. The company supports wind farms, biogas generators, solar installations, and methane capture projects. Many companies partner with *Native*Energy to help their customers participate in the offsetting program, including CLIF Bars, Stonyfield Farms, and the film *An Inconvenient Truth*. It costs $12 to offset 1 ton of CO_2 with *Native*Energy.

> **Going Green**
>
> You can use *Native*Energy's travel calculator to determine your own travel offset balance: www.nativeenergy.com/travel/

CLIF Bar, the popular natural energy snack bar for hikers, adventurers, and sports enthusiasts, helps their customers go green by selling "cool tags." Each $2 cool tag offsets 300 tons of CO_2—about as much as a tank of gas emits, they say. CLIF Bar sends the $2 directly to *Native*Energy in support of their programs.

Use the *Native*Energy online calculator at www.nativeenergy.com/lifestyle_calc.html.

Carbonfund.org

Carbonfund.org is a nonprofit organization that charges $5.50 for one climate tag per ton of carbon dioxide offset—they estimate each of us produces 10 tons of CO_2 emissions per year. How do they calculate your impact? They consider many factors in their carbon calculator. They estimate that if you drive a car that gets 41 or more mpg, such as a hybrid, your car emits 6,000 pounds of CO_2, costing you $4.96 to offset. If you drive an SUV, you're looking at 10 to 18 mpg, emitting 20,000 pounds for $49.89. Adding all our carbon-emitting activities together, Carbonfund estimates we produce 23 tons per year per person, and they'll offset that for $8.25 per month—or offset your family's emissions for $33 per month.

Carbonfund invests in wind, solar, and methane power projects as well as initiatives to help low-income communities by providing lower-cost renewable energy and clean air and water. Their projects are located around the United States. In Michigan, an electrical generating station uses methane from landfills; in California, a biomass digester converts farm animal wastes into methane, which is then used to power a desalination water plant to provide community drinking water.

Carbonfund also buys GHG credits from the Chicago Climate Exchange and supports responsible forestation projects, managed to ensure that mature trees remain onsite.

Use the Carbonfund online calculator at carbonfund.org/site/pages/calculator/.

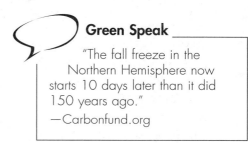

Green Speak

"The fall freeze in the Northern Hemisphere now starts 10 days later than it did 150 years ago."
—Carbonfund.org

Climate Trust

Climate Trust is a nonprofit organization based in Portland, Oregon, and located online at www.CarbonCounter.org. Funding projects to provide electric power so diesel trucks needn't idle to keep systems running when not driving, among other projects, the fund charges $10 per ton of CO_2 emissions offset.

Mass Transit: Planes, Light Rail, Rapid Transit, Trains, Buses

While air travel is a big greenhouse gas producer, there are times in today's fast-paced world when it is the only solution to our travel needs. Finding ways to balance out the environmental cost of that convenience is one way to lessen the negative impact of airplane emissions. Utilizing other mass transit options which are more energy efficient than automobiles whenever possible is another way to reduce your overall global warming contribution.

Planes

In recent years air travel has become much less expensive, and thus the airline industry has grown remarkably. Paired with global trading, the earth truly has grown smaller in the sense that the farthest reaches of the globe are much more accessible to so many more citizen travelers who desire to explore the world beyond their home base.

Alas, airplanes are high-emission vehicles, so the increase in air travel has resulted in a dramatic increase in airline emissions. Many companies have arranged to offset the travel needs of their employees by partnering with green tag companies such as those described above. Individual travelers can also make similar offset trades to "neutralize" the impact of their travel.

To date, one airline has taken responsibility for offsetting its flights. Nature Air of Costa Rica is a small airline with eight small planes serving the cities, rainforests, and volcanoes of Central America. The privately owned company took the initiative to offset its carbon output by calculating emissions based on the amount of gasoline burned each year. Working with the Costa Rican government, the company determined the cost of its emissions at more than $12,000, which it then reinvested in reforestation and habitat restoration projects across the country. Although perhaps unrelated to its ecofriendly investment, the company boasted a 25 percent growth in its first year of emission-free service.

In September 2006, Richard Branson, founder of Virgin Records and a host of Virgin companies including Virgin Atlantic Airlines, announced that all profits from his airline and train companies would be diverted to Virgin Fuel, a firm devoted to researching alternative renewable fuel choices for the transportation industry. Branson said that transportation and energy companies must take the lead in developing environmentally friendly business strategies. The Virgin Fleet operates as efficiently as possible, such as by reducing the weight of cargo and by towing planes as near the runway as possible to avoid extending engine idling. A carbon offset program for Virgin customers is expected to be released in 2007.

Richard Branson pledged $25 million as prize money for a contest designed to spur creativity in addressing global warming. The Virgin Earth Challenge will award the individual or group that comes up with a commercially viable design that will remove human-caused greenhouse gases from the atmosphere for 10 years without producing any harmful effects. The end result must contribute to the stability of Earth's climate. For more information, visit www.VirginEarth.com.

As 2006 drew to a close, the European Union was wrestling with a controversial proposal to charge airlines for their carbon emissions, similar to the taxlike charges imposed on other industries as a result of the Kyoto Protocols. The United States government was among those opposed to the idea, preferring instead a global-wide standard which is expected to take years to develop and expressing concern that the surcharge would add a burden to the airline industry, but advocates said the cost would likely be passed along to passengers.

> ### Green Speak
>
> "We must rapidly wean ourselves off our dependence on coal and fossil fuels. By launching the $25 million Virgin Earth Challenge, the largest ever science and technology prize to be offered in history, we want to encourage scientists and individuals from around the world to come up with a way of removing lethal carbon dioxide from the earth's atmosphere. By competing for this prize they will follow in the footsteps of many of history's greatest inventors and innovators, but in this case potentially save the planet. It is our hope and belief that the winner of the Virgin Earth Challenge will help to reverse the collision course our beautiful world is currently on. They will not only make history but preserve history for many, many generations to come."
>
> —Sir Richard Branson

Europe has been trading greenhouse gases very effectively, in keeping with the Kyoto Protocol, which it supports. The European program is called the EU Emissions Trading Scheme.

Light Rail

Light rail is similar to trolleys from the 1940s and 1950s. Light rail transit cars are much like electric streetcars, but today's versions operate with more speed and efficiency than those in the past and are more efficient because they carry more passengers, according to Light Rail Now in Austin, Texas. However, some transportation specialists believe better alternatives exist.

"Light rail is very expensive," said Chapin Spencer, founder of Local Motion of Burlington, Vermont, a nonprofit company that promotes bicycle use as well as walking, running, and skating. The company works in the local community to create pathways for two-wheel and pedestrian traffic for safety, fun, health, and environmental reasons. Chapin says that *light rapid transit* is preferable to light rail transit, at least in his community.

def•i•ni•tion

Light rail refers to electric transit cars that are similar to trolleys.

Light rapid transit refers to buses with minimal stops along dedicated traffic lanes to provide faster, more efficient service to passengers.

Light Rapid Transit

Chapin described a system of buses that move through traffic in dedicated lanes with fewer stops and facilitated ticket systems to reduce the time for passengers to get on and off the vehicles. The systems are streamlined so they can serve riders in a faster, more efficient way, thus making them a more attractive mass transit option than buses which sometimes offer ominously long routes and consequently have markedly low passenger rates. Another appreciable feature is that the system can be implemented without the expense of new vehicles or developing new transit lines—both are already in place. Light rapid transit is currently being used in many cities in the United States and around the world.

Other light rapid transit systems are similar to monorail lines such as those serving multiple terminals at many airports—above-ground electric trains with one or more cars that glide *Jetsons*-like from station to station.

Nearly 200 cities in the world provide urban underground mass transit systems that convey hundreds of thousands of residents to and from metro areas daily in a cost-efficient and timely manner. Interestingly, cities worldwide have discovered that creating ambient subway tunnels for their underground transit systems increases passenger volume and perception of safety. The Soviet Union boasts the most beautiful transit tunnels, with mosaics and elaborate marble architecture—the system is used as a showcase for public art displays.

Hazard

The Natural Resources Defense Council reports that about half of all school buses in the United States operate on diesel fuel, exposing more than 23 million children to deadly exhaust fumes that are responsible for more than 125,000 cancers nationwide each year. Clean diesel and hybrid electric buses provide safer transportation.

Although most major cities in the United States have well-established metro systems, most more than 100 years old, such as those in Boston, New York, and Washington, D.C., most Americans can't make use of such public systems because their urban development does not effectively support the use of mass transit. Our cities and towns were built to accommodate the auto, and our roadway system took precedence over public transportation in a push, enhanced if not generated, by the auto and oil industries with the support of the government through the mid-twentieth century.

Trains

Beyond the urban mass transit systems, diesel powers most trains rather than electricity. Trains that run between cities and across the country are spewing even more CO_2 than previously documented, which means that suddenly we must regard trains as a potential environmental hazard. Major rail line companies are attempting to address this problem with emission modifications.

Whenever you're planning a trip, choose the most efficient method of travel to reduce the ecological impact of your trip.

In addition, traveling provides a good example of a reasonable opportunity to purchase carbon offsets or green tags to counterbalance the emissions produced by your own transport needs. The green tags should go to balance the pollution we now know spews out of trains and planes, which will hopefully feed money toward the green energy applications currently underway.

Eco Vacations

While most people consider the perfect vacation a week or so of lying inert on sun-drenched beaches and sipping tropical concoctions until it's time to stir one's self out for a delicious dinner prepared by someone else, the traditional vacation is beginning to look a bit boring to a small but growing segment of travelers. These people want to explore far reaches of the earth; discover native cultures and hidden grottoes; savor exotic flavors; and meet, learn about, and perhaps help people in faraway places.

Incorporating these interests along with careful protection of natural features and habitats of a region are all part of the increasingly popular ecotourism industry. Positioned to open up perhaps previously inaccessible areas to tourists yet in such a way as to protect the area from becoming damaged by increased visitation, we offer several criteria that really help classify an eco destination.

When you think about some of the most popular tourist meccas, such as South Beach in Miami or Cancun in Mexico, you realize that the influx of tourism has shaped and changed the nature of these places. Instead of the once bare and scenic beaches, hotels line the waterfronts; many are so tall they cast shadows on the beaches by afternoon, taking away an important feature once treasured by visitors. Shops and restaurants are abundant, all hawking goods to capture tourists' dollars. Monies flow out of the communities and into the coffers of the multi-national corporations that own the lodging, dining, and shopping establishments. Quite often, the locals not only don't benefit from the revenue raked in by the tourist industry, but they also lose access to the most appealing parts of their local landscape, their beaches, their parks, and their mountaintops. In the ecotourism industry, special care is taken to preserve the natural environments and to involve the local communities so they benefit from the tourist trade.

Begin your search for ecological destinations using one of the organizations that are dedicated to promoting ecotravel, such as Sustainable Travel International (www. sustainabletravelinternational.org) or the International Ecotourism Society (www.ecotourism.org). Both nonprofit organizations strive to protect natural destinations from tourism damage and help local communities provide ecofriendly education and lodging to travelers interested in exploring natural regions. Another resource to find green lodging is www.Greenhotels.com, which provides tips to hoteliers on ways their businesses can operate in a more ecofriendly fashion and referrals for travelers who want to support such initiatives.

> **Green Gamut**
>
> *The New York Times* called ecotourism the "buzzword of the year" in 2006 and said that 38 percent of U.S. travelers are willing to pay more for a greener trip.

You will find many variations of ecofriendly accommodations, from green hotels, which might reduce their water usage by washing towels less frequently; to ecoresorts, which can be luxurious yet also offer nature tours and respect for indigenous populations; to ecolodges, the purest form of environmentally friendly lodging.

Ecolodges

If you're seeking that intense native experience, perhaps an ecolodge is the choice for you. An ecolodge is a place that has been built and operates in a way that respects the local environment, including the local people and their economy. Natives are on staff to introduce you to their community and to help keep revenue from the business within the community. Local people will guide you through their wilderness and introduce you to local customs and culture. It's a wholly different experience from typical tourism, but it's a wonderful chance to learn about people from around the world.

One of the newest ecolodges on the market is Crosswaters Ecolodge in Guangdong Province, China. Built on the Nankung Mountain amid vast bamboo forests, the lodge remains hidden by the lush greenery of the forest and surrounded by the creeks and waterways of the mountainside. The lodge was built using local materials, such as the bamboo that grows quickly onsite, with recycled railroad ties used to create walkways through the trees. A feng shui master—someone well versed in the ancient Chinese art of placement, based on energy flows of an area—helped architects plan the best use of space. So when you choose to have a massage or take a meditation break, you'll know that you're taking advantage of the best energy available for the job. One way or another, Crosswaters seems to guarantee a restful stay in a relatively undisturbed natural setting.

An ecolodge hidden in the forests of China's mountains.

(Hitesh Mehta)

An ecolodge or ecoresort might utilize alternative energy resources such as wind or solar power, process its waste through a natural wetland filtering system, recapture grey water for reuse in irrigation, or use organic fabrics for linens and upholstery and low VOC paints for interiors.

Ecoresorts

Ecoresorts provide some of the same benefits—they are built in a way that respects and protects the local environment rather than being a drain on natural resources and involve local people who benefit in some way from the business in their community. However, ecoresorts are also designed with the high-end tourist in mind, one who has money and expects a bit of luxury when traveling. Some environmental concessions might be made in the effort to cater to these well-heeled high rollers, although since they like to feel that they are helping local communities with their visits, some benefits do trickle down. This is the largest market for ecotourism today.

Green Hotels

Green hotels are an option you can often find in cities where environmental considerations and opportunities are limited. Hotel owners incorporate as many ecofriendly practices into their business as possible—they may recycle waste or purchase recycled materials, ask guests to reduce laundry requirements, and refill soap and shampoo bottles instead of distributing sample sizes that are discarded half-full after a day's stay.

All of these choices are steps in the right direction and can add to your own eco-friendly low-impact goals when traveling.

The Least You Need to Know

- ◆ Carbon offsets are not a solution to global warming or to your personal pollution problems, but they can help to turn us toward less-polluting activities.

- ◆ Companies trade carbon and other greenhouse gas credits on a large scale as commodities on the exchange market.

- ◆ You can choose low-impact travel options, or you can buy carbon offsets to lessen the impact of your traveling choices.

- ◆ You can select hotels that are also trying to lighten their impact on the environment, or you can fully immerse yourself in environmental studies in the wild.

Part 4

Green Living in Your Daily Life

The American Lung Association reports that an estimated 26.3 million Americans have been diagnosed with asthma, more than a third of them children. The disease accounted for 3 million adult sick days from work and 12.8 million lost school days—it is the leading chronic illness in children.

The fourth leading cause of death in children is poisoning, and 90 percent of all poisonings occur in the home, usually in the kitchen or bathroom—where we store our household cleaning agents.

This part covers many of the issues related to indoor air quality and the chemicals, smog, and other threats to your healthy home.

"Green is like totally the new black."

Chapter 11

Chemicals in Foods

In This Chapter

- ◆ Chemicals used in food production
- ◆ Chemicals found in our groceries
- ◆ Choosing organic
- ◆ The natural medicine cabinet
- ◆ Choosing organic for our furry friends

Many of us grew up with food from the big grocery store around the corner. With each passing season, the apples got redder, more perfectly shaped, and never appeared with bruises. The same went for peaches, pears, and tomatoes. Our produce was pretty. We've been trained to think beauty and perfection equals good nutrition, but unfortunately that isn't always the case.

In this chapter, we'll learn which chemicals are in our foods and how those chemicals are used to grow our food. We'll learn how to find and choose organic foods, produce, and meats for our families and pets. Finally, we'll discuss ways to get the worst chemicals out of our medicine cabinets.

Chemicals Found in Food Production and in Us

What many of us don't think about are the pesticides, herbicides, and fertilizers it took to bring us such beautiful bounty. What started out as a way to preserve the product on its journey from the farm to the market ultimately has proved harmful to our health. Decades after farmers decided it was a great idea to use those poisons, we're learning about the harmful effects, which may show up as cancer or fatal diseases.

> **Green Speak**
>
> "Laboratory studies show that pesticides can cause health problems, such as birth defects, nerve damage, cancer and other effects that might occur over a long period of time."
> —U.S. Environmental Protection Agency

And yet, if you ask people who really love their food, this method of farming ended up harmful to the very flavor the food is supposed to be packed with.

Unfortunately, the big business of farming with pesticides is still in practice. Farmers continue to use chemicals to increase yields and lengthen the shelf life of a wide variety of produce. The bottom line is hard to move—few producers are willing to alter lucrative standard practices without being forced by legislation or regulatory measures. However, as the detrimental health effects of using synthetic chemicals on our food become better understood, it's likely that consumer demand will help to tip the balance and catch the attention of both our legislators, who will enact the laws that the public wants, and the food providers, who want to make sales.

def•i•ni•tion

Integrated pest management (IPM) is a method of pest control that includes planting to suit the environment; encouraging beneficial insects (such as praying mantises); watering correctly; using organic fertilizer correctly; and using physical means to control pests, whether it means plucking beetles from leaves or covering delicate plantings with row cover (lightweight fabric) to protect them from insects.

Hopefully, farmers will begin to decrease their use of pesticides, herbicides, and synthetic fertilizers, and begin using *integrated pest management (IPM)* instead. A study by the Leopold Center for Sustainable Agriculture in Iowa has produced some surprising and encouraging statistics indicating that farmers who switched from conventional farming methods to organic produced a 52 percent increase in gross sales revenue and other economic benefits.

But this is the information age, and more and more people are educating themselves about the dangers of these practices. As people take advantage of the information that abounds in the world around us, more and more consumers are choosing to go organic, which means they can avoid the pesticides and insecticides used in those big business farming practices.

All About Organics

Organic is not a casual designation. The official USDA Certified Organic label means products have not been genetically modified and have been grown (or raised, in the case of livestock) on land free from chemicals for at least three years. No antibiotics or hormones are allowed in the livestock certified organic, and foods are not allowed to be irradiated or fertilized with sewage sludge.

Do be aware, though, that some farms which have used organic practices for many years have resisted paying for USDA certification although their product would certainly qualify. These farmers, who are the grandparents of the industry and who helped create the boom in organics today, object to some of the criteria established for USDA certification because they feel it isn't stringent enough. If you're familiar with the supplier and confident of its practices, you may choose their organic products even if they don't bear the certification label.

It pays to be vigilant about the status of the USDA organic designation. From time to time, the government, under pressure from the agricultural industry, has considered weakening the requirements for the organic designation. Until now, the organic industry has managed to maintain the integrity of the label, but it requires constant vigilance as the USDA and the organic industry don't always see eye-to-eye on what should be allowed the organic designation. The Organic Consumers Association (www.organicconsumers.org) provides bulletins on its website to keep up to date on what you need to watch for.

Reeducating consumers raised on those unblemished apples is part of the process of increasing the demand for organic foods and products. Your apples may not be uniformly red and exactly the same size and weight. Skin blemishes on produce do not affect the quality of the fruit or vegetable and are not harmful. The shelf life of some products may be much shorter than those "protected" with pesticides. Enjoy that fact. That means you eat the food when it's truly at its peak of freshness.

Hazard

Imported foods don't have to meet the same standards in their own countries to be labeled organic. Unless a product has the USDA green and white Certified Organic label, it doesn't hurt to question whether a product truly is organic.

Chemicals Found on the Grocer's Shelves

The produce section isn't the only place chemical, pesticide, and insecticide use may show up. Many of the products we buy are made from nonorganic ingredients. The end result, unfortunately, is the same: we are consuming too much of the bad stuff.

Always read the labels. You may be surprised by what you find—or don't find—in the foods you're feeding your family. Kraft Foods made big headlines when people started talking about its avocado-free guacamole dip. That's right. There's plenty of hydrogenated vegetable oil in there, some color, and a smidgen of avocado (so it's not *really* avocado free, just *nearly* avocado free). Doesn't that sound appetizing?

Junk food is called junk food with good reason. Going back to those labels, look for strawberry syrups with no real strawberries (red dye and artificial flavor) or juice boxes with little real fruit juice in them. It is amazing what scientists can make by combining artificial flavors, scents, and textures. It's amazing, but it's not food!

The reality is: it pays to educate yourself on how to read a label. People suffering from food allergies have long known this. And sometimes you will need to be a translator.

Did you know carmine is a dye made from the ground-up husks of beetles? There's a good chance carmine is on the label of anything in your pantry that is red. How do you like eating bugs? Although bugs are a delicacy in some societies, it does seem creepy and cruel to many Americans. But in terms of nutrition, bugs are undoubtedly healthier than synthetic dyes!

Sodium nitrite is used in meat and fish products to protect the meat's lovely color and to preserve it. But that ingredient may react with stomach acids to create N-nitrosamines, which are carcinogens. To prevent that reaction, manufacturers add ascorbic or erythorbic acid. Read the label on your bacon; you'll probably find sodium nitrite and one of those acids. Wouldn't you rather just be eating bacon? Bovine growth hormone is often found in milk; it's added to increase milk production in cows, as are antibiotics and other hormones. The list goes on.

Unless you're in a natural/health food store, most of the products you pick up from the shelves will have additives in them. Organic products ban the inclusion of these synthetic chemicals.

Luckily, there's something you can do about that.

Chapter 11: Chemicals in Foods **129**

The Green Market Explosion: Welcome It into Your Home

The organic food industry is one of the fastest-growing segments of the food industry right now, accelerating at about 20 percent annual growth and increasing each year. Whole Foods, the grocery chain that carries only foods without additives, preservatives, artificial colors, or sweeteners, is the fastest-growing food store chain in the nation.

And there's no evidence that the boom in the industry is slowing down.

Ten, maybe even just five years ago, to find produce, meats, and grocery products without any unwanted additives, consumers most likely had to trek to a health food store. Maybe it was a little bit "hippy-fied," and the conservative, suburban mom or dad might not have felt comfortable shopping in those surroundings.

But times are changing. These days, many urban dwellers can walk into the smallest branch of a local grocery chain just minutes (no longer a special trip) from home and find an organic produce section (outweighed by the regular produce, but there), a small section specifically dedicated to "green" products (organic sauces, pastas, grains, breads, mixes, cereals, drinks, even cookies), gallons and half-gallons of hormone- and antibiotic-free milk (whole, skim, and 1 percent) right with the other gallons of milk, several choices of hormone- and antibiotic-free eggs, and meats and poultry raised without the addition of synthetic chemicals. The freezer case has some frozen, prepared meals that are certified organic, too.

Realistically, it wouldn't be fiscally wise to throw out the contents of your pantry to replace those things with organic products and produce, but you can replace products one by one. The next time you need eggs, go for the free-range, chemical-free eggs. Instead of reaching for the gallon of store-brand milk, buy organic milk.

You will pay more for these products, but in the long run, you may well pay less for healthcare; your body will be happier without those chemicals; and the earth, our air, and our water will be better off for fewer chemicals. Gradually, as you incorporate buying organic products into your regular

Going Green

If you drink organic juices, read the labels to make sure the juice has been pasteurized. Some pathogens, such as E. coli, can live in nonpasteurized juices. Those pathogens have been known to cause illness and even death in small children or adults with compromised immune systems. Pasteurization kills harmful bacteria and is an accepted safe food practice in the organic and nonorganic industry.

Going Green

You can get a wallet-sized card to take with you to the market. This guide from www. foodnews.org is an easy way to decide which fruits and vegetables are the safest to put into your cart if they are not organic. It identifies a "Dirty Dozen" and the "Cleanest 12."

shopping habits, you will wean the products with additives and preservatives out of your diet.

Some foods you might consider buying from your grocery store's organic shelves are peaches, apples, and green bell peppers, which top the list of fruit and vegetables with the highest pesticide loads. Mango, pineapple, avocados, sweet corn, and onions are at the bottom of the list, and are therefore your best choices with the lowest pesticide load.

Another way to participate in the organic food movement is to take part in a Community Supported Agriculture (CSA) program in your area.

CSA participants purchase a share of a local farmer's (or of a group of local farmers') harvest. For one season's fee, buyers get whatever is harvested and in season at the local farms. In the northern climates, this may start out as early lettuces and peas and lead into bountiful summer crops, including strawberries from the fields in late May or June, peaches, truly vine-ripened tomatoes in August, hardier cabbages, sprouts and greens later, and ending with winter squashes as autumn sets in. Products, timing, and quantities vary with the region and the weather. You may even get produce you never would have bought at the store, but what better way to try something new than have it appear in your basket? It's a true culinary adventure. What CSA participants *do* know is that they are getting fresh-from-the-farm, unpreserved, and untainted produce. And they are supporting the small farm tradition at the same time.

Green Gamut

There has been some discussion among those already buying organic about whether it makes sense to buy organic grapes from Chile in the middle of our winter; after all, an awful lot of fossil fuel was needed to get those grapes from point A to point B in the name of going green. The average piece of fruit travels 1,500 to 2,500 miles before landing on your plate, according to a study by Rich Pirog of Iowa for the Leopold Center for Sustainable Agriculture in Iowa. So what is the best advice? *Buy local.* It didn't have to travel far, and it's fresher. And what are you doing eating grapes in the middle of the winter? Eat with the seasons!

Where's the Beef? And Poultry?

You may also want to consider buying only meats and poultry, eggs and milk from animals not treated with hormones or antibiotics. As with produce, chances are good you will pay more for these meats, but studies show good reason to pay a bit more for these products.

Hormones are given in extra large doses to animals in order to promote growth (recombinant Bovine Growth Hormone—rBGH). In the case of dairy cows, artificial hormones are given in order to stimulate greater milk production. A report in *Science Times* states that 80 percent of U.S. cattle are given artificial hormones. Additional antibiotics are often required to counteract the negative effects of the hormones, such as when the nearly constant milk production causes a weakening of the cow's nutritional and immune systems. Today's cows produce 18,000 pounds of milk per year, compared to about 5,300 per year in 1950.

Our USDA and FDA claim this practice causes no risk to humans, but a study by the European Union's Scientific Committee on Veterinary Measures Relating to Public Health (concluded in 2002) states the use of a variety of hormones may pose a risk to human health. Hormone residues may lead to early onset of puberty in young girls as well as potential problems (including possible increased cancer risks) later in life resulting from hormonal imbalance brought on by ingesting foods with hormone residues.

Going Green

Don't know where to start in the search for healthier food? Online web searches can make it as easy as one click of the mouse. Visit www. eatwellguide.org to enter your zip code. The site will quickly identify restaurants and stores/retailers offering organic and natural products.

Antibiotics, given to treat or prevent diseases in animals living in feedlots, may only help build drug-resistant strains of certain diseases in humans.

There is enough cause for concern that the prudent choice would be to look for meats from animals that have not been treated with growth-promoting hormones or antibiotics.

Swimming with the Organic Fishes? Maybe Not

When it comes to choosing organic fish, your choices are tougher if not impossible. Fish in the ocean are accumulating poisons from their own environment—pollutants we're dumping into our oceans and waterways. If you think farm-raised fish is the answer, you may well have to think again. The runoff into farmed fish holding tanks is very often contaminated, leaving farmers no real way to prevent chemicals from reaching their fish.

Shoppers may, however, see fish labeled "organic" (although not Certified USDA Organic) at their grocers. But the U.S. label applies only to land animals and crops. So what's the story behind those organic fish labels?

Fish Labeling

In the case of "organic" salmon, the fish most likely come from Canada or Scotland, where they may come from farms with more room to swim, fed with organic feed, and not given extra growth hormones or antibiotics. But because the Certified USDA Organic label doesn't apply, there may be additives. It pays to ask the fishmonger about where the fish came from. A well-educated person behind the counter may put your mind at ease about what was used to raise those fish.

Consumers may also want to educate themselves about which fish have higher levels of contaminants. Because we have allowed pollution to freely dump into our oceans for years, now even the wild fish may have unhealthy levels of heavy metals, especially mercury, which causes birth defects in unborn fetuses and can cause developmental heart and brain problems in infants and young children.

More recent studies show the metals to be harmful to an average, healthy adult who consumes a lot of the contaminated fish. Problems may include fatigue and headaches, some loss of memory, and joint pain. The study subjects (people who already consumed a lot of fish) proved to have mercury levels higher than the EPA's safety threshold.

Going Green

Are you consuming too much mercury? You can test your own mercury levels using a hair sample and a $25 kit provided by Greenpeace. You'll get the results back in two to three weeks, and your data will contribute to a national study of mercury exposure among humans. Go to secureusa.greenpeace.org/mercury/.

Because humans store these metals in their bodies in the same way the fish do, even women just *considering* becoming pregnant would do well to avoid consuming the fish on the list below. A Centers for Disease Control and Prevention (CDC) study found 16 percent of women of childbearing age have levels high enough to warrant concern about developing fetuses.

Mercury exposure is more dangerous for children and fetuses than adults because it can cause permanent damage to developing organs, the brain, and the nervous system. While mercury does cause damage to adults as well, when an adult ceases to consume mercury, the metals wash out of the body after a few months, leaving minimal damage behind.

Selecting the Safest Fish

While the EPA recommends limiting fish consumption to one to two meals a week, other groups recommend consuming none of the fish from what it calls the "high-mercury" fish and limiting the "moderate-mercury" fish to one meal per month. (Most contaminants are stored in the fatty parts of animals, so avoiding the skin of these fish is a good idea, too.)

The EPA advises women of childbearing age and children to avoid shark, swordfish, king mackerel, and tilefish (golden snapper) because of their typically high concentration of mercury. Other fish with high levels of mercury that should be avoided include Atlantic halibut, oysters (Gulf Coast), pike, sea bass, and tuna (steaks and canned albacore).

Fish acceptable for moderate consumption, with moderate amounts of mercury, include Alaskan halibut, black cod, blue (Gulf Coast) crab, cod, Dungeness crab, Eastern oysters, mahi-mahi, blue mussels, pollack, and tuna (canned light).

These fish have low mercury levels: anchovies, Arctic char, crawfish, Pacific flounder, herring, king crab, sand dabs, scallops, Pacific sole, tilapia, wild Alaska and Pacific salmon, farmed catfish, clams, striped bass, and sturgeon.

The other category of fish to avoid is the "high-POP" category. POP refers to *persistent organic pollutants* and includes polychlorinated biphenyls (PCBs)—neurotoxic, *hormone-disrupting* chemicals banned in the United States since 1977. A 2004 study in the journal *Science* showed PCB levels seven times higher in farmed salmon (most of the salmon sold here in the United States) than in its wild counterpart.

def•i•ni•tion

Persistent organic pollutants (POPs) are chemicals which don't dissipate in the environment or in the body and may accumulate, causing increased levels of exposure over time. Some POPs are also carried genetically from one generation to the next and may cause genetic damage and disease.

Many chemicals are now being recognized as **hormone disruptors**—they mimic estrogen in the body and cause related hormonal changes. Amphibians in the wild have been identified as changing from male to female, and several studies indicate that male births are declining, probably as a result of this influx of estrogen and hormone-disrupting chemicals into our environment.

PCBs are showing up in farmed salmon because the fish are fed a diet of ground-up small fish that have accumulated PCBs in their fatty tissue. While salmon might eat some of these fish in the wild, their diet is more diverse and the concentration of PCBs is much lower. The Environmental Working Group (EWG) conducted a study of PCBs in salmon and found that the FDA approval level is much higher than the EPA's recommended safety level of PCBs in fish because the FDA levels were set decades ago, before PCBs, a by-product of the plastic and synthetic chemical industries, inundated our environment. EWG recommends that the FDA reevaluate its standards. Meanwhile, EWG suggests that consumers choose wild salmon or canned Alaskan salmon when available and eat farmed salmon no more than once a month. You should cut fatty tissue off of fish before cooking and prepare it by broiling, baking, or grilling instead of frying so fats will drain away from fish.

> **Green Speak**
>
> "... farmed salmon are likely the most PCB-contaminated protein source in the U.S. food supply. On average farmed salmon have 16 times the dioxin-like PCBs found in wild salmon, 4 times the levels in beef, and 3.4 times the dioxin-like PCBs found in other seafood."
>
> —*Environmental Working Group: PCBs in Farmed Salmon*

> **Going Green**
>
> The U.S. FDA and EPA have compiled a list of fish to avoid—or at least to limit—because of high levels of mercury or POPs. You can download all this information on The Green Guide's Fish Picks Card at www. thegreenguide.com/gg/pdf/ fishchartissue97.pdf.

The EPA and several countries worldwide have taken action to limit the production and use of some chemicals identified as POPs, and studies are underway to determine how to isolate or remove these chemicals, some of which are now endemic throughout our air, water, soil, and bodies, from the environment.

It stands to reason that fish pulled from contaminated bodies of water will have similar problems. Check updates from local fish and wildlife organizations and pay attention to local news advisories, if you should go fishing for dinner or when buying fresh local fish from the market.

Consider Becoming a Vegan ... or at Least More of a Vegetarian

Maybe you are already driving a hybrid car, taking the bus when you have to, and walking or biking to work as often as you can. You're moving in the right direction.

But if you haven't gone *vegan*, you can still do more for yourself and the planet.

Our consumption of meat is a significant factor in the global warming equation. A University of Chicago study published in the April 2006 issue of *Earth Interactions* suggests that people can do more to reduce greenhouse gas emissions by changing their diets than they can by changing what they drive.

def•i•ni•tion

A **vegan** diet is one that includes no animal or animal by-products. Vegetarians eat no meat, but may consume some animal products such as honey, cheese, and eggs. Ovo-lacto vegetarians consume dairy products and eggs, but no other animal products.

Food production and farming, as well as the non-CO_2 emissions from livestock and animal waste, are a big part of our global warming problem, say the authors of the study, Gidon Eshel and Pamela Martin, assistant professors in geophysical sciences at the University of Chicago.

According to Eshel and Martin, a typical American omnivore contributes a ton and a half of carbon dioxide in addition to methane and other gases, all produced because of that American's food choices.

Green Speak

"We neither make a value judgment nor do we make a categorical statement. We say that however close you can be to a vegan diet and further from the mean American diet, the better you are for the planet. It doesn't have to be all the way to the extreme end of vegan. If you simply cut down from two burgers a week to one, you've already made a substantial difference."

—Gidon Eshel, assistant professor in geophysical sciences, University of Chicago

In 2002, fossil fuel used to produce food accounted for 17 percent of all the fossil fuel used in the United States, which added three quarters of a ton of CO_2 to the atmosphere for every person in the United States.

Add to that 17 percent the emissions from livestock waste ("manure lagoons," for example, which are typically part of large-scale pork production), mostly methane and nitrous oxide, a pound of which equals the greenhouse effect of 50 pounds of carbon dioxide. That's a significant effect on the atmosphere!

The same study compared five diets: vegetarian, fish, red meat, poultry, and the average American diet. The vegetarian (one that included eggs and dairy) diet produced the least impact in terms of greenhouse gases, and the fish and red meat diets proved to be nearly equal in their inefficient use of energy (therefore, producing the most greenhouse gases).

The inefficiency of the fish diet surprised Eshel and Martin, but they noted that fishing for some of the popular species, such as swordfish or tuna, requires large fishing boats at sea for long periods of time, trips which use a lot of fuel. And serious health concerns are related to diets based on animal fats and protein.

"The adverse effects of dietary animal fat intake on cardiovascular diseases are by now well established," Martin and Eshel conclude in their report. "Similar effects are also seen when meat, rather than fat, intake is considered. To our knowledge, there is currently no credible evidence that plant-based diets actually undermine health; the balance of available evidence suggests that plant-based diets are at the very least just as safe as mixed ones, and most likely safer."

The simple conclusion: a vegetarian diet is healthier for the consumer *and* for the earth. In other words, your mother knew what she was talking about when she told you to eat your vegetables.

And ultimately, if you are worried about the extra expense of going green in the kitchen, remember that you'll have more money to spend on organic fruits and vegetables if you decide to give up meat.

The Greening of Your Medicine Cabinet

There's no question that our quality of life has improved greatly with the advent of modern medicine. But there are plenty of times when it is unnecessary to turn to chemicals or pharmaceuticals to treat minor ailments and complaints. In fact, our overuse of antibiotics for what were probably minor (perhaps even nonexistent) reasons has already been proven to have led to the development of *super bugs*, resistant to the antibiotics we have to treat those bacteria.

def•i•ni•tion

A **super bug** is an organism that is able to fight off the effects of an antibiotic. These organisms have mutated over time— evolved—as they built resistance to antibiotics that previously had killed them.

But nature provides many remedies for our ailments. So instead of heading to the drugstore or the doctor for a prescription, you might want to take some time to learn about the ancient art of healing with natural substances: herbs. In fact, many of the synthetic compounds we know as pharmaceuticals were derived from these natural substances, already known for their healing powers.

As modern society moved away from the knowledge of these herbs, the general consensus somehow became that herbal healing was nothing but old wives tales and ineffective nonsense. An industry developed around the *petrochemical*-based synthetic pharmaceuticals, and soon doctors and patients alike adopted the belief promoted by the industry that science was superior to Mother Nature.

def•i•ni•tion

A **petrochemical** is a petroleum-based synthetic chemical.

But when the late Varro Tyler, Ph.D., and Dean Emeritus of the School of Pharmacy at Purdue University, decided to investigate, he opened the door to a new generation of scientists who came to realize that herbs hold powerful healing powers. Tyler believed that more adequate research and standardization will bring more benefits to light, as it has in Europe, where herbs are commonly prescribed by doctors for a number of ailments. That door has not been shut, and today many doctors approach healing holistically, using a combination of modern drug therapy and herbal treatments.

While scientists continue to isolate powerful characteristics of various herbs, Tyler maintained that the healing abilities of herbs are attributed to the working together of the many chemical constituents in each plant. Identifying a single powerful element is valuable, but often the single is not as effective as the whole.

Tyler, who died in 2001, left behind plenty of scientific literature attesting to the healing powers of medicinal herbs. Some of his favorites include the following. (Please note that you should thoroughly research these herbs and their effects for yourself, and be sure to consult with your medical doctor about how best to use these.)

◆ *Cranberries:* Scientific evidence dating back to the 1920s proved cranberries prevented urinary tract infections. Then in 1994, the Journal of American Medicinal Association showed how: cranberries prevent infection-causing bacteria from clinging to the urinary tract. You may want to eat them whole (too tart for some, perhaps), brew a tea, drink the juice (pure cranberry juice, not cranberry juice cocktail), or make your favorite compote. They'll help keep you clean—literally.

◆ *Black Cohosh:* Women suffering from hot flashes due to menopause may want to age more gracefully by downing a daily dose of 40 milligrams of black cohosh. "There is a great controversy over how it works," said Tyler, "but it does help women feel much better, reducing and eliminating hot flashes, irritability, anxiety, depression, and sleeplessness, and it enhances concentration." A sure sign it works? Black Cohosh has been adopted by GlaxoSmithKline and is marketed as Remifemin.

◆ *Chaste Berry:* In 2000, the *Journal of the American Pharmaceutical Association* reported that this Mediterranean tree berry is effective against PMS by preventing its causes; better, said Tyler, than simply masking and treating the pain resulting from PMS. Tyler suggested 20 milligrams a day during the two weeks before your menstrual cycle begins, which is typically when the worst PMS symptoms strike.

◆ *St. John's Wort:* Europeans believe that this herb helps fight depression, though studies in the United States have not corroborated the claims. Many people have chosen to try this over pharmaceuticals. "People really like St. John's Wort because it doesn't give them the heebie-jeebies the way Prozac does," said Tyler.

◆ *Kava Kava:* "Nature's Valium" is how Tyler referred to kava kava. It can help calm you down if you are anxious, although too much may put you to sleep. The advantage of kava kava is that you won't get hooked. Tyler did warn that car accidents had been known to happen when people take too much kava kava, and pregnant or nursing women should avoid it, as should anyone who is feeling depressed. It also should not be combined with alcohol or when operating machinery or driving.

◆ *Feverfew:* Feverfew has been used to prevent migraines since the first century. A study released by the University of Exeter in the United Kingdom confirms its effectiveness and safety. Take 125 milligrams or eat the fresh leaves as a preventive to reduce the frequency and symptoms of migraine.

◆ *Valerian:* Get some extra sleep with the help of valerian, although no one has quite proven why this works. "It's been used for more than 1,000 years," said Tyler, "and yet we don't know the active principals. I think that's sad." He doesn't like valerian tincture or tea because it smells so bad; he recommended taking valerian only in capsule form.

◆ *Hot Peppers:* Scorch your pain away with capsaicin, the active ingredient in hot peppers. Mix capsicum, cayenne, chili powder, or crushed red pepper into a lotion or soak a cloth with a hot pepper tea (not for drinking!) to use on your skin as relief from arthritis, shingles, and vascular headaches, or following surgical trauma such as mastectomy or amputation. It takes a few days of continued use to become effective, and the pepper lotion or pepper tea may sting at first—that means it's working!

◆ *Milk Thistle:* This has been found to be effective in preventing hepatitis and cirrhosis. It shields liver cells and helps promote the growth of new, healthy cells. Tyler recommended taking 12 to 15 grams of milk thistle (capsule form) before and after drinking binges.

◆ *Chamomile Tea:* Chamomile has been a tummy soother for centuries. Tyler recommended it for those who are not allergic to its pollen (nor allergic to other ragweed allergens). The tea is soothing and fragrant, but a capsule will pack a bigger punch. "I personally think there is nothing better for an upset stomach than a cup of chamomile tea," said Tyler.

Going Green for Fido or Muffy

Another segment of the organic market growing by leaps and bounds is the organic pet food industry because what are our pets if not part of our families?

The Organic Trade Association (OTA) projected a steady 17 percent annual growth in this category each year for the years from 2004 to 2008. The OTA firmly believes that pet food should conform to human food standards (while acknowledging the benefits of certain added nutrients for specific species). Again, more pet owners are thinking that what is good for them is good for their pets.

In the spring of 2007, hundreds and possibly thousands of pets were sickened and many suffered fatal kidney failure traced to the chemical melamine used in the production of more than 100 pet foods. A sudden surge in the organic pet food industry and in home-cooked pet meals followed. Further studies are underway to determine whether the same chemical might also have found its way into human foods.

A study done by veterinarian Michael W. Fox, former science director and senior scholar for The Humane Society of the United States, identified something called endocrine-immune disruption syndrome (EIDS) in animals, which he links to chemical compounds in food known as endocrine disruptors (also called hormone disruptors).

Fox attributes a number of symptoms to EIDS, but posits that the causes to these hormonal imbalances lie in an animal's surroundings, most likely in its food, where *endocrine disrupting compounds* (*EDCs*), when

def•i•ni•tion

> Endocrine disrupting compounds (EDCs) are endocrine or hormone disrupting chemicals that interfere with the development and processes of bodily hormonal systems. These EDCs are prevalent in industrial pollution and plastics, including many persistent organic pollutants, PCBs, and phthalates (chemicals used in many plastics to soften them).

ingested, become concentrated in the animal's fatty tissue, brain, mammary glands, and its milk. EDCs can cause behavior, neurological, and developmental problems.

Because EDCs are turning up in household products, flooring materials, clothing, and in the food and water we eat and drink (and share with our pets), Fox encourages veterinarians to educate animal owners to provide their pets with pure water and organic food. It is also wise to avoid the indoor use of pesticides and to keep pets off of lawns treated with pesticides. Avoid PVC plastic toys and feeding bowls, too.

Other problems have been related to common ingredients that have for years been used in the making of pet food. Ash, for instance, has been linked to urinary tract infections and stones in animals. Sugars in pet foods may contribute to the onset of diabetes in your pet.

Hazard

"According to the Association of American Feed Control Officials, pet food can and does include spray-dried animal blood, hydrolyzed hair, dehydrated garbage, unborn carcasses, and many other things." Additives in pet food can include dead and diseased animals, too. (*Green Living: The E Magazine Handbook for Living Lightly on the Earth*, by the editors of *E/The Environmental Magazine* [Plume, 2005]).

As with the food in your cupboard, you should become a label reader of your pet's food, too. Make sure there's plenty of protein, vegetables, the right nutrients—all from the right, organic sources (Newman's Own, for example, uses Bell and Evans organic chickens for its pet food products). If you have any doubts, ask your vet to have a look at the label.

You can make your own pet food, too, if you wish. Dr. Michael Fox provides recipes on his website, and you can find many more online. But do be aware that your pets' diet needs are different from yours, and cats have different needs than dogs. While dogs might be able to eat a carefully planned vegetarian diet, a cat is likely to become ill without meat. Both animals are natural meat eaters.

The Least You Need to Know

- Most foods on the grocery store shelves have any number of artificial additives and preservatives. You can learn to avoid these by reading labels and choosing products with natural ingredients.

- You can decrease your intake of chemicals and pesticides in foods by choosing USDA Certified Organic products.

◆ Even the meats, poultry, fish, eggs, and milk in stores may contain artificial additives, such as synthetic hormones, antibiotics, chemical flavorings, and dyes.

◆ Eating more vegetables and less meat has a significant impact on the atmosphere by reducing the amount of fossil fuel needed to produce meats and by reducing the amount of animal waste being produced: fewer animals = less waste.

◆ Consider traditional herbal remedies for your medical complaints when modern pharmaceuticals are not called for.

◆ You can give your pets organic food, too; if it's good for you, it's good for them.

12

The American Lawn and Garden: Making It Safe

In This Chapter

- ◆ Benefits of lawns for everyone and the environment
- ◆ Facts about pesticides
- ◆ Starting an organic lawn
- ◆ Growing an organic garden

First, let me give you some statistics: of the 27.6 million acres of turf grass in America, about 21 million of those acres are household lawns. The planting and maintenance of lawns across America annually generates as much as $40 billion for the national economy. About 80 percent of homes in the United States have private lawns.

That's a lot of grass! Unfortunately, we Americans seem to love green carpets better than true yards. Green carpets are lawns without a sprig of clover, a violet, or a dandelion. These lawns may feel luxuriously soft to the bare feet, but you'd be better off not walking on them. They're likely hazardous to your health because of all the pesticides used to get them looking like pretty green carpets.

Lawns Are Good for What Ails the Earth

The good news is that we're doing well to have lawns at all, and the more we have green space around us, the better off our environment is. According the World Group for the Evergreen Foundation, 93 percent of American homeowners value green space and more than 90 percent of homeowners see a nice lawn as a way to increase the value of their property.

James Beard, Ph.D., an expert on turf and chief scientist at International Sports Turf Institute, has listed some of those ecosystem benefits:

- Lawns help cool hot air through evaporation, and the grass produces oxygen and keeps dust and pollutants out of the air.

- Organic matter decomposes in a balanced lawn, adding to the health of the soil.

- Trees, shrubs, and bushes are also great sound insulators, filtering out traffic roar and street noise from our living space.

- Lawns and other plants also contribute to erosion control, keeping soil from slipping away as dust down hillsides or into waterbodies.

> **Green Gamut**
>
> According to Paul Tukey, host of www.SafeLawns.org and author of *The Organic Lawn Care Manual,* Americans dump some 30 million pounds of weed killers on their lawns each year.

But rather than looking for a swath of solid green with every blade in place, we need to learn that what nature intended is slightly different than what much of suburban America strives for (and, unfortunately, what much of suburban subdivision America expects through its deed restrictions).

When you cross the street and look back at your lawn, is it all green, with no big patches of brown and not too many errant dandelions? Then you're doing okay. Sometimes when you examine the turf too closely, you can be bothered by tiny flowers (that aren't grass) such as clover, violets, and an occasional dandelion (maybe you can teach your kids to pick these for you before they go to seed). But the long view can still be pleasing even with these so-called imperfections. Clover, violets, and other native plants also are natural pest repellents, too.

The switch to an organic lawn requires a fundamental shift in the way we Americans view our lawns. So let's adjust our thinking and get ready to apply organic principles to our lawn and garden.

Pesticides and Poisons

The very definition of pesticides means that they are poisons. *American Heritage Science Dictionary* refers to pesticides as chemicals "used to kill harmful animals or plants," in agriculture *and* in areas where humans live. Pesticides comprise the variations fungicides, herbicides, insecticides, and rodenticides. This forward-thinking dictionary at least acknowledges that some are harmful to humans and the environment. But plenty of places tout the benefits of pesticides. After all, it's undeniable that we don't want to live with bugs, and bugs can ruin crops and the livelihoods of farmers.

And so the fact that pesticides are poison doesn't stop us from using them. In fact, American lawn owners have made pesticides big business. According to the Safer Pest Control Project (www.spcpweb.org), whose mission is to find safe alternatives to the poisons we put on our lawns, Americans spread 67 million pounds of pesticides on lawns each year, and because most lawn owners are amateurs, we manage to spread heavier pesticide concentrations on our own lawns than commercial agriculture does on its fields.

Pesticides: Some Sobering Facts

We must acknowledge many other sobering facts about pesticides. The New York State Department of Law Environmental Protection Bureau reports that studies have shown that exposure to many of the most commonly applied lawn pesticides have produced cancer, birth defects, reproductive complications, and problems in the nervous system, the livers, and the kidneys of lab animals. The *Toxicology and Industrial Health Journal* reports that even ingesting low doses via a water supply source led to aggression and damaged immune systems in lab animals.

Pesticides tend to kill whatever they touch, both harmful and beneficial plants and insects that help a natural lawn system maintain a healthy balance. So the poison sprayed on one plant to kill cut worms will also kill the ladybugs and the praying mantises that keep a pest population down through natural methods.

Yet nearly 1,000 species of insects, plant problems, and unwanted weeds don't succumb to the pesticides used, which leads to evolution of pesticide-resistant strains of all of the above. This then leads to stronger toxins or heavier (and often incorrectly used) applications of the same pesticides. It's a circular problem that only weakens the natural defense mechanisms nature started with, as reported by Anne Platt Mcginn in Phasing Out Persistent Organic Pollutants, Society for the Advancement of Education.

Nearly 1,400 pesticides, herbicides, and fungicides can be found in more than 34,000 different household products we use in our homes today.

Children and Pets

Anthropologist and research scientist Elizabeth Guillette discovered in a long-term landmark study started in 1967 (and still continuing) that Mexican children exposed to farming chemicals—fertilizers, pesticides, and herbicides—demonstrated slower mental and physical development than children who were not exposed. Dr. Guillette expressed concern about the lack of creativity and imaginative play among the children of the chemical farmers and about the long-term effects on their reproductive abilities. These children were developing less mammary tissue than their counterparts, which raised concern about their ability to nurse their offspring. Finally, Guillette noted that although all of the children seemed normal before the testing took place, studies have proven that the chemicals in the pesticides will lower I.Q. levels.

Green Speak

"It's been projected that if I.Q. decreases just five points across a community, you lose roughly two-thirds of your geniuses, and increase the number of children who are mentally retarded by two-thirds. This has huge consequences in terms of education, care and medical needs. Also, it's the children of today who are going to be responsible for our communities, nation and world tomorrow. If we lose them, what are we going to do?"

—Anthropologist Elizabeth Guillette, during an interview for *E/The Environmental Magazine* (July/August 2006)

Comparison of children's drawings—those on the right were done by children exposed to agricultural chemicals, those on the left were not.

(Courtesy Dr. Elizabeth Guillette, University of Florida)

FOOTHILLS

VALLEY

60 mos
female

71 mos
male

71 mos
female

71 mos
male

Keep in mind that children are especially susceptible to the effects of pesticides, as they are smaller, their bodies are still developing, and they're more likely than adults to run barefoot through a pesticide-treated lawn, roll on the grass, and even ingest pesticides from unwashed hands that played in the yard.

Sadly, studies show that pesticides even reach into the womb. One such study from the Environmental Working Group and Planet Ark is titled "Body Burden, The Pollution in Newborns, A benchmark investigation of industrial chemicals, pollutants and pesticides in human umbilical cord blood" (July 2005). This study found an average of 200 industrial chemicals present in the placental fluid of 10 infants. The chemicals found are known to cause birth defects and to affect development. To quote from the study, "Now we know that at this critical time when organs, vessels, membranes and systems are knit together from single cells to finished form in a span of weeks, the umbilical cord carries not only the building blocks of life, but also a steady stream of industrial chemicals, pollutants and pesticides that cross the placenta as readily as residues from cigarettes and alcohol. This is the human 'body burden'—the pollution in people that permeates everyone in the world, including babies in the womb."

Pesticides from the yard travel quite conveniently into the home on shoe soles. One EPA study found 23 types of pesticides in dust and air of interior environments.

Pets spend plenty of time in yards. A study done by the National Cancer Institute found dogs from homes using the common pesticide known as 2,4-D had double the occurrence of malignant cancer. Dogs diagnosed with CML (canine malignant lymphoma) were 30 percent more likely to have come from yards treated by the owners with 2,4-D, or from yards treated by lawn care companies (Hayes, HM et al. [1991]: "Case control study of canine malignant lymphoma: positive association with dog owner's use of 2,4-D." *J National Cancer Institute*, Vol. 83, pp. 1226–1231).

The United States Geological Survey has found all types of garden pesticides, especially commonly used weed killers, in waterways around city centers.

If you had any doubt about the presence of these chemicals in your surroundings before you started reading this chapter, you shouldn't doubt it now. These toxins are in our environment.

The good news is that you can take steps to make your immediate surroundings safer, and your small steps only bode well for the greater environment.

> **Green Gamut**
>
> An interesting University of Washington study reported in *Environmental Health Perspectives* in 2006, found that children whose urine showed contamination with some pesticides showed dramatic reduction in pesticide levels after just two weeks of being fed an organic diet.

What It Takes to Get Started

We've already addressed the immediate need to change the way we look at lawns, but it bears repeating here. You need to give up the notion that your yard will be nothing but soft, gentle blades of grass—weeds are simply a fact of nature. You won't be letting them overrun your yard, but you will have to deal with them on a case-by-case basis. Look at it this way—who decided those little yellow and purple flowers are weeds, anyway?

> **Green Speak**
>
> "You can't be afraid of weeds. People have to let go of their dandelion phobia. When the dandelion disintegrates, it adds nutrients (to the lawn)."
>
> —Rachel Rosenberg, executive director of Safer Pest Control Project

You don't need to give up on the notion that your yard will be green, but now it will have some clover, maybe some violets, a dandelion or two, but best of all, it will have no pesticides. So for an instant change, simply stop using any of the commercial pesticides you have on hand. Just cutting the lawn before weeds go to seed will prevent them from spreading.

> **Going Green**
>
> When disposing of pesticides and chemicals you no longer wish to use, do it in the safest way possible. Contact local waste management facilities to inquire about hazardous waste collection programs. Call 1-800-CLEANUP (1-800-253-2687) to find out hazardous waste collection sites in your area. Be aware that local requirements may vary from town to town, and check with state and local agencies before you do anything.

Exercise patience while you are learning to see all the green in your yard as a good thing. Because you will no longer be using instant gratification chemicals, the changes taking place will be more gradual as well.

First Steps

A good first step to growing an organic lawn is to have your soil analyzed by the local extension office. This analysis will let you know what your lawn and soil lack and what you should focus on planting. Typically, you'll test for nitrogen, potassium, and phosphorus.

As far as grasses go, choose grass seed that is specifically suited to your region and doesn't require excessive watering. It's also worth noting that just 50 years ago, most lawn seed mixes had clover, but because broad-leaf pesticides destroy clover, it's no longer in most lawn seed mixes. So add some clover seed yourself. It resists drought, is green, and even flowers. What more could you ask from a lawn?

> **Green Gamut**
>
> Reseeding annually will keep weeds at bay by keeping the grass growth thick and adding nutrients to your soil.

To control pests in the lawn, you must be vigilant. Pay attention and watch for evidence of insect damage or disease. Clues can be anything from leaves that seem to disappear overnight (ravaged by beetles) or patches of lawn that look wilted or inexplicably brown.

Watch how sunlight hits your lawn. Be aware of areas that get no direct sun and areas that seem to get all sun all the time. Make sure your yard mixes good areas of lawn with shrubs and trees.

When you choose groundcover (including grass), shrubs and trees, look for native species. These are suited to your environment and climate and will be less trouble to establish and maintain and more resistant to native pests. By diversifying, you add strength to the lawn.

Pay attention to the seeds you buy. You can find disease free, certified seeds at lawn centers. Read up on plant types, and select those that are disease resistant.

Managing Pests

To manage pests that do arrive—and they will, after all, this is Mother Nature—practice integrated pest management (IPM). Use row covers. Handpick eggs and insects off plants. Mulch all bare spaces—nature abhors a vacuum, but weeds love that space! Mulch both suppresses weeds and preserves moisture in the soil. Remember some insects, like praying mantises that eat aphids, are good for lawns!

Invite in the good insects. Plant flowering shrubs that invite birds, bees, and butterflies. Plant plenty of yellow flowers, which seem to attract good insects, such as ladybugs and lacewings. Learn which plants are native for your region, and choose those—they'll use less water and require less attention.

Many other natural substances may help as well. Insects don't appreciate herbs and spices that pack a punch, such as lavender, clove, citronella, ground red pepper (cayenne), or cedar. Some gardeners fight pests by mixing up a spoonful of cayenne with water in a spray bottle, then lightly spraying plants; others choose a dollop of liquid Ivory soap in water, applied the same way.

Watering, Mowing, and Weeding

Learn to water your lawn correctly. The most common advice is to water early in the day so the lawn has a chance to dry before night time. Watering before the worst heat of the day lessens evaporation, and a dry lawn discourages fungus from developing. Water deeply, too, really saturating the root system. Deep, thorough watering should be sufficient once a week.

And learn to mow your lawn correctly. Keep the blade sharp so it makes clean cuts. Blunt cuts weaken the health of the lawn. Leave the mower blade high, and never cut the grass shorter than three or four inches high, which protects lawns from drying out (meaning you don't have to water as often).

Do no more bagging of lawn clippings, either. Happy organic lawn keepers use those clippings for their compost pile. And if there's no compost pile cooking in the yard, grass clippings return vital nutrients to the soil if you just let them fall where they are cut.

Rediscover the joys of hand weeding. You may still want to get rid of those hardy dandelions. If you must, learn to remove weeds by using lawn tools. The simplest is a long, sturdy piece of steel with a fork-like tip. Push the steel into the ground at the base of the plant, lever it back, and you have a good chance of removing the weed right down to the taproot. Remember, hand weeding isn't an instant fix. Consistent work on a regular schedule will reduce weeds over time.

You may also want to try an organic product, such as corn gluten, to cut down on weeds in your garden. Apply it before the soil gets too warm. It, too, may take a season or two to really affect the lawn, so just be patient.

And if, after reading all this, you feel you really can't go it alone, more and more organic lawn services are starting up or being offered by already established lawn care companies. You can call companies and discuss your options, but be aware that many companies still may resort to chemical solutions in the face of strong infestation problems.

Getting the Word Out

Okay, you're improving your little corner of the world. But suddenly you realize the chemicals your neighbors are using are drifting into your yard. Or even worse, your kids are running over (barefoot, no less!) to play in the just-treated backyard.

You don't want to lecture your friends and neighbors, so you might need a plan of action to at least get a discussion started. One simple way to start that discussion is to post a sign from the Safer Pest Control Project. This organization sells ($10) eight-inch diameter aluminum signs declaring your yard a "Pesticide Free Zone."

Pesticide Free Zone sign.

(Courtesy Safer Pest Control Project)

By putting up the sign, you invite your neighbors to start a discussion just by asking about it. The more you can offer in the way of alternatives to pesticides, the more likely someone will be to trying something new. You've done the homework for your neighbors. Now you just need to give them the road map to their own pesticide free zone.

The other place we need to get the word out is in our schools. When we talk about lawns, few of us think right away about the lawns surrounding our children's schools.

The Healthy Schools Project of the Center for Health and Environmental Justice tries to minimize the risk to our children in school by reducing the amount of pesticides used in schools. Already more than 27 school districts in 19 states are aiming to improve school environs by practicing Integrated Pest Management. The initiative, Safer Schools, provides information and resources for schools to use on the way to implementing IPM.

Some pesticides have been linked to the increased incidence of asthma in school-age children. One effort encourages parents to send the schools postcards discouraging the use of pesticides. Many schools notify parents of children with asthma before spraying so they can avoid exposure to potential irritants.

Planting an Organic Garden

Of course, anyone thinking about an organic lawn naturally likes to envision a thriving vegetable garden—organic vegetable garden, that is—as part of the whole, happy healthy ecosystem. The same principles apply: no synthetic fertilizers or pesticides.

Growing your own vegetables in your organic garden ties you to the earth in a way nothing else can.

The Kitchen Gardeners realize this (www.kitchengardeners.org), and the group actively encourages food appreciation by encouraging home growing and home cooking. Kitchen Gardeners, "by seeking an active role in their own sustenance, are modern-day participants in humankind's oldest and most basic activity, offering a critical link to our past and positive vision for our future."

According to the group's site, home food production is declining to near nonexistence, and the average distance traveled for the ingredients making up our meals is between 1,000 and 2,500 miles, which means for the food to reach our tables we need as much as 17 times more fossil fuel than we did just two decades ago.

Hazard

While you are out in the yard enjoying your oh-so-green lawn, don't fire up the grill with lighter fluid, which contains petroleum distillates. It makes the food taste bad, and some petroleum distillates have benzene, a carcinogen. Learn how to start hardwood charcoal using a "chimney starter" at en.wikipedia.org/wiki/Chimney_starter.

Foodies might quibble about whether a blind tasting will reveal an organic tomato to be tastier than a non-organic tomato, but few people will argue against the merits of a tomato just picked, still warm from the vine, sliced, and enjoyed within minutes of its harvest. That alone is good enough reason for many to plant a few tomatoes in an already organic yard. I've found that there is indeed a distinct taste difference between a conventional carrot and an organic one—try your own taste test of your favorite fruits and vegetables! Remember that locally grown fare will be much fresher than supermarket varieties and those imported from far away.

Gardeners should learn to *compost*, and there's plenty of information to educate them. *Organic Gardening*, one of the classic organic gardeners' guides, publishes instructions, tips, improvements, and reader solutions to building a better compost bin.

It also pays to learn what plants like to be next to each other and how they can benefit growth. This is known as companion planting. For example, basil is said to improve the flavor of tomatoes as it encourages the tomatoes' growth and repels flies and mosquitoes. Corn and tomatoes don't mix well—worms may seek out tomatoes and, in turn, infest the corn. A bit of research into companion planting for your own garden will show you extensive lists of good combinations, as well as combos to avoid. Organicgardening.com has a wealth of information on this, too.

def•i•ni•tion

Compost is a mixture of organic matter (leaves, grass, vegetable and fruit scraps from the kitchen) that "cooks" into a nutrient-rich soil. By building a compost pile (no fancy turner needed, although that keeps the pile neat), you can recycle your yard waste into rich soil for your garden, your flower beds, and your yard. Find instructions at www.organicgardening.com.

The Bigger Picture

Sustainable, organic gardens aren't just for the backyard gardener, though. These days, small organizations are working to help farmers in less-developed countries establish hardier crops by replenishing soil nearly ruined by agricultural expansion. By teaching farmers how to care for the land and replenish it and to fight deforestation and erosion by planting trees, organizations such as Sustainable Harvest International is giving farmers and their families food and income without harming their surroundings.

Other individuals are working to prevent loss of seed varieties. According to Annie B. Bond, executive producer of *Care2 Healthy Living Channels*, our population relies on just 20 varieties of plants for 90 percent of our food. If something were to happen to the supply, the results could be disastrous, along the lines of what happened when the potato crops in Ireland failed in the 1840s, leading to the Irish potato famine.

Bond encourages her readers to start saving seeds from their own crops in order to "protect the health and biodiversity of the plants we grow."

That's not a bad idea.

Hazard

Speaking of seeds, we should mention some of what big business is doing to our seed supply. Several of the world's largest seed suppliers are succeeding in getting regulations passed around the world preventing farmers from collecting seeds from their own crops to replant for the coming year. By patenting their genetically modified seeds, these companies are laying claim to the seeds, thus disrupting a centuries-old practice that helped small farmers earn a living without having to buy seeds each year. Lawsuits are being filed and honored against farmers who save their own seeds. In India in 2004, farmers lost their crops to drought, had no seed to replenish their fields, and could not afford to buy new seed. More than 16,000 farmers committed suicide (some by drinking the pesticides!), according to an article by Margot Ford McMillen in the *Progressive Populist* magazine (February 2007).

The Least You Need to Know

- Everyone—humans, pets, wildlife—benefits when we care for our lawns without using pesticides.

- Making your lawn organic is not as daunting as it may sound, although patience is required because it may take several seasons before you see permanent results. You have to accept that it won't look like an artificial green carpet.

- Organic gardening is a pleasant pastime, a way to use your own kitchen and lawn waste, and a productive way to use some of your yard, so learn to eat what you sow.

- Organic gardening practices help communities fight the ravages of agribusiness by restoring the health of the soil and allowing local farmers to become self-sufficient.

- It's a good idea to save and replant any seeds you encounter from your own garden or from fruits and vegetables at your table.

Chapter 3

Chemicals in Cosmetics and Body Care Products

In This Chapter

◆ Skin treatments penetrate into our cells

◆ Daily exposure to chemicals through the use of cosmetics and personal hygiene products

◆ Cosmetics and the menacing unknown of nanoparticles

◆ Fresh, safe cosmetics in your kitchen

Chemicals have proliferated since the advent of petroleum ingredients in the mid-1900s, and in some cases our rush to apply these new miracle ingredients surpassed our cautionary safety studies. The practice to use some substances with the assumption that it was safe until proven otherwise became routine. Today many such chemicals are being traced to health and contamination problems. In this chapter, we'll take a look at which chemicals are potentially dangerous, where to find them, and how to avoid them.

Cosmetics: Color at What Cost?

Was Cleopatra safe? Probably not—chances are her elaborate makeup came from powders and pigments made with heavy metals. Lead, cadmium, and mercury are all common coloring agents used in paints, even today. And traces of some of these toxic materials are still turning up in some cosmetic products, which are only loosely regulated.

But consumer knowledge is leading to improvements. Kohl, for example, which is made of lead and commonly used in some cultures, was recently banned from U.S. cosmetics. The use of crushed beetles as a coloring agent is still allowed, though its use is being examined because of allergy reports and even some incidents of anaphylactic shock caused by exposure to the dead bugs in food and cosmetics. (Look for *carmine* on the label to avoid this toxin.)

Coal-tar coloring agents are commonly used in cosmetics, hair dyes, and foods, but they must be batch-certified by the FDA. Watch for ingredients labeled FD&C #XXX, D&C #XXX, or External D&C #XXX, and you'll find petroleum-based coal tar dyes. They're everywhere, but try to avoid them whenever you can.

Antibacterial soaps were once the darlings of the kitchen, but they quickly found their way into the doghouse because of concerns that as we overprotect ourselves from bacteria, we provide them with the impetus necessary to fortify themselves against our attacks—thus creating stronger and more resilient strains of bacteria that we may be unable to conquer in the future. We're already seeing mutant strands of staph germs and bacterial infections in hospitals, where antibiotic treatment is the standard. We're better off helping our bodies to develop immunity to these attackers in our environment without using artificial ammunition against them.

Going Green

Find out what's in the products you use and whether their manufacturers have agreed to help protect your health: www.safecosmetics.org/companies/signers.cfm.

Reserve the use of antibacterial soaps for those situations when you feel it's really necessary for your family's health rather than as a daily use soap. For example, bacteria from raw poultry sometimes can be contaminated by unsanitary processing conditions, so cleaning up the kitchen with antibacterial soap or spray after preparing a chicken or turkey dinner could be warranted. Or use the soap when someone in the family has the flu. But you don't need to use the antibacterial hand soap every time you wash your hands. The active ingredient in many antibacterial products, Triclosan, has been indicated as potentially harmful to the human liver and can form carcinogenic chlorine gas when mixed with tap water and endocrine-disrupting dioxins and exposed to sunlight.

Women of today use an estimated average of 12 body care products daily, each with an estimated 10 different chemicals, resulting in daily doses of more than 200 chemicals. The Environmental Working Group (EWG) reports that only 11 percent of the 10,500 ingredients in these products have been tested for safety; one third are known carcinogens and stay in the body. Young women pass their lipstick on to future children. Many chemicals are absorbed into the body through the skin, and the average woman is said to ingest 4 pounds of lipstick over her lifetime. That's a tasty snack. And all this delicious beauty costs an average of $650 per year, per woman.

Today cosmetics have evolved into a $35 billion international industry, positioning this industry as a powerful lobbying force against government regulatory agencies such as the EPA and FDA. Yet strides are being made. In January 2006, a landmark agreement was struck when 500 cosmetic firms agreed to voluntarily remove harmful and potentially unsafe ingredients from their products.

The EWG reports that many cosmetics contain potential and known carcinogenic chemicals, including formaldehyde. Typically, industry advocate groups deny such claims, citing with disdain research indicating that rats prenatally exposed to certain chemicals developed sexual organ ambiguity—some were born with male and female characteristics. These malformations resulted from particularly high doses of the chemicals, say industry proponents, and are not accurate indicators of danger posed to humans using cosmetics with such ingredients.

> **Going Green**
>
> Is your makeup safe? Look up your favorite products, and see how they rank on the scale of toxicity: www.ewg.org/reports/skindeep2/index.php.
>
> The Environmental Health Association of Nova Scotia provides yet another list of common beauty care products and their chemical constituents: www.lesstoxicguide.ca/index.asp?fetch=personal.

A wealth of information is available to help you make your own decisions about whether you're willing to engage in daily use of a product that is known to cause abnormalities and disease at certain doses.

And Now Nanos

Just as cosmetic companies are recognizing the need to provide safety information for their customers, a new wave of cosmetic development is coming from the scientific community—*nanotechnology*. And it presents a whole host of new concerns about product safety.

def•i•ni•tion

Nanotechnology is the study of microscopic subatomic particles called nanoparticles. It explores their uses and safety.

Exciting discoveries are happening in the field of molecular science. Scientists have discovered how to manipulate the tiniest known elements of matter—microscopic subatomic particles—to surprising outcomes. Resulting compounds are being integrated into cosmetics, pharmaceuticals, and other industrial uses, in spite of the fact that the nanotechnology is still in the discovery phases of science, with many unknowns outstanding. Nanoparticles have been rushed to the market as possible healing agents, but their use goes far beyond medical consultation. Many cosmetic companies are incorporating nanoparticles into their cosmetic products, in spite of the fact that questions about safety have not been resolved, and evidence is mounting that nanoparticles may be toxic to humans, according to in-depth reports by Friends of the Earth and the EWG.

Hazard

Nanoparticles can enter the bloodstream through the skin and circulate throughout the body. The safety or danger of such infiltration of the body has not been established.

The EWG analyzed 25,000 personal care product labels and found more than 250 products with 1 or more of 57 different types of nano-scale or micronized ingredients. Another 9,500 products contain ingredients that are available in nano-form, but were not identified specifically as nano-sized on the label.

No regulations exist for the labeling or use of these products at this time. One of the biggest concerns about nanoparticles is that since they're so small, they may be able to penetrate the skin easily, and many products have additives that push the particles into the body and toward the bloodstream at an accelerated rate. Once in the bloodstream, these particles can move all about the body, into the brain, heart, lungs, liver, kidneys, everywhere—and we're not sure how much damage they can or will do in these organs. But we do know that some nanoparticles have caused liver damage in humans and brain damage in fish and are suspected of causing lung damage in humans, which may be related to asthma.

This is another instance where the proposed Precautionary Principle, which asks manufacturers to withhold releasing any products until safety has been established, should be applied.

Friends of the Earth, a nonprofit organization that studied nanotechnology, has filed suit against the FDA demanding that commercial release of personal care products containing engineered nanomaterials be curtailed until scientific safety studies have been completed. You can read their full report online at www.foe.org/camps/comm/nanotech/nanocosmetics.pdf.

> **Green Speak**
>
> "Manufacturers seem to be following the pattern they established with conventional chemical ingredients—put poorly tested chemicals into personal care products and do the science later if at all."
>
> —Jane Houlihan, vice president for research at EWG, and author of the EWG assessment

The EWG has compiled a list of cosmetic products that contain nanoparticles. Micronized titanium dioxide and zinc oxide are particularly popular in sunscreens, but remember that only the nano versions of these elements are being questioned, so while your sunscreen may list these natural ingredients, they're not suspect unless they are nanoparticles, though that could be ambiguous on the label. Microparticles of titanium dioxide and zinc oxide have been found to produce free radicals which cause DNA damage to skin cells when exposed to UV light—perhaps more damaging than the skin cancer they're supposed to prevent!

Revlon, L'Oréal, and even Jason's Natural Products are listed as containing nanoparticles by EWG. Check for your favorite products at ewg.org/issues/cosmetics/20061010/table2.php.

So what do we have to do, give up using makeup now? No, we promised that going green didn't mean we'd have to go back to cave days, although it is worth noticing that many women of science choose to forego the beauty enhancements of makeup …

Nasty Nails

You've noticed that noxious smell when someone's polishing her nails in your vicinity—or even worse when nail polish remover comes out. Sure enough, both fumes signal poisons in the air that you should avoid. Nail polishes often have dibutyl phthalate (DBP), a reproductive toxin that has been identified as a cause of birth defects and banned in Europe. The EWG report Skin Deep found DBP in all of the test subjects, with highest levels present in women of childbearing age—those who most love nail polish are also the ones most likely to suffer the worst effects, on their unborn babies. Think, too, about the nail technicians breathing these fumes all day, every day.

The EWG project and Campaign for Safe Cosmetics helped score a healthy win for these women and others when two top nail manufacturers, Orly International (OPI polishes) and Sally Hansen, both agreed to remove DBP from their polish formulas.

Acetone in nail polish removers is toxic, too. Small doses can damage liver, kidneys, mucous membranes, and the corneas of eyes (on contact); large doses can be fatal. Many polish removers today are nonacetone; they still may be toxic but are preferable to the acetone products. Be sure to use these in a well-ventilated area, away from children.

Cruelty-Free Cosmetics

Since it's been illegal and immoral to test potentially harmful substances on humans, common scientific practice has been to subject animals to testing procedures to try to determine ill effects on humans. Millions of animals have been maimed, poisoned, tortured, and killed in the name of science.

Most of us have been inured to this tragic reality, and we've learned not to think about it, just as we avoid concern for animals while downing steak or Thanksgiving turkey. But let's rethink that position. Do you have a pet? I've found that my little Yorkie's leg is about the same size as a chicken leg, and when I touch her leg, I remind myself that I certainly wouldn't want to eat it! And I love her far too much to be able to subject her to torture just to make sure I'm safe from anything. Those laboratory and farm animals aren't mindless automatons with no feelings of pain. Remember that they're living creatures just like you and your pet, and then decide how you think they should be treated.

Look for cruelty-free labeling, and buy products that have not been tested on animals.

Make Your Own Makeup

Long before phthlates and nanoparticles existed, women were finding ways to paint their faces—sometimes with similarly toxic materials, such as the lead and mercury mentioned earlier. But now that we know about such dangers, we can still use nature's bounty to enhance our beauty. Not surprisingly, many cosmetics today are inspired or derived from natural botanicals, which often impart true healing qualities (as opposed to healing claims).

Growing your own organic herbs or ferreting them out at the local health food store or apothecary is challenging, and blending them to create a unique, fresh, and healthy product is fun! Here are a few ideas to get you started.

You've heard of a milk and honey complexion? Egyptians are said to have used milk to sooth and moisturize their skin, and both milk and honey do serve as excellent moisturizers. Egg white can be whipped up (or not) and used as a natural facial mask; sugar, salt, and/or baking soda make a great scrub for face and body, sloughing off dead skin, polishing, and deodorizing at the same time.

Crushed strawberries and cucumbers are joyful to dry or distressed skin, and we all know that earthen clay or mud can pull dirt and grime out of pores—many commercial products tout natural mud from the Dead Sea or other waterholes renowned for their health-giving properties.

Create an herbal bath soak/scrub by combining your favorite herbs (lavender, rose petals, orange peel, rosemary, or sage) with oatmeal and salt. Add a few drops of natural essential oil—your favorite fragrance. Tuck a few tablespoons of the mixture into a square of natural cotton (preferably organic) fabric, and tie the bundle with a piece of twine or ribbon. Hang it under the bathtub tap so water passes through the sachet as it fills your tub, and then use the packet to scrub your body and to clean and refresh your skin.

Make a facial steam by combining your favorite herbs—mint, lavender, sage, or thyme—and boiling them in a pot of water. When the water begins to boil, hold a towel over your head and lean (carefully!) over the pan to let the herbal steam soak into your pores, opening them and imbibing your skin with the natural healing qualities of the herbs.

Use diluted lemon juice to wipe your face clean of oil and close the clean pores opened by the steam.

Aromatherapists—those who use natural scents to help relieve stress and promote health among their clients, often through the use of naturally scented oils and massage therapy—say that certain herbs have different effects.

Lavender is supposed to be calming; rosemary is stimulating; and basil is said to help lift depression. Sage is used to clear and refresh the energy of a place or person, citrus oils are stimulating, and jasmine and rose are aphrodisiacs.

Buy henna—which has been around since prebiblical Ancient Egyptian times—at a middle-eastern grocery or the drug store as a natural alternative to dying your hair.

Want to lighten your hair or add highlights? Squeeze fresh lemon juice on wet hair; then sit outside in the sunshine for awhile. Be sure to shield your face and skin from the sun to avoid UV rays—remember that zinc and titanium dioxide are good natural sun-protective agents, but commercial sunscreens sometimes have enough dangerous chemicals in them that their health preventive qualities are outweighed by potential dangers.

Many new products are coming on the market today to compete with commercial powdered and liquid foundations. Made from natural minerals blended together to create various colors, these natural mixtures of crushed stone are said to feel silky and to be pure enough to safely leave on your skin all night long. Some include titanium dioxide and zinc—not micronized nanoparticles—and serve as natural sunscreens.

Disinfectants and antibacterial qualities are said to be found in tea tree oil, myrrh, and goldenseal. Lemon and other citrus oils have disinfectant qualities, and their acidity lends astringent properties as well.

Commercial Products with You in Mind

Some manufacturers put your health and your continued patronage above profits of the moment. The following cosmetics companies apply at least some knowledge of chemical hazards when making their products (look for their contact info in Appendix B):

Burt's Bees, Aubrey Organics, Lavera, Dr. Hauschka, Ecco Bella Botanicals, Dr. Bronner's Magic Soaps, The Body Shop International, barefaced Minerals, Jason's Natural Products (which were found to use nanoparticles in sunscreen). Also, there's Peacekeeper, whose advertisement says, "No Nasty Anything!" We love that, but carmine is a listed ingredient. Bugs don't qualify as a nasty ingredient in lipstick? What about being cruelty free? We appreciate their stance, but as in all environmental arenas, there's still a long way to go.

You can find many more safe cosmetic companies at www.safecosmetics.org. Although some of these companies have been known to use questionable ingredients, all are among the more than 500 that have now signed the Compact for Safe Cosmetics, a pledge to replace ingredients linked to cancer, birth defects, hormone disruption, and other negative health effects within three years.

Twenty-First-Century Chemicals and Cosmetics

As in many other cases, we can't help but note that many of the ills wrought upon the chemical industry have evolved from the synthetic chemicals derived from petroleum—petrochemicals. The good news is that our supply of petroleum is coming to an end, so chemical companies are already hard at work finding alternatives to the petrochemicals, whose dangers we are now recognizing.

The Center for Green Chemistry at the University of Massachusetts–Lowell, was founded by John Warner, a scientist whose child died of liver disease, leaving the father to wonder whether chemical toxicity might have been the cause. Warner has been instrumental in developing this new field, the parameters of which are to create policies and chemicals that are sustainable—within one generation. It's a tall order, but it is clearly the best possible direction for the chemical industry to take in the face of unexpected endemic pollutants already present in our air, water, soil, and bodies. Most encouraging is the fact that this is not only an academic venture. Many chemical companies, including Dupont, Pfizer, and SC Johnson are active participants in this movement, and the American Chemical Society has founded the Green Chemistry Institute to help further research.

Many large companies are working together to change from using chemical pollutants to healthier and more energy efficient alternatives. Are they motivated by safety issues and fear of lawsuits? That is unlikely. Consumer demand drives these business innovations. As public awareness of the dangers of chemical pollutants and the importance of energy efficiency grows, businesses are rushing to give buyers what they want. Perhaps our economy is moving us in a win/win direction for all.

> **Green Gamut**
>
> Currently, environmentally benign alternative technologies have proven to be economically superior and function as well as or better than more toxic traditional options. When hazardous materials are cut from processes, all hazard-related costs are cut as well, significantly reducing hazardous materials handling, transportation, disposal, and compliance concerns (Center for Green Chemistry).

The Least You Need to Know

◆ Cosmetic ingredients are only loosely regulated, allowed and considered safe until proven otherwise.

◆ Many cosmetic ingredients are being found to pose significant safety dangers to our health.

◆ Many cosmetics contain nanoparticles, which can penetrate the skin and may be dangerous to the body.

◆ It's wise to learn more about dangerous ingredients and to read the label of products you're interested in before buying and using them.

◆ Many cosmetic and chemical companies are working hard to create healthier products.

14

Chemicals in Cleaning Products

In This Chapter

- ◆ Toxic cleaning products
- ◆ Products to avoid and why
- ◆ Natural cleaning agents
- ◆ Tips for natural green cleaning solutions

Most of us want our homes to be clean and free of germs—safe, healthy havens for our families. It's not surprising that when the chemical industry comes forward with a great new product that kills germs or restores whiteness, we want to use it! But after decades of applying some household miracle magic, we've learned that there can be a high price to pay for getting our homes squeaky clean.

Many of our favorite cleaning products are toxic. By using them, we're polluting our homes, waterways, and air and creating potential health hazards for our families, pets, neighbors, and communities. Children are particularly susceptible to the dangers posed by cleaning products and other chemicals in the air because their lungs are still developing and damage to them can be life-long. But we don't have to sacrifice clean living for a healthy environment. We can follow guidelines on which products to avoid and how to replace them with human- and earth-friendly substitutes.

Bypass Toxic Products

When you learn a little bit about some of the various cleaning agents commonly used around the home and their ingredients, it becomes much easier to create a healthier environment for your family. Let's take a look at some of the items often found under the kitchen sink.

Chemical Cleaning Agents to Avoid

Be aware that labels on products that say "Caution," "Warning," or "Danger" indicate that a product can be fatal at some dose, whether by a taste, sip, gulp, or gasp. Avoiding products with these designations will be better for you, your family, and your pets.

def•i•ni•tion

Volatile organic compounds (VOCs) are toxic substances in gases emitted from many caustic chemicals, paints, adhesives, formaldehyde, and common building materials. If you must use VOC-containing products, keep the area well ventilated.

Hazard

Never combine cleaning chemicals. Many different chemicals can interact in dangerous ways.

The most dangerous cleaners in most homes are the corrosive cleaners containing lye or acid—drain cleaners, oven cleaners, and some toilet bowl cleaners. These can burn if they come into contact with your skin, eyes, and throat—and sometimes contact can be airborne. Many such cleaners contain *volatile organic compounds* (*VOCs*), which can irritate and damage lungs and respiratory systems when they become airborne.

If your drains are clogged, use the old-fashioned methods of running a metal snake through the drain to dislodge hair and solids or try a plunger. If those methods fail, call the plumber instead of pouring corrosive fluids down the drain and into the waste stream!

Chlorine bleach and ammonia are both toxic on contact, when airborne, and to ecosystems when they migrate from wastewater. When the two are combined, they form a very poisonous gas—chloramine—that can cause lasting damage to your respiratory system.

Most public water supplies are disinfected with chlorine—and while its use can be invaluable when it comes to making contaminated water safe for drinking, it is not something you want to drink or saturate your body with. Remember that your skin is the largest organ of your body, and it absorbs many substances it comes in contact with. You can purchase a filter for your shower or for your whole house to help remove the chlorine and fluoride intentionally added to your water supply as well as metals and some microbes that could contaminate your supply. Reverse osmosis is one of the most effective and popular water filtration systems.

Another ingredient to avoid is Naphtha, a carcinogenic petroleum distillate found in cleaning fluid, shoe polish, lighter fluid, solvents such as for painting, and lantern fuel.

Perchlorethylene, a commonly used dry cleaning chemical, is a probable carcinogen and a neurotoxin that can damage the brain, liver, kidneys, and reproductive and nervous systems. Even the bags used to protect newly cleaned garments can carry the toxic chemical into your home.

Search for "green" cleaners who will safely launder your "dry clean only" fabrics using a gentle wet method instead, or ask your dry cleaner if they can safely wet-wash your clothing items so you don't have to bring these toxics home or wear them. You might even find that you can safely wash some items and line dry them at home instead of dry cleaning them.

Green Speak

"Regrettably, REACH (Registration, Evaluation, and Authorisation of Chemicals) does not have all it takes to adequately protect us and future generations from further contamination—far from it—but now for the first time a law is in place that can, if properly enforced, help reduce our daily exposure to chemicals that can cause cancer, birth defects and affect reproductive health. The EU decided to give the chemical companies up to 11 years to come forward with safety data, which is irresponsibly slow. But despite all its scandalous shortcomings, REACH could be the beginning of a new era."
—Jorgio Riss, Greenpeace European Unit Director who fought for EU legislation to test chemicals

Laundry detergents are often made with phosphates. While some claim that phosphates enhance cleaning power, their devastating effect on the environment far outstrips their value in the laundry machine. Some states have outlawed the use of phosphate detergents to protect their waterways. Phosphates serve as a nutrient to water-borne algae, causing overgrowth of algae in waterways. The green plant draws oxygen out of the water, curtailing the oxygen supply for marine life, which results in fish kills. Algae floating on the surface of water also prevents sunshine from reaching into the depths of streams and water bodies, preventing other natural plant life from growing, and robbing the water-based ecosystem of a natural food source and nesting protection. This contamination affects whole water bodies, creating dead zones where sea life once provided food and recreational values for local economies. Please choose phosphate-free laundry detergents.

Fabric softeners contain many dangerous chemicals, including chloroform, benzyl acetate, and pentane, known carcinogens, neurotoxins, and lung irritants. Although they seem fragrant, that's a cover for chemicals that can cause headaches, stomachaches, dizziness, breathing difficulty, and fatigue.

Carpets are difficult to clean, so carpet-cleaning detergents often contain a cocktail of potentially harmful chemicals. Some contain cleaning solvents similar to dry-cleaning chemicals (perfluorcarbons) or acids, disinfectants, and fragrances, any of which may be dangerous to inhale or ingest. Actors Kelly Preston and John Travolta's son Jett became ill after crawling on recently cleaned carpets, and the couple suspect the chemical exposure caused his illness, Kawasaki Disease. Preston became a spokesperson for Children's Health Environmental Coalition (CHEC) for several years to help alert other parents to the dangers of chemicals in the environment.

Stain-repellant chemicals once applied to protect carpets and upholstery from soiling were also dangerous. A main ingredient in these products was perflouro-octane sulfonate, a persistent organic pollutant and suspected hormone disruptor; however, the main manufacturer of these products, 3M, discontinued using PFOS in 2000 because of concerns about its persistence in the environment. Today 3M products are made with chemicals of lower toxicity and which are more degradable thus less persistent in the environment.

A study released in 2007 found that the testosterone levels of Massachusetts men declined 17 percent from 1987 to 2004. A decline in male births has been reported and scientists have documented sex abnormalities among amphibians—males have female organs—particularly those exposed to chemicals such as those in agricultural areas. An increase of male sterility has also been documented in some regions. All of these changes may be linked to the prevalence of hormone-disrupting chemicals in the environment, including some POPs (persistent organic pollutants) and phthalates, a chemical used in production of PVC (polyvinyl chloride) and plastics—including the soft rubber toys given to teething children—that has been found to be ubiquitous both in our environment and in our bodies. We are only beginning to explore and discover the health effects of low doses of these toxics.

Women Know That Clean Means Green

One woman has taken her environmental concerns to the level of action. Lois Marie Gibbs gained fame as the most outspoken and indefatigable resident of Love Canal in Niagara Falls, New York, when the local school was built on a hazardous waste site where dioxin—a POP—had been buried. Gibbs' son and other school children became ill, and the government finally bought out homeowners and declared the area the first Superfund site. Gibbs founded the Center for Health and Environmental Justice (CHEJ), which helps communities address environmental problems. Among other environmental activities, CHEJ has organized a campaign to fight PVC, which has been successful in getting several companies to stop carrying PVC and phthalate-containing products. (For more information, visit www.chej.org.)

Another woman whose experience has led her to fight environmental pollution is Nancy Chuda, who co-founded the Children's Health Environmental Coalition (CHEC) with her husband Jim when their daughter Collette died of Wilm's Tumor, a cancer they believe was caused by a termite treatment Nancy was exposed to during pregnancy.

CHEC provides a comprehensive website (www.checnet.org) with a wealth of information about the chemicals we commonly use in our homes and that are prevalent in our environment, with details about the detrimental effects suspected and known to be caused by these substances. The website also provides many resources for reducing exposure to chemicals.

CHEC has the support of many scientists and celebrities and has been successful in influencing legislation to protect children from chemicals. Science and governing agencies are just beginning to recognize the importance of the fact that children are smaller than adults and their developing cells are at greater risk of being affected by poisons.

The CHEC newsletter provides monthly briefs on environmental concerns geared to their child's age, such as the dangers of microwaving formula in plastic containers (such as baby bottles!) or hazards at floor level for kids in the crawling stage, such as pesticides in the home, cleaning products, and fertilizers and other poisons carried in on shoe soles. Leave those shoes at the door!

Going Green

To learn more about the Children's Health Environmental Coalition, visit www.checnet.org, where you can read how to keep your house free of pesticides.

"You have to just become aware," Nancy Chuda told me for an article in *South Florida Parenting Magazine* in 2004. "But when you see this unbelievable growth in the organic industry, which has just exploded, you know it's working. Every time a mom goes into a store and makes a decision, we're making the change."

Easy Alternative Cleaning Solutions

I read recently that the average American home has nearly 200 different chemical cleaning products tucked under the sinks, in the shower, and in the garage. The companies that manufacture these products and the business majors who market them to us must be given credit for these numbers. They have us believing that every single application requires a different product (priced anywhere from a few bucks to tens of dollars and more). But the truth is a little acidic action, abrasive action, or microbial action can clean most things. Vinegar, baking soda, and essential oils can meet these needs without *off-gassing* any toxic fumes or draining poisons into the water supply.

def•i•ni•tion

Chemicals in products dissipate into the air—a process that can take years to occur in some materials. When the chemicals produce toxic fumes, it's referred to as **off-gassing**.

I'm cleaning out my bathrooms, kitchen, hall closet, and garage to see how many of these toxic products I can purge from my household. I'd like to whittle my cleaning collection down to a few essentials that can handle the entire job.

Have you noticed how many cleaners today are orange-scented and boast citrus power for better cleaning? These claims are based in reality. But you don't need to buy the cleaners to get the benefits—you can use the fruits and their oils themselves. The natural essential oils of citrus fruits and many other botanicals have bactericidal powers—the same qualities that protect the plants they're derived from against attack from bacteria and other creatures. And the fragrance from lemon, orange, grapefruit, lime, or pine oils aren't synthetic concoctions designed to numb your senses or mask unpleasant odors—they fight and eliminate the odor-causing bacteria without emitting toxic fumes.

Hazard

Beware: some essential oils are toxic, so read up on a specific oil before you use it, especially if you have pets or young children. But few are the potent poisons that conventional cleaning products pose. Here's a good resource: www.aromaweb.com/essentialoils/default.asp.

Experts suggest dissolving a few drops of essential oils, which are available at health food stores—be sure the label says "natural essential" and not "fragrance"—in vinegar, honey, or alcohol, and then diluting mixture with hot water. I just sprinkle a few drops of oil into the hot water bucket for mopping the tile floors, and my home is sparkling and fragrant in minutes. I like the citrus oils, but when I'm tackling ants, I use cedarwood oil, which acts as a fragrant repellent—remember the cedar chests our grandmothers used to protect their linens from moths?

Essential oils are also said to offer other advantages when their fragrances are inhaled and waft to the brain. That's the basis of aromatherapy, which can provide an added benefit on your cleaning day. Lavender is said to have a calming effect, orange blossom and chamomile help to lift spirits, and rosemary works as a stimulant and relieves headaches, arthritis, aches, and pains.

As a cleaning agent, baking soda has many valuable properties. A naturally occurring mineral called sodium bicarbonate, its abrasive quality can serve as a scouring powder that's gentle enough that it won't scratch your kitchen surfaces or tile. It deodorizes while it works and is also popular for cleaning refrigerators. Keep a small bowl of it in the corner of the fridge to continually combat odors (refresh every few weeks). You can sprinkle baking soda on carpets before vacuuming to absorb odors, and add it to laundry to soften the water and help remove stains. Wash some down the drain if you detect foul odors. Remember making volcanoes in science class as a kid? If you pour half a cup of baking soda down a clogged drain and chase it with half a cup of vinegar, that same bubbly reaction might help move your clog along and out of the drain.

Hazard _____

Don't pour vinegar in the drain if you've already used commercial drain cleaner—the chemical reaction could cause dangerous fumes.

Steel wool and elbow grease can tackle rust stains and lime buildup, saving you from using corrosive chemicals. Baking soda and steel wool are a good team for cleaning the oven.

Vinegar's acidity makes it a popular kitchen aid because it helps dissolve calcium buildup in coffee pots, dishwaters, and around faucets. It cuts through grease and soap scum, and, stinky as it is, it helps carry away foul odors as it evaporates. It also cleans windows, and when cleaning carpets, add a bit to your rinse water to help remove the soap sediment often left behind that causes carpets to get dirty faster. You can also mix vinegar with salt and water as a cleaning compound.

Lemon juice can lighten or brighten whites in the laundry or the kitchen and will also help remove stains. Its acidity fights odors, and it works as a glass cleaner as well.

Borax, another naturally occurring mineral, is useful as a cleaning agent. Add it to your laundry load to boost the power of your laundry soap. Sprinkle a bit of borax in the bottom of garbage pails to fight mold and bacteria and their odors. Mix it with water and use to disinfect as you clean.

Use vinegar, baking soda, lemon juice, or borax to clean and disinfect toilets.

For the laundry, remember that soap is made from natural oils but can discolor light-colored clothes. You can buy natural soap and biodegradable detergents at health food stores, and many commercial detergents are now limiting the chemical content by eliminating colors and fragrances—particularly good for those who are chemically sensitive.

If you'd rather not mess with mixing your own cleaning agents or are just more comfortable using commercially prepared products, many are available. CHEC provides a Safer Products Store at its website (CHEC's Safer Products Store), and you can find more products at www.ecomall.com.

If you want to avoid cleaning agents altogether, you might try the microfiber mop. Just dampening this mop enables it to collect the tiniest dust particles from wood and tile floors. Microfiber towels and brushes do the same for tables, countertops, fan blades, and window shades, and they last forever if properly cleaned and cared for. Visit www.bluewondercloth.com.

As you can see, it's surprisingly easy to swap your routine caustic cleaning agents for natural alternatives. Your family will breathe easier and your home will smell and feel fresher than ever when you clean with citrus oils and other nontoxic products!

The Least You Need to Know

- Some chemicals in commonly used products can be fatal or cause developmental, brain, or nervous system damage. Small children and pets are more susceptible to these dangers than adults.

- You can use many safe alternatives to toxic cleaning agents and save money at the same time.

- Vinegar makes a fine household disinfectant when used instead of bleach.

- Baking soda can be used as a whitening agent and scouring powder.

- Citrus oils can help disinfect, repel insects, and freshen the air when a few drops are added to water and used for cleaning and mopping.

15

Creating a Green Home Interior

In This Chapter

◆ Toxic chemicals in our homes

◆ Recognizing the poisons

◆ Ways to eliminate home poisons

◆ Choosing toxic-free interiors to improve your indoor air quality

The EPA tells us that we spend as much as 90 percent of our time indoors, and quite often the air we breathe inside our homes, schools, and offices is more polluted than the outside air. Many of our furnishings, paints, carpets, and even the walls and floors are built from composite materials that include glues and adhesives, ammonia, formaldehyde, and other toxic chemicals that can poison the air for years. Today's tightly designed, super-efficient buildings can trap these poisons as they continue to multiply during years of off-gassing.

For those of you who wish to go green as well as those with allergy concerns, we've checked in with some interior designers who have health in mind. Read on for some of the wisdom they've shared with us.

Chemicals in Fabrics, Furniture, and Paints

Since petrochemicals (chemicals derived from petroleum) came on the scene in the mid-twentieth century, many thousands have been developed, and many applications have come into the marketplace, creating whole industries (plastics, cosmetics, pharmaceuticals, and many more) based on the formulations of these synthetic chemicals. These industries form a substantial chunk of our economy, so we have many vested interests in keeping synthetic chemicals in the field.

Strangely, in December 2006 the EPA approved new rules that increase by four times the amount of toxic pollutants a company can release before it is required to reveal the emissions to the public. Because companies are not required to disclose information about these levels of toxic chemicals before they release them into our environment, communities will be unable to consider whether such substances might be causing environmental problems. In addition, companies won't be motivated to find safer ways to dispose of toxic chemicals if they're allowed to simply dump them into the waterways, air, and landfills in such large quantities.

> ### Green Speak
>
> "The EPA has severely limited the public's right to know today. What communities don't know can hurt them. Critical possible threats will be hidden from view."
>
> —Tom Natan, research director for the National Environmental Trust, *The Delaware News Journal*, December 18, 2006

At the same time, the Union of Concerned Scientists (UCS) reports that the EPA is closing its nationwide network of libraries, destroying contents or shipping uncatalogued material to warehouses where they will be inaccessible and unsearchable. Scientists, the public, and the media will not have access to years' worth of studies the EPA has conducted and collected. While the government claims this is being done in an effort to cut the expense of maintaining its libraries, the UCS and many other groups are concerned that eliminating access to this data will enable known dangerous practices and exposures to continue. And it will also eliminate any evidence that such practices have been allowed despite evidence that they posed known dangers to the public.

Clearly, it's up to citizens to educate themselves and to protect themselves from such potential dangers.

Hazard

Candles and "air fresheners" with synthetic fragrances can numb olfactory organs so you don't smell anything. They also decrease the ability to taste and enjoy food. Does that smell like fresh air to you?

Creating a Healthier Home

"There are so many things to be cautious about in the home—the body can only take so much toxins," said green interior designer Bernadette Upton when I interviewed her for *The Palm Beach Post's First Sunday Magazine*. "Creating healthier interiors is a whole new way of thinking—it affects every decision I make."

Chances are you and your family have already absorbed high levels of many chemicals which have become endemic in our environment. You may not have noticed any ill effects, or maybe you or your children have developed asthma, or someone has come down with cancer, yet no one knows why. Now that you're learning more about chemicals and their effects on our bodies and our environment, you know that it pays to avoid them whenever possible. You can reduce your family's exposure to chemicals in the environment by creating a healthy home with a focus on eliminating toxic chemicals wherever possible. Here are some tips and starting points for you.

Floor Coverings

Which should you choose: carpet, tile, or wood floors? Think local, honest materials for flooring. Natural interior designers eschew many carpets which are made with formaldehyde and which use heavy adhesives to secure the carpet in place. For healthy interiors, choose natural wool carpets or others made without toxic chemicals, because the chemicals tend to continue off-gassing into your home for years after installation. Some of the gases common in carpet manufacture are considered harmful to developing lungs in children and could aggravate respiratory conditions, such as asthma, even in adults. If you buy conventional carpet, ask the installers to allow it to rest outside or in an open area for a day or so to allow some of these toxics to emit before bringing them into your home. Also ask installers to use tacking strips during carpet installation instead of glue. Keep windows in the room open as long as you still smell the odor of the carpet and any installation adhesives, if used.

You can buy carpet made from recycled soda bottles, too. This is better than carpet made from raw synthetic materials, but it's really just delaying the need to dispose of the plastic bottles. We'll all be better off when we stop creating plastic since its after-life is, well, forever.

Carpets made with natural fabrics can safely biodegrade, but it's far better to recycle them instead. The Carpet America Recovery Effort (CARE; www.carpetrecovery.org) is a consortium of carpet industry representatives and government leaders working to make carpet disposal more environmentally friendly. The organization reports that in 2002, some 4.7 billion pounds of carpet was disposed of, 96 percent in landfills. Because most elements of carpets are recyclable, the organization has established a goal of diverting 40 percent of that trash away from landfills through recycling by 2012. The group is on track with 224.6 million pounds of carpet diverted from the landfills in 2005, with 194.3 million pounds being recycled, twice as much as the year before. When you buy carpet, ask the seller if he can remove your old carpets for recycling instead of going to the curb for waste pickup.

Tricycle Inc. is a design firm that specializes in sustainability and has created digital versions of many designer samples to reduce waste. According to their research, one carpet sample, a swatch a designer might show to a client, uses 1 quart of oil in manufacturing. When that sample is discarded, it contributes 1.5 pounds of waste to the landfill. Tricycle says they sent 37,700 digital samples to designers in one year—no waste, no oil used—preserving 942,000 gallons of oil and preventing 56,500 pounds of carpet samples from being dumped in landfills.

A leader in sustainability in the carpet industry is a company called Interface, run by CEO Ray Anderson, who has made a name for himself and his company in industrial ecology. Anderson wants his company to be the world's first environmentally restorative company by 2020 and is pioneering management and manufacturing processes to achieve this goal.

Another carpet company that's taken initiative in environmental business practices is Milliken and Company, which was the first carpet company in the United States to replace chlorinated solvents with organic alternatives in 1990 and introduced PVC-free carpet in 1986. Since 1999, Milliken has operated a zero-waste business and offsets its carbon emissions through investments in forests and alternative energy facilities. Milliken is a founding member of the U.S. Green Building Council.

> **Green Speak**
>
> "Hard surface flooring is another example of a healthy material and will not only reduce dust mite exposure, but pesticide exposure as well. Studies show that there is up to 100 times more pesticide exposure in carpet dust than in the average lawn!"
>
> —Denise Robinette, HealthyLiving Interiors

If you choose tile, select local materials rather than fancy Italian marble that must travel around the world to find you (unless it's for your Italian villa, of course!). New, ecofriendly materials include tiles made from recycled glass and recycled light bulbs and Marmoleum, a natural linoleum-type material made from ground flax seeds and linseed oil with no petrochemicals and a long life span. Popular in the 1950s, the material is reemerging as a healthy option for home interiors today.

Denise Robinette created her own exotic floor using broken pieces of marble granite and slate from tile yards—extra pieces she collected from their refuse piles over time. When she had enough, she pieced them together into a beautiful slate mosaic for her entry foyer.

Interior designer Denise Robinette used pieces of broken, discarded granite to create this beautiful mosaic granite foyer floor.

(Denise Robinette, Courtesy HealthyLiving Interiors)

An interesting new flooring material is leather floor tiles such as those offered by Ecodomo. These floor tiles and wall coverings are made of 65 percent recycled leather mixed with natural rubber and bark from the Acacia tree which, the company says, regrows without damaging the tree and is similar to cork bark. These tiles emit low VOCs (volatile organic compounds) when installed with recommended adhesives, and the leather is maintained with periodic natural wax treatments.

Wood floorings are warm, but they come from trees, and we now realize that our forests are not a sustainable resource if we're using them faster than they can replenish themselves. However, you can recycle wood from any number of previous uses and it will still provide its natural glow to your home. Polish up some old barn siding, or look for refinished chestnut (no longer available fresh because of a blight) or timber dredged from river bottoms after tumbling from mill barges a century ago—the underwater treatment renders this wood nearly impervious to pests and rot.

Tiles made of recycled leather.

(Courtesy Ecodomo)

Faux wood and laminate products are composed of many synthetic materials and may pose off-gassing and allergy problems in the household. Many of the synthetic chemicals used in applications such as this have never been tested for health safety, and evidence is mounting that some chemicals can contribute to respiratory and other health conditions.

Bamboo flooring is gaining in popularity because it's both warm and sustainable. Bamboo grows very quickly and is being farmed around the world as a hardwood substitute, although there is some concern that western demand for supplies in eastern countries may outpace production, causing Asian farmers to dedicate more land to bamboo farming and production than feasibly sustainable. Look for a local source if this is your flooring material of choice.

Robinette says that bamboo flooring is 25 percent harder than red oak and more dimensionally stable. This fast-growing "grass" derives from managed growth areas; it grows a foot per day and takes just five years to reach maturity. By contrast, hardwoods take from 50 to 200 years to reach their prime. Bamboo is also harvested by hand, minimizing the impact on the local environment.

Another innovative new flooring material is cork, created from bark peeled from cork oak trees. New bark is said to grow back in nine years without killing the tree. Cork provides sound proofing and insulation, and as a natural material it's somewhat nonallergenic and actually has microbial properties to fight bacteria as well as repel insect pests. Expanko creates high-quality cork flooring as well as recycled rubber flooring.

"Cork is being reintroduced after being used hundreds of years ago in libraries in the Northeast," says interior designer Denise Robinette of HealthyLiving Interiors. "There are so many flooring options now available such as bamboo, reclaimed woods, recycled glass, and even recycled leather tiles."

Fabrics and Furniture

Fabric coverings for furnishings can pose similar off-gassing hazards, having been drenched with toxic chemicals, such as cotton frequently receives during the growing process, or treated with toxic substances such as fire-retardants and stain-resistant compounds. Fabrics may be secured to furniture frames with a heavy dose of formaldehyde-containing adhesive, also a potential problem. Choose your furnishings and fabrics carefully, and try to avoid heavy chemicals. Let new items sit outside in the breeze for several hours to air out chemical gases before bringing them into the house.

> **Green Gamut**
>
> Antique and second-hand furniture is often toxic-free. It may be old enough to pre-date the use of synthetic petrochemcial materials such as formaldehyde, adhesives, and composites; or it may have already released the toxic fumes associated with these substances through years of off-gassing.

"Childhood asthma has risen 72 percent in the past 10 years," says Bernadette Upton, who designs ecofriendly homes for the American Lung Association and is co-author of their healthy nursery interiors guide, *A Baby's Breath*. Lung disease and breathing problems are the leading killer of children during their first year of life, and Upton believes that the increase in respiratory ailments among children is directly related to chemicals off-gassing in their home environments. Upton owns a store, EcoDecor, in North Palm Beach where designers and consumers can find information and supplies for green design.

Fabrics and carpets also harbor dust in the home—posing a real danger to those with asthma and allergies. Denise Robinette, owner of HealthyLiving Interiors and co-founder of the HealthyLiving Foundation, suggests using furniture made with leather upholstery which can easily be cleaned and maintained dust-free. Avoid vinyl or plastic upholstery as both are toxic forever and essentially nonbiodegradable.

To also cut down on dust in your home, choose easy-to-clean blinds instead of fabric draperies. Rice paper blinds and shades provide a nontoxic alternative to fabric as do bamboo stick shades.

Paints

Paints have high concentrations of VOCs, toxic chemicals that can cause havoc when airborne, and pose another serious threat to the developing lungs of infants and children. Paints can cause asthma and allergies and are just another noxious pollutant that healthy bodies should not be subjected to.

> ### Green Gamut
>
> When I requested Sherwin Williams Harmony brand no-VOC paint for my home interior painting, the cost of painting 1,200 square feet increased by less than 10 percent, and the odor decreased by more than 90 percent!

Pay extra for low- or no-VOC paints; many manufacturers offer them, but you may need to ask for them. If you can't find them at the neighborhood building supply store, check stores that specialize in paints.

When selecting the paint, don't confuse low- or no-odor paints with low- or no-VOC paints. Often the low-odor paints are just as toxic or even more toxic because they've added more chemicals to mask the offensive odors that alert you to the poisons. Also remember that just because a paint, adhesive, solvent, or other product is VOC-free, it may still have toxic chemicals in the mix. Continue to check labels for ammonia, formaldehyde, and other chemicals that could be toxic, even if they don't qualify as a volatile organic compound.

Whether you use products with VOCs, low- or no-VOC paint, or any other product, always paint with doors and windows wide open and let the room aerate frequently for years after application.

Toxic paint fumes can persist for years and can irritate respiratory systems, triggering asthma and other reactions in the chemically sensitive. For more information on healthy paints, sealants, caulks, and other building finishes, check out American Formulary Manufacturing, the makers of SafeCoat paints, at www.afmsafecoat.com. This company makes products that are pollutant free, not just no/low VOC.

When it comes to improving efficiency, an interesting new paint has been developed to help keep homes cooler in summer by reducing the surface temperature of the house by as much as 40 degrees. Using technology developed and applied by the U.S. military, Textured Coatings of America produces a thicker paint that's mixed with tiny pieces of reflective pigments that help modify the temperature by redirecting sunrays when they hit the house. The paint is also stronger and more durable than conventional exterior paints, and the company claims the paint can last up to 40 years—making the investment a money saver with reduced repainting and energy costs.

Retrofitting an Older Home

You can apply many of the same principles to your renovation and redecoration projects that you would consider when building a new home. There are many ways to increase efficiency and cut costs during home upgrades. A bonus in working with an existing home is that you may find that many of the materials used in construction of homes built before the 1950s are more environmentally friendly than materials developed since the advent of synthetic chemicals. Or if they were built with particle board or laminates, they have already had the chance to off-gas most of their toxic fumes.

And check with the IRS or your accountant to see whether you may be eligible for state and federal tax credits to offset the cost of your energy-saving home improvements. New credits and incentives are frequently available. You may even be able to get a credit from your utility company when you replace old appliances with more energy-efficient models.

As you can see, whether you're buying a new house or retrofitting an older one, there are may things you can do to make your home environmentally friendly, energy-efficient, and healthier for you and your family.

> **Green Speak**
>
> "Chemicals have replaced bacteria and viruses as the main threat to health. The diseases we are beginning to see as the major causes of death in the latter part of (the 1900s) and into the 21st century are diseases of chemical origin."
>
> —Dr. Dick Irwin, toxicologist, Texas A&M University, from *The Guide to Less Toxic Products*

The Least You Need to Know

◆ Both furnishings and finishing products are often created with toxic chemicals.

◆ Toxic chemicals come into your home with the furniture, cabinets, paints, and carpet that you buy.

◆ The fumes of these chemicals are toxic and can contaminate the indoor air of your home for years.

◆ You can avoid many of these toxics when you know what to buy—and what not to buy—for your home.

◆ Choosing hard surface flooring and nonporous upholstery helps prevent dust and allergen buildup.

◆ Sometimes special chemical treatments, such as for flame or stain resistance, present toxicity problems.

Part 5

Going Green at Work

Many businesses are leading the way into the green revolution, designing green buildings that are energy efficient with alternative power supplies from windmills and solar panels, having zero-waste (or close to it) streams thanks to recycling, and reusing of building materials and office supplies.

Other companies are incorporating green principles into their business practices, such as the way Interface carpets will come back to collect their product when you're done with it (and recycle it into a new product) or Starbucks coffee will give you a 10¢ discount if you bring your own cup for java. Some businesses are building their own solar panels and windmills for the ultimate energy efficiency projects.

"It's the new low-energy paper shredding program."

Chapter 16

Green Buildings LEED the Way

In This Chapter

◆ The popularity of green building in commercial design and construction

◆ Builders can earn green building certification

◆ Green buildings can save money as well as energy and resources

◆ Green building principles improve employee morale and performance

Often referred to as high-performance buildings or sustainable buildings, structures that genuinely earn such labels are designed, built, and managed with a greater emphasis on protecting the environment than conventional practices.

The varying standards for green buildings generally involve practices and products that conserve natural resources; reduce waste; recycle; avoid pollutants; and promote fresh, healthy air.

In this chapter, we'll learn details about an array of buildings that earned accolades for their environmental facets.

All About LEED

The U.S. Green Building Council is generally regarded as a key authority in setting standards and guidelines for sustainable buildings. The organization offers a voluntary certification program for structures that meet its standards. The program, Leadership in Energy and Environmental Design (LEED), evaluates participating buildings and offers prestigious certification at levels that include Certified, Silver, Gold, and Platinum.

> **Green Gamut**
>
> A $4 investment per square foot in building green nets a $58 benefit per square foot over 20 years (U.S. Green Building Council).

The areas addressed in the ranking include the site, water efficiency, energy efficiency, materials and resources, and indoor environmental quality.

Whether renovating an existing structure or building from scratch, builders are drawn to environmentally sound practices for protecting the environment as well as other benefits including reduced management costs, higher lease rates, and happy, healthy workers. Let's visit a few examples of green office buildings around the country.

Wind Facility Takes Gold

Wind NRG Partners in Hinesburg, Vermont, designed its facility to promote the use of renewable energy sources and provide its staff of about 45 people with a beautiful and healthy workplace. The project, with its rustic barnlike building, earned a LEED Gold rating.

NRG Systems designs and manufactures wind-measurement systems for the wind power industry. Fittingly, the facility generates about 80 percent of its electricity on site through a blend of solar and wind power. The primary fuel for heating is pellets from wood waste, according to information from the business.

The three-story building is on about 10 acres of the 56-acre property. While respecting existing ecosystems and allowing for wildlife habitats, the location and angling of the structure is designed to maximize solar exposure and cooling breezes and minimize heat loss and exposure to winter winds.

A pond multitasks as a recreation area and a feature of the cooling system. In the summer, heat from the building is removed through floor tubing and redirected to 2 miles of tubing in the bottom of the pond. The tubing in the concrete floors (8 miles' worth) is part of the heating and cooling system. Warm water circulates through the tubing in the winter, and cool water circulates in the summer.

Indoors, low-flow toilets and other water-saving plumbing fixtures enhance water conservation. It's estimated that NRG uses about 113,000 fewer gallons of potable water a year than a comparable conventional building.

Along with high-efficiency motors and other features, the building itself is designed to be energy efficient. Built to be airtight, windows are plentiful and open manually. Light pours into the building through the windows and skylights and flows through the open floor plan.

To promote healthy indoor air, NRG avoided carpets and uses nontoxic cleaning products. Other products include low-emission paints and caulk joint sealants and solvent-free construction adhesives. Attention to recycling and waste reduction also was part of the building process. The products used include recycled-glass tiles.

To help limit auto travel, the site was selected, in part, because it is near the homes of existing employees. Other employees are recruited from the local area. To encourage walking and biking, the project includes a pedestrian path, bicycle racks, and showers. Local materials selected during construction also worked to limit auto travel. In other gas-saving techniques, the firm offers a financial incentive for employees to purchase hybrid vehicles and also provides electric outlets for electric vehicles.

Green Speak

"Wind energy is a particularly appealing way to generate electricity because it [is] essentially pollution free. ... Wind farms can revitalize the economy of rural communities, providing steady income through lease or royalty payments to farmers and other landowners."

—American Wind Energy Association

Wind NRG Systems Building.

(Courtesy of U.S. Green Building Council)

Project on Old Industrial Site Nets Top LEED Rating

The Alberici headquarters in Overland, Missouri, a construction firm, earned a LEED Platinum certification for its relocation project which reused a structure that previously was a metals manufacturing plant on a site of about 14 acres. The Alberici headquarters, which houses a staff of about 200, also was recognized as one of the American Institute of Architects' Top Ten Green Projects.

The project involved both renovation and new construction. To take advantage of natural light and allow it to penetrate through the interior, the building offers perimeter windows, three atria, and an open design. Ninety percent of the staff members are able to look directly outdoors. Also, windows open to allow for natural ventilation.

On site, the green practices included limiting pavement area and adding natural drought-resistant landscaping. Rainwater from the garage roof is gathered and filtered for use in the cooling tower and sewage system. The reuse of rainwater along with water-efficient fixtures contributes to saving about 500,000 gallons of water annually.

Energy efficiency also is emphasized in this project. In addition to efficient products, traditional energy is supplemented by renewable sources generated on site. A 125-foot-tall wind turbine helps power the building and solar panels that preheat hot water.

Reducing waste from the construction process included grinding drywall for use as a soil amendment. Also materials selected for the décor included such environmentally preferable products as cork flooring and recycled rubber flooring.

Alberici Corporation head-quarters.

(Courtesy U.S. Green Building Council)

According to a case study for the Alberici corporate headquarters for the U.S. Green Building Council, "Indoor air quality is not just beneficial to the final occupants, but also creates a healthier construction site. Workers were going home feeling better, not dizzy from the typical construction materials, products, and processes."

Manhattan Gold

The Hearst Tower in New York, which incorporated an existing historic structure as its base, touts a LEED Gold rating. The 46-floor skyscraper was built to bring together the staffs of several magazines and some of the other enterprises run by the publishing firm.

The tower's distinctive appearance in the metropolitan skyline is based on its unusual diagonal grid pattern, which wraps the building in a framework of giant diamond-shaped segments. The unconventional structural technique required about 2,000 tons less steel than a traditional frame would need, according to Michael Wurzel, a partner with Foster and Partners, the architectural firm on the project. More than 90 percent of the structural steel contains recycled content.

Another feature that's both visually spectacular and environmentally functional is the waterfall that cascades over sculpted glass in the atrium. The waterfall provides an energy-efficient tool that helps cool and humidify the atrium. Other energy-saving features include efficient heating and air-conditioning, as well as the emphasis on natural light, which enters the building through about a mile's worth of tall glass windows. Sensors are used to adjust the amount of artificial light to the level that's necessary.

The water conservation techniques include collecting rainwater on the roof for various uses, including providing water for the waterfall in the atrium. An emphasis on low-emission paints and other products help protect air quality. Reducing waste also was part of the project. In addition to using materials with recycled content, the project team sent off about 85 percent of the construction debris for other uses.

> **Green Speak**
>
> "Green buildings are better for the environment. But what's becoming more and more apparent is that they're better for the bottom line. Energy-efficiency is one reason, but greater workforce productivity is proving to have an even more significant effect on company profits. Simply put, green buildings are cleaner, fresher and take advantage of natural lighting. They often establish a connection to nature. They're more comfortable and offer healthful amenities such as gyms, casual meeting rooms and colorful dining areas."
>
> —The Green Building Initiative

Environmental Agency Goes Platinum

The California Environmental Protection Agency Headquarters Building in Sacramento earned several environmental honors, including a LEED Platinum rating in 2004. The Environmental Protection Agency's Energy Star program also named it the "Most Sustainable Building in North America" in 2003.

The 25-floor office tower includes various energy-saving features, including motion detectors that turn lights on and off at workstations. Another noteworthy feature is a floor-by-floor fresh-air ventilation system that uses two intake ducts on each floor, rather than a central duct system.

Adding water-efficient fixtures and using native drought-resistant landscaping reduced water usage by 20 percent indoors and 50 percent outside.

Recycling construction debris and using recycled products also played a key role in the project. Carpet tiles and ceiling tiles each are made with recycled content. In addition to recycled content and salvaged materials, other criteria for selecting products included durability and flexibility.

The various energy-efficient, water-efficient, and waste-reducing efforts are providing a financial advantage in maintenance expenses. Among the waste-reducing measures that also save money are the practice of eliminating liners in the garbage cans and opting for reusable cloth bags in recycling bins. Those two relatively simple techniques save about $80,000 a year, according to a case study of the building issued by the U.S. Green Building Council.

> **Going Green**
>
> Jumpstart a green building project with a financial incentive. The U.S. Environmental Protection Agency provides links for various programs that offer grants, tax credits, loans, and rebates for qualifying projects. To see if your project fits, log on to www.epa.gov/greenbuilding/tools/funding.htm.

Some of these noteworthy green measures in the EPA building were part of a $500,000 project aimed at boosting efficiency through upgraded equipment, operations, and employee practices. The improvements are returning about $610,000 worth of savings yearly, according to the case study.

Computer Center Uses Solar Energy

The U.S. EPA National Computer Center in North Carolina earned a LEED Silver rating from the U.S. Green Building Council. The data-processing equipment in this building significantly boosts energy demand. A fraction of that is offset by electricity generated onsite from solar panels on about 15,000 square feet of the roof.

Among the energy-efficient devices are sensors that automatically dim the electric lights when natural light is available through the vertical glass panels and atrium. Occupancy sensors keep the high-efficiency fluorescent lights off in vacant areas, and manual switches allow workers to select a lower lighting level, if they prefer.

Builders used materials containing recycled content in different facets of the project, including the structural steel and acoustic ceiling tiles. Carpet tiles made from recycled fibers feature a random pattern that doesn't need to match exactly at the seams, thereby reducing the amount that would otherwise be wasted during installation. Rubber floor tiles in the kitchen contain material from recycled tires.

For its own waste, construction debris was sorted, allowing about 82 percent of the construction material (by weight) to be recycled.

Going Green

The U.S. Department of Energy offers a wealth of information related to designing, building, renovating, and maintaining high-performance structures. To peruse these tools, guidelines, and links, log on to www.eere.energy.gov/buildings/about/index.html.

Green Gamut

Buying one block of green power (100 kilowatt-hours) for a year replaces enough coal-fired power to prevent 2,207 pounds of carbon dioxide (CO_2), 6.64 pounds of sulfur dioxide (SO_2), 4.78 pounds of nitrogen oxides (NO_x), and 0.024 grams of mercury (Minnesota Office of Environmental Assistance).

Law School Saves Energy

Vermont Law School Oaks Hall in South Royalton, Vermont, with 23,500 square feet, built in 1998, was designed to accommodate eight classrooms, a courtroom, a student lounge, and an outdoor deck. The building uses significantly less energy than another building on campus of similar size.

The energy-efficient features in the three-story building include occupancy sensors that automatically turn off the high-efficiency fluorescent lights when a room is empty. The walls and roof are well insulated. The ventilation system, which offers fresh air, is activated where needed, based on the push of a button in the specific room that allows outdoor air to be supplied only to occupied rooms.

Also enhancing air quality are accessible windows that open and the selection of paints, flooring, and other materials with no or low toxicity. In addition to a focus on healthy indoor air quality, the project team selected materials that were durable and featured recycled and recyclable attributes. Among the products with recycled content are bathroom partitions made from recycled plastic, gypsum board drywall, and acoustical ceiling tiles and track. The wainscoting is made from straw-based wheat board.

The building's achievements earned several awards, including a Quality Building Council Award of Excellence for Sustainable Construction Design and a Vermont Governor's Award for Excellence in Pollution Prevention.

Shared Border Office Shares Environmental Responsibility

U.S./Canada Shared Port of Entry, about 100,000 square feet in seven structures, is a joint LEED-certified project of the U.S. General Services Administration and Canada Border Services Agency. The neighboring governments both use the site that covers 22.8 acres.

The project's design and management is geared to achieve water and energy efficiency. Water-conserving fixtures indoors contribute to reducing water use by about 20 percent. Natural light shines through an atrium. Another technique to allow natural light to penetrate the interior is the use of glass partitions in areas near windows.

Ceiling tiles are made with 90 percent recycled content. To help reduce waste, the project emphasized salvaging materials during construction. Also salvaged were some of the structures slated for demolition. Eighteen buildings on the site before construction were relocated to other areas for reuse.

The facility encourages alternative modes of transportation for employees. On site are bicycle racks and showers. Preferred parking is available for carpoolers, and fueling stations are provided for charging electric cars. Also, the site is near bus lines for commuters who want to use public transportation.

To boost indoor air quality the project team designed an entry that would remove dirt before people walk into the building. Also, designers selected paints, carpet adhesives, and other products with low or no volatile organic chemical (VOC) emissions.

Green Speak _____

"Employees benefit from the use of daylighting [the use of windows and skylights to bring sunlight indoors] and nontoxic chemicals, plus better temperature control, ventilation, and indoor air quality. With the high cost of labor, payback on energy features is shortened even further when savings from reduced absenteeism are combined with energy cost savings. Energy-efficient building features also help building owners attract and retain tenants."

—U.S. Department of Energy, Office of Energy Efficiency and Renewable Energy

Learning Center Showcases Environmental Exhibits

Westcave Preserve Environmental Learning Center in Round Mountain, Texas, is a 3,000-square-foot facility built in 2003 for educational programs at the 30-acre nature preserve and canyon in south Texas. It's listed as one of The American Institute of Architects' Top Ten Green Projects.

Designed to be simple and flexible, the building showcases some environmental features as part of the educational tools. Among them are a rainwater collection and filtering system and a solar energy panel.

Another feature is an interactive educational tool that allows users to help keep energy use in the building below the level that's supplied by the on-site solar panel. When someone switches on the lights, fans, or air-conditioning, monitors display the amount of energy used.

The insulated building is designed to function with little or no supplemental energy. Open windows, fans, and window overhangs for shade generally control indoor air quality and temperature. An open floor plan takes advantage of breezes from windows that are placed in areas that provide natural ventilation. Parking is limited and dispersed.

Air Quality Emphasized in Environmental Office

The Pennsylvania Department of Environmental Regulation Cambria Office in Ebensburg, Pennsylvania, received a LEED Gold rating. The 36,000-square-foot building features efficient floor-mounted air-distribution diffusers that allow workers to set and vary the air flow in their individual workspaces.

Other measures to enhance air quality include providing workers access to windows that open and installing mats at the entrance for collecting debris. To reduce indoor pollutants, the paints, sealants, and adhesives selected feature low or no VOCs.

In other environmentally preferable practices, solar panels on the roof provide a renewable energy source, push-rod automatic faucets in the rest rooms reduce water consumption, and window features are designed to allow natural light to filter into the building. Energy efficiency is accomplished through various measures including attention to insulation, lighting components, and air-handling units.

Gasoline-saving measures are encouraged though preferred parking for carpoolers and a bicycle rack and showers for pedestrians and bikers. Also, the building is near a bus line.

The construction process on the 8.3-acre site included emphasis on waste reduction and recycling debris. The selection of materials for the building also included items with recycled content, which include recycled-rubber flooring, recycled structural steel, recycled steel roofing shingles, and toilet partitions made from 50 percent recycled plastic. The high-reflectivity ceiling tiles are made with 75 percent recycled material.

Students Enjoy Fresh Air

Ben Franklin Elementary School, in Kirkland, Washington, is named among the American Institute of Architects' Top Ten Green Projects for 2006. A main focus of the project is a design that provides classrooms with natural lighting and natural ventilation. The ventilation system supplies the rooms with fresh air functions without conventional air-handling equipment.

The building's angle, window placement, skylights, and high ceilings are all designed to allow natural light to penetrate through the open interior. Electric lights are equipped with occupancy sensors and automatic dimming controls to reduce unnecessary energy use when natural light is plentiful.

Taking advantage of its woodsy location on a narrow 10-acre site, the 56,000-square-foot school features landscaped courtyards that double as outdoor classrooms.

Material selection also was a key factor in this project, with an emphasis on non-toxic, durable, and low-impact products. Among them are paints with low emissions of VOCs and rubber resilient flooring. Surfaces were selected that allowed for easy cleaning without harsh products.

With green building practices a hot and desirable trend, more and more businesses are eager to participate. They're devising ways to reduce adverse effects of their construction and remodeling projects and incorporating techniques that allow buildings to function with less waste and less pollution. The investment in protecting the earth often pays off in other ways, including happy, healthy employees and customer loyalty.

The Least You Need to Know

◆ The U.S. Green Building Council, a nonprofit organization, is a well-respected authority on environmentally friendly design, construction, and management.

◆ Buildings that meet the U.S. Green Building Council's various standards may qualify for prestigious certification in the organization's Leadership in Energy and Environmental Design (LEED) program.

◆ Buildings constructed and maintained with environmentally preferable products and practices often reap an extra benefit in related cash savings. Water and energy efficiency saves on utility fees. Recycling, reusing, and reducing waste might drop disposal fees.

◆ Businesses that emphasize healthy air quality and other green practices often enjoy greater worker productivity and loyalty.

◆ Various government agencies and nonprofit organizations offer a wealth of information for boosting the environmental standards in a building project.

Chapter 17

Companies That Have Gone Green and How

In This Chapter

◆ Green businesses: from simple mom-and-pop establishments to global enterprises

◆ Activities aimed at minimizing environmental impact

◆ Popular areas of focus for green business

◆ Financial incentives or other rewards for participating in businesses' environmental programs

Some businesses start out with an environmentally responsible attitude as part of the basic principles. They sell items produced with recycled products and work in an energy-efficient, nonpolluting building. They want their profits to be associated with deeds that help protect the environment. Some established businesses modestly tack on ecoappropriate practices tailored to their particular industry. Others write out elaborate environmental policies, appoint staffers to work on environmental issues, and showcase their philosophies and achievements on their websites.

Either way, all sustainable activities that take into account such factors as social justice and the planet's well-being are valuable. They also are valuable to the business itself. A business that promotes its sustainable activities draws shoppers and other businesses happy to support such principles. Some businesses include shoppers in their environmental efforts by providing incentives such as rebates or handy recycling services. Businesses that are taking an environmentally responsible approach are enjoying a wealth of benefits, including recognition from various governmental agencies and environmental organizations. In this chapter, we look at some examples.

Businesses Based on Recyclables

Recycline uses old yogurt cups and other recycled plastic for the handles of its Preserve brand toothbrushes, razors, and other products. The used toothbrushes and other products also are recyclable, as is the packaging. To encourage users to recycle their old toothbrushes and other grooming products, Recycline requests their return and offers prepaid envelopes and postage labels. The company then recycles used toothbrushes and other products into plastic lumber (not toothbrushes!).

Hanger Network in New York also promotes a product that's recycled and recyclable. This firm prints advertising on EcoHangers that are made from 100 percent recycled paperboard. They distribute the hangers free to participating dry cleaners, and the dry cleaners send them out to their customers with the freshly pressed attire. While serving as a backdrop for advertising, the EcoHangers reduce waste associated with discarded wire hangers. If customers don't want to reuse their EcoHangers, they can recycle them.

Green Speak

"Producing new plastic from recycled material uses only two thirds of the energy required to manufacture it from raw materials. Aluminum can be recycled using less than 5 percent of the energy used to make the original product."

—The U.S. Environmental Protection Agency

Aurora Glass of Eugene, Oregon, uses 100 percent recycled glass for its bowls, accent tiles, field tiles, table lamps, and other handmade home décor and architectural accents. The St. Vincent de Paul Society of Lane County owns and runs the glass foundry, which is part of the nonprofit organization's recycling initiative. Artisans make the various decorative products from old windows and glass tabletops brought in by residents and builders. The tiles and other items are sold in the retail shop in Oregon as well as internationally online. Proceeds from the sale of those items go to St. Vincent de Paul's social service programs.

Powered by Wind and Sun

Affordable Internet Services Online (www.aiso.net) of Romoland, California, just east of Los Angeles, provides Internet services and web hosting from a facility that's 100 percent solar powered. Solar panels generate electricity to its office and data center. And the building features other environmental aspects as well. *Solar tubes* bring in natural light; a recycled paper product provides the insulation that boosts the structure's energy efficiency. The staff is working toward adding a green roof of dirt and plants designed to reduce heating and cooling requirements.

Another project in the works is switching from fluorescent bulbs to energy-efficient and mercury-free *LED lighting*. Products such as paper and cleaning supplies are selected based on their environmental attributes—recycled, recyclable, and chlorine-free. Some paper products are even tree-free, and cleaning products do not have toxic ingredients.

def•i•ni•tion

Solar tubes are cylinders usually about 8 to 12 inches in diameter that bring sunlight into interior rooms. The tube is capped with a dome on the roof, which allows light into the chamber, which is lined with reflective paint or material to enhance the light as it comes down into the room.

LED (light emitting diodes) lights have emerged in recent years as the next best bulb since compact fluorescents. The bulbs have a low glow intensified and directed by a tiny mirror—so light goes only where it's needed instead of flooding the area and adding to light pollution.

New Belgium Brewing Company, which brews Belgian beers in Fort Collins, Colorado, switched to wind power to supply energy to its facility. It also receives energy returned via the facility's wastewater system. Various techniques are incorporated into the building design and functions to reduce energy use. These techniques include taking advantage of natural light, sun tubes, motion sensors for electric lights, and the reuse of heat in the brewhouse. A sustainability coordinator is on staff. In waste-reducing tactics, keg caps are reused as table surfaces, and the firm buys recycled paper and recycled office furniture.

Going Green _____

Some businesses are reducing the amount of single-vehicle transportation by offering incentives for workers to use public transit, bicycles, carpools, or other commuter alternatives. Some firms allow employees to work from home—to "telecommute." For ideas and information, log on to the Best Workplaces for Commuters Program at www.bwc.gov, sponsored by the U.S. Environmental Protection Agency and the U.S. Department of Transportation.

Buying Renewable Energy

Whole Foods Market, the natural products retailer based in Austin, Texas, with dozens of stores throughout the nation, supports wind power by purchasing Renewable Energy Credits (RECs) in amounts about equal to the energy used in its various facilities. The publicity related to Whole Foods' purchase of RECs provided the added benefit of promoting wind power.

For direct use of renewable energy, several of the stores receive some of their electricity from their own solar panels. Other stores offer various environmentally responsible features. The Whole Foods store in Sarasota, Florida, achieved a prestigious Silver rating from the U.S. Green Building Council's Leadership in Energy and Environmental Design (LEED) program (see Chapter 16 for more on LEED). That store features recycled materials, nontoxic low-odor paints, a reflective, energy-saving roof, and skylights that draw natural light. Vehicles also are part of Whole Foods' environmental focus. Some of the trailers at a distribution facility were retrofitted to reduce drag and improve fuel economy. To encourage shoppers to participate in reducing waste, Whole Foods offers a nickel rebate for each bag they bring in to pack up their groceries.

ThinkHost, a web hosting company based in Portland, Oregon, supports renewable energy through the purchase of wind and solar power. The business determined the energy use of its offices and servers, then purchased that amount in green energy certificates. Other environmentally valuable aspects of the business include members working from home offices, thereby reducing auto travel and encouraging the use of notebook computers, which are more energy efficient than desktops. The company also offers free hosting services to some nonprofit environmental organizations.

Teaming Up to Reduce Waste

Some businesses offer their own recycling programs to help reduce waste associated with their industry. Among them are computer companies. Dell, based in Austin, Texas, provides various drop-off and pick-up programs—some of them free—for people who want to discard their old laptops, printers, and other electronic equipment.

Some of the equipment is recycled; some is donated. Generally, the recycling programs accept items from any brand of electronics. Dell was among *Business Ethics Magazine*'s 100 Best Corporate Citizens and received awards and recognition from several organizations, including the U.S. Environmental Protection Agency.

Hewlett-Packard (HP) also offers take-back and trade-in programs—some free, and others that cost $13–$34 per item—for computer hardware and its other products. The items are sent off for recycling in facilities that meet its standards. HP also offers free recycling for its printer ink cartridges, although consumers find new ink cartridges are heavily packaged. Among its various other environmental aspects include setting social and environmental responsibility standards for the suppliers that manufacture parts. Hewlett-Packard buys green power.

Their various awards and recognition include EPA's Fortune 500 list of Green Power Partners, Recycling Council of Ontario Platinum Waste Minimization Award, the Idaho Association of Commerce and Industry's Environmental Excellence Award, and an EPA Evergreen Award for Pollution Prevention.

> **Green Gamut**
>
> According to Hewlett-Packard, plastics and metals recovered from products recycled by HP have been used in new HP products, as well as a range of other uses, including auto body parts, clothes hangers, plastic toys, fence posts, serving trays, and roof tiles.

Stonyfield Farm, which sells organic yogurts and other dairy products, offers a program to accept clean yogurt cups and lids back from its customers for recycling. Stonyfield offers free recycling because its containers are made of a type of plastic, polypropylene #5, that's not accepted by some residential recycling programs. Stonyfield states on its website that it opted for that particular packaging because it uses less plastic, and less plastic needed for yogurt cups decreases the amount of plastic manufactured and disposed.

Other environmental facets include giving 10 percent of its profits to organizations and projects working on various types of environmental activities, purchasing green power, and installing a solar energy system at its facility.

Eat, Drink, and Be Merrily Green

Hot Lips Pizza, in Portland, Oregon, a family-owned business established in 1984, stocks its kitchens with produce, often organic, bought from local farmers. The business runs several pizza restaurants in the Pacific Northwest. To take advantage of freshly picked local fruits, Hot Lips handcrafts its own apple, pear, blueberry, raspberry, and strawberry sodas. The delivery fleet includes five electric vehicles. The business earned a Seal of Business Sustainability from the Sustainable Business Institute, a nonprofit organization based in Saratoga, California.

Elixir, a bar in San Francisco, offers organic wines and organic beers among its selection of beverages. Some of its mixed drinks also are organic, made with organic vodka and organic produce. Elixir hosts Sustainable Business Happy Hour events and is recognized by the San Francisco Green Business Program.

Elixir serves organic brews.

(Courtesy of Elixir)

The owner of several Subway franchises in Norman, Oklahoma, reduced energy expenses by about 40 percent by installing energy-efficient lighting, heating, air-conditioning, and other appliances.

Starbucks Coffee Company, based in Seattle, Washington, set a program offering a 10¢ discount to folks who bring in their own mugs. That incentive helps reduce waste from disposable cups. The burlap bags that transport beans are recycled and reused in other industries, including furniture and carpet pad manufacturing. And stores sell coffee grounds to be used as garden mulch. Other environmental aspects of the business include purchasing green power credits and buying from vendors with responsible environmental farming practices.

> **Green Gamut**
>
> The restaurant industry (#1 electricity consumer in retail sector) accounts for 33 percent of all U.S. retail electricity use (the Green Restaurant Association).

Appreciating Recycled Paper

Inkworks Press, a worker-owned and worker-managed print shop, stocks its supply shelves with recycled paper. The business, in Berkeley, California, also uses vegetable oil inks and offers discounts to social justice organizations. The shop is among those certified though the Bay Area Green Business Program and is a member of Co-Op America's Business Network. Another bonus: the recycled paper is chlorine free.

The Pacific Bell Directories in San Francisco are produced with recycled paper and also are recyclable. The outdated books are recycled into paper for various products, including envelopes, telephone books, home insulation, cereal boxes, and packaging.

Nomad Café uses recycled paper products for its menus and napkins. Promoted as an Earth-friendly arts and Internet café, the business in Oakland, California, serves its customers on reusable dishes. For to-go orders, the packaging is biodegradable and nonpetroleum based. It's said that 95 percent of waste produced at the café is composted or recycled. Appliances and fixtures are energy efficient and water efficient, and items used for housekeeping and general business are selected for low-impact attributes. Coffee products are organic and Fair Trade Certified. Some employees walk to work, and staff transportation is pedal powered. They also provide bicycle racks for customers.

Reducing Waste

Walser's, a family business that sells art supplies, offers shoppers store displays that it no longer needs. Also, the employees of this business in Torrance, California, recycle cardboard, paper, plastic, glass, and cans. From money earned through recycling, the business holds a party for the employees and their families. The recycling efforts were at work even when collection services were not available in that area. The owners took the discards home and added the items to the residential recycle collection. It's estimated that those efforts diverted nine tons of solid waste and provided a cost savings estimated to be over $3,000. Walser's is a winner of the California Waste Reduction Awards Program (WRAP).

Another business acknowledged by WRAP is Vallejo Insurance Associates, in Vallejo, California. The insurance agent and brokerage business reduced its paper waste after hiring a consultant to increase efficiency with its computer programs. When relocating to another office, the firm purchased some of its furniture, file cabinets, and partitions from a used office furniture dealer and through auctions.

Other WRAP winners include Safeway, Inc., for composting green waste at its retail grocery stores and Byers' LeafGuard Gutter Systems, in Grass Valley, California, which uses low-emission, fuel-efficient sales vehicles. Byers' also works with a firm that picks up metal gutters from clients' homes and recycles them.

Nike's Reuse-A-Shoe program recycles old athletic footwear to produce sports surfaces. Nike grinds the shoes into different types of materials that are used in football fields, soccer fields, basketball and tennis courts, and running tracks. Other environmental aspects of the global business based in Beaverton, Oregon, include energy efficiency, the restoration of wetlands and wildlife habitats, and production of catalogs with chlorine-free recycled fibers. The Beaverton site takes advantage of natural light and uses occupancy sensors to keep electric lights off when not required. Window frames and wall framing are built with recycled aluminum, and the wall panels and roofing materials minimize cooling requirements and heat gain. The in-house recycling program accepts about 20 types of products, including videotapes, batteries, and different types of plastics.

The U.S. Environmental Protection Agency also reports these other waste-reducing efforts:

◆ The U.S. Postal Service Alabama District established an Online Swap Shop for excess materials, such as forms, office supplies, and furniture. In 2005, the swapping effort reportedly saved the Alabama District more than $40,000 worth of supply purchases.

◆ The Los Angeles Unified School District reduced wasted food through its "Offer Versus Serve" program in school cafeterias, which allows students to decline items they don't want rather than throwing away what they don't like. That effort helped avoid $600,000 in food disposal costs in one year.

◆ The Limited Brands, Inc., reduced packaging waste by revising its design standards for the cardboard boxes used for apparel. That project prevented 87 tons of cardboard from being thrown out.

> **Green Gamut**
>
> As one of the world's largest recyclers of aluminum beverage containers, Anheuser-Busch Recycling Corporation recycled 804 million pounds of cans in 2004—more than 125 percent of the number of cans that the company's breweries use to package their products (The U.S. Environmental Protection Agency).

It has been noted that some companies tout small yet visible contributions for environmental health, yet other company practices may be damaging to the environment. This is called "greenwashing" and is fairly common, especially among larger corporations. Nonetheless, change begins with small steps, and while this may be considered somewhat deceptive, it is also a clear indication that companies realize that consumers want to see corporate environmental responsibility. We see this as a move forward, however small.

> **Going Green**
>
> Whether you are an eco-entrepreneur or simply someone who loves to shop, your purchases add financial weight to supporting businesses with environmentally preferable practices. Select vendors who respect the planet, and tell them the environmental reasons behind your shopping decisions.

Hotels and Resorts Go Green

Forever Resorts, based in Scottsdale, Arizona, with lodges and houseboat rentals in various parts of the nation, established a rating system that gives preference to vendors and suppliers with environmentally focused business practices and products. Its various environmental practices at different resorts and other business ventures earned recognition from the Green Restaurants Association, the U.S. Environmental Protection Agency Performance Track, and the Integrated Waste Management Board of California.

Grand Targhee Resort in Alta, Wyoming, purchases green energy credits that support wind power. To help reduce waste and pollution associated with typical transportation, the resort offers free bus service for employees in local communities. Also, the resort set a policy that aims to reduce idling buses and other vehicles in its fleet. They hired a staff person to work on implementing sustainable initiatives and provide environmental education programs and training at the resort and in the community. Buses and snow removal equipment are powered by biodiesel fuel. Other measures that promote sustainability include switching from traditional beverage cups to products made of nonpetroleum plastic, installing water-saving low-flow shower fixtures, and providing recycling centers for staff and guests.

Green skiing at Grand Targhee Resort.

(Courtesy of Grand Targhee Resort)

Xanterra South Rim, which is a lodge at the Grand Canyon, is part of Xanterra Parks and Resorts, which sets environmental standards for various aspects of the business including waste, water conservation, pollution prevention, and design. The lodge's activities include using 100 percent post-consumer recycled copy paper, switching thousands of lightbulbs to a more efficient product, promoting recycling, and allowing guests to opt for reusing sheets and towels. Xanterra also establishes employee green teams at its various locations to provide suggestions.

Businesses Based on Reuse

In building and remodeling projects, extra supplies are frequently left over and often the hardware or other items being replaced are perfectly usable. Offering a business that serves as venue for redistributing excess building materials is a valuable way to prevent waste and promote reuse of what's already available.

The RE store in Bellingham, Washington, sells usable building products, including windows, doors, hardware, and tiles brought in from other projects. The RE store, which was established by the RE Sources nonprofit educational organization, also recycles motor oil for resale and sells items such as pianos, sewing machines, and lighting. Its yearly take includes more than one million pounds of salvage. Shoppers simply go through the stuff and buy what they need.

Another business that takes advantage of leftover supplies is MetroPaint. The paints, available in an array of hues, are produced from 100 percent recycled latex paint by the Metro regional government in Portland, Oregon. The Metro Solid Waste Recycling Department blends and filters good quality leftovers dropped off by residents. About 15 different colors are sold at the MetroPaint Store in Portland and at some other retail stores in the area. The paints are suitable for indoor and outdoor uses and work with rollers, sprays, and brushes.

 Green Speak

"Reusing products, when possible, is even better than recycling because the item does not need to be reprocessed before it can be used again."

—The U.S. Environmental Protection Agency

Promoting Efficient Transportation

Flexcar is a business that offers low-emission, fuel-efficient vehicles for rent by the hour in a fast-growing repertoire of urban areas, including Philadelphia; San Francisco; Washington, D.C.; Los Angeles; and Seattle. The car-sharing service and its competitor, Zipcar, are a handy option for folks and businesses that want occasional access to vehicles. The Flexcar fleet includes hybrids, pickup trucks, sedans, and mini-vans. Zipcar doesn't promote itself as fuel efficient or boast hybrids at press time.

Also working to promote efficient vehicles is Hyperion Solutions, a software business. The company, based in Santa Clara, California, established a program offering $5,000 reimbursements to eligible employees who purchase vehicles that achieve at least 45 miles per gallon. About 175 workers from different locations in the world have taken advantage of the program by press time.

Pedro's Planet in St. Louis, Missouri, which sells office supplies, figures it would do something for the environment when it drops off orders at businesses. It offers to take waste paper, aluminum cans, phone books, and some other recyclables from their clients, and transport them using the truck that's already on site. Then, they sell the paper and aluminum for recycling and use that money to support nonprofit environmental groups. The business, also in Denver, Colorado, includes an array of recycled products among its selection of office supplies. They include paper clips made from metal auto parts (when available), recycled paper, pencils made from newspapers, and pens made from recycled plastic.

Selling Green Goods and Services

Eco-Wise in Austin, Texas, sells green building supplies, such as recycled glass tiles, and various other ecopreferable and fair trade products. Among the selection are outfits for babies and grownups in organic fabric, an energy-efficient tankless water heater, and backpacks made with fabric produced from recycled plastic bottles.

Natural Built Home in Minneapolis, Minnesota, offers sustainable and safe building products, including kitchen and bath sinks of recycled aluminum, recycled glass and recycled aluminum tiles, low- and no-VOC paints, and recycled landscaping glass.

Wildrose Farm in Breezy Point, Minnesota, produces organic apparel and hand-woven rugs. The family-owned business uses organic cotton for its made-to-order jackets, skirts, shirts, and pants. The rugs are woven from organic cotton and recycled fiber. The Mixed Berries rug features organic cotton, recycled denim, and hemp warp yarns. The business recycles all of its fabric scraps; some are woven into rugs while others are used to produce paper. Other environmentally focused aspects of the business include an in-floor hot-water system as a fuel-saving technique to heat the company's sewing studio and the use of nontoxic, water-based inks to print designs on the apparel.

> **Green Gamut**
>
> Eastman Kodak saved more than $8.6 million in operating costs in 2002 from its energy management efforts. Ford Motor Company has saved more than $75 million through effective energy management (U.S. EPA Energy Star).

Baltix Sustainable Furniture in Long Lake, Minnesota, produces furniture from environmentally preferable natural sources without harmful adhesives and VOCs. The materials include recycled papers and sunflower husks.

Showcasing successful businesses that focus on the environment, employees, and social justice is energizing for businesses and their employees and informative for other businesses eager to implement their own ecoresponsible practices. And for like-minded shoppers, it's great to know where best to spend money.

The Least You Need to Know

◆ All types of businesses, including independent family-owned shops, are adopting procedures aimed at protecting natural resources and reducing pollution.

◆ Incorporating environmental equipment and practices into a business offers added bonuses, such as reducing utility and waste disposal expenses.

◆ Because several organizations and government agencies publicly acknowledge businesses that meet environmental standards, businesses are eager to showcase that prestigious recognition, which tends to draw employees, shoppers, and other businesses eager to support such practices.

◆ Businesses that promote sustainable activities often use their purchasing power to support like-minded vendors and suppliers.

Chapter 18

Working with Our Employers to Green the Workplace

In This Chapter

- Applying green practices at work
- Going green can save money and boost morale
- From recycled paper to ink cartridges and more
- Setting up an office recycling center
- Working with your bosses and co-workers to fight global warming

You bike to the beach and tote groceries in a reusable bag. That's great. Now keep it up while on the job. Showcase that eco enthusiasm and join forces with the folks who share your office. Perhaps they're equally gung-ho or just need a gentle nudge. Working as a team, you'll be even more likely to accomplish some of your grander goals. Also, the synergy is exhilarating.

So grab the bosses and the staff, sit down with some fair-trade organic snacks, and discuss ideas for establishing a healthier workplace and environmentally responsible business practices. This chapter gives you plenty of ideas to talk about.

Green the Office Routine

Work toward enlisting the support of managers. Backing from the bosses elevates efforts to boost the environmental standard to a higher priority. With their help draft guidelines for policies, practices, and products that are less wasteful and less toxic. Management might even be open to establishing a staff position, such as Environmental Practices Coordinator or Eco Supplies Buyer.

The Pennsylvania Department of Environmental Protection, in a set of guidelines relating to school administration, suggests management appoint a Pollution Prevention Coordinator and establish a Pollution Prevention Task Force. The task force would include representatives from key divisions among the staff. Participants would hold regular meetings to discuss, among other things, opportunities to incorporate pollution-prevention measures, such as switching to less toxic, environmentally preferable cleaning products and installing windows that open for fresh air according to those guidelines.

Sharing resources is a simple way to reduce excess waste and unnecessary duplication. Set up bins for staffers to toss magazines, staplers, leftover notebooks, pencils, and other supplies they don't use. Rather than throwing unused desk-cluttering items in the trash or tucking them away in the back of a filing cabinet, offer them up to co-workers who might otherwise be buying duplicates. Sharing saves money and reduces the related environmental impacts associated with production and disposal of excess products.

Reducing auto travel is another technique for boosting environmental responsibility at the workplace. When appropriate, set up conference calls instead of traveling to in-person meetings because conference calls save time, gas, and money. If driving is required for staff meetings or group training sessions, encourage officemates to drive together.

Paper Cuts

Paper is a staple of the workplace. It's so available, so easy to use, and so easy to toss into the trash. It's also one of the simplest areas to focus on when working toward a more environmentally responsible office.

Think before you tear a new sheet from a notebook. Sometimes you might be able to accomplish the same objective without grabbing a fresh piece of paper. When jotting down a phone number or an informal reminder note, use the back of an old letter or that scratch paper where you were doodling. To keep all those informal notes neat and handy, make your own scratch pads. Cut out clean sections from partially used paper you'd otherwise throw away and staple the sheets together. Tada—you have a simple way to reuse and recycle paper.

When communicating with a colleague, determine if an e-mail memo would do just as nicely as the paper version. Or skip the written version entirely and go verbal by picking up the telephone or sticking your head in your co-worker's office.

With notices intended for the entire staff—whether it's announcements, jokes, or party invitations—skip the trip to the photocopy machine and don't waste a ream of paper. Simply set up an office bulletin board and post any items there.

When office presentations include visual displays, use a less wasteful alternative to paper flip charts. Opt for erasable boards, overhead projectors, or electronic software presentations.

One of the most effective ways of reducing paper in the workplace is using both sides of each sheet. Make it a habit. Buy copiers and printers with a duplex feature for double-sided printing. Gather up paper previously printed on only one side and use the backs for faxing, scratch paper, or copying drafts or other informal documents.

Also print just what you need. Scrutinize drafts and fix mistakes before pressing the "print" button.

Call or e-mail businesses that send catalogs or advertising flyers and ask them to remove you from their lists. According to The Twin Cities Green Guide, www.thegreenguide. org, two departments in the Itasca County Courthouse in Minnesota decreased their junk mail by 90 percent, from about 100 pieces to 10 pieces per week. They used preprinted postcards asking that their names be taken off mailing lists.

> **Green Gamut**
>
> The average office worker uses 10,000 sheets of copy paper each year, according to the Minnesota Office of Environmental Assistance.

> **Going Green**
>
> More than 17 billion catalogs—3.5 million tons of paper—are sent out each year, many to businesses as well as homes. Help save some of the 60 million trees that go into this junk mail by joining a "Do Not Mail" list. Write to: Mail Preference Service, Direct Marketing Association, P.O. Box 643, Carmel, NY 10512, or register online at dmaconsumers. org/cgi/offmailinglist.

Reduce Waste

Rather than nonchalantly dropping items into the trash bin, take a break and think about how you might limit the environmental impact. Determine if any of these products are suitable for reuse, recycling, or replacing with nondisposable versions.

The snack room offers a terrific opportunity to reduce waste. Equip the food service area with washable plates and utensils. Encourage staffers to bring in their own mugs so they're not tossing away plastic, foam, or paper cups.

When shopping for office products, look for items that are durable, reusable, or returnable through stores that offer take-back services. Toner cartridges are a prime example of a product that's easily recycled. Take the used ones back to a store that collects the empties and replace that one with a remanufactured version. Remanufactured toner cartridges work just as well as new ones and are significantly less expensive, according to Steve Baker, president of GreenLine Paper Company in York, Pennsylvania.

Another way to reduce waste is to take advantage of items already available, such as packaging supplies. Rather than tossing out shipping cartons sent to the office, reuse them. And don't forget to save and reuse the packing material.

Redecorate with Green

Other waste-reducing efforts involve the selection of office décor and furnishings. The Minnesota Office of Environmental Assistance suggests buying sturdy and durable products that you won't need to replace quickly. The tips also include using flexible interior features, such as moveable walls. Flexible elements are adaptable and reusable and reduce the amount of waste generated if the office is renovated.

Green Speak

"Healthy doesn't have to be the sterile white clinical look. I'm actually trying to make people's space healthy without them knowing it."

—Denise Robinette, HealthyLiving Interiors

Recycling office furniture is another tool for avoiding waste. Send old desks, chairs, and other pieces to businesses that do refurbishing and remanufacturing work. Consider shopping for remanufactured furniture when replacing office décor.

Denise Robinette of HealthyLiving Interiors recently created a green office for an accounting firm. She used cork for the flooring and also on columns for aesthetic appeal and to improve acoustics in the tax office (cork absorbs noise). She used nontoxic paints and formaldehyde-free cabinets and reused most of the existing furniture. She had some cabinets resized to fit the newly designed workspace and selected glass doors and glass partitions to allow natural light to filter throughout the space, which cut electricity costs. Solar window shades helped reduce air conditioning costs without compromising the view. Before completing her work, Robinette helped educate her clients about the use of nontoxic cleaners to maintain their healthy new office.

A green office.

(Courtesy HealthyLiving Interiors)

Energy and Water Efficiency

Slimming down on excess energy and water use is a key element in raising environmental standards in the workplace, and money saved on utility fees also makes management happy.

Some waste-cutting efforts are simple and available to anyone on the staff. Take notice of leaky water faucets and report them to the building maintenance officials. Turn off lights and other electrical office equipment when leaving the office. And use energy-saving features on computers and other equipment, such as low-power settings when the product is not being used.

In a broader scope, businesses that are adding or replacing appliances and fixtures should take advantage of energy-efficient models. Some utility companies offer rebates or other incentives for energy and water efficiency. Reaping such a financial incentive may help make the switch to a more energy-efficient office extra appealing.

Going Green

Leaks inside the toilet can waste up to 200 gallons of water a day. You can detect a toilet leak by adding a few drops of food coloring to water in the tank. If the colored water appears in the bowl, the toilet is leaking (American Evergreen Foundation, www.usagreen.org).

As an example of a financial perk, the cash incentives from the California Solar Initiative combined with federal tax incentives can cover up to 50 percent of the total cost of a solar system, according to the California Energy Commission.

When buying or replacing plumbing fixtures in restrooms and kitchens, seek those with environmentally preferable features, among which are low-consumption toilets and low-flow aerators for faucets and showerheads.

Green Office Supplies

Make a point to buy paper and office supplies made with recycled materials. Using paper with recycled content for stationery, brochures, and other office documents is a great way to highlight that your business puts a priority on environmentally preferable practices. Recycled paper is impressive. It's hip. It's available in an array of hues and styles and textures. You can choose from bright white to a more natural, earthy tone. Some recycled paper includes flecks of color from the inks on the old paper that was recycled.

When shopping for recycled paper, note the specific amount of recycled content, which generally ranges from 30 percent to 100 percent. Opt for the 100 percent versions if possible, to reduce the demand for virgin pulp.

Also in the selection of environmentally preferable papers are those that blend recycled paper with tree-free fibers, such as sugarcane waste, said GreenLine Paper Company president Steve Baker.

Hemp is another paper source that is gaining in popularity.

While converting from paper pulp to hemp fiber would require major changes in milling and farming practices including the development of new technologies for processing, establishing this resource could go a long way toward protecting our valuable forests. Unfortunately, growing industrial hemp is illegal in the United States because it is related to marijuana, although the hemp plant used for fiber does not have the hallucinogenic qualities that would classify it as a drug. It is, however, legal to make hemp products in the United States if the hemp is imported from other countries. The Industrial Hemp Farming Act of 2005 has been introduced to Congress, H.R. 3037, in an effort to amend this rule.

Green Speak

"On less than 5 percent of our arable land, we could produce enough hemp fiber to replace all the pulp now produced in the United States."

—Bob Schildgen, "Mr. Green Column," *Sierra Club Magazine*

Various other typical office products also are produced with recycled content. GreenLine Paper Company, for example, sells rulers made with a blend of recycled plastic and old blue jeans. They also sell trash bags made of 100 percent recycled content.

The Sustainable Group in Seattle, Washington, offers presentation folders with pockets among its products made with recycled material. The firm also offers custom screen printing using the client's logo.

The accessories from Green Earth Office Supply in Redwood Estates, California, include ball-point pens made from post-consumer rubber tires and recycled plastic, paper clips made from recycled steel, lamps made from computer circuit boards, and chlorine-free telephone message pads made with 100 percent recycled content.

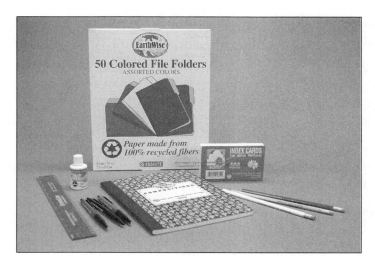

A recycled blue jeans ruler and other recycled products.

(Courtesy GreenLine Paper Company)

Green Lunch

Whether you're nibbling at the desk, ordering take-out, or going out to a restaurant with work friends, take advantage of opportunities to be kinder to the earth.

Lots of folks bring lunch from home. It's economical, handy, and allows workers to eat exactly what they want, which is especially nice if they're devotees of organically grown produce and other foods. A packed meal offers the environmental advantage of access to food without auto travel. To enhance the green value of bringing lunch from home, opt for reusable, washable food containers. Buy a durable lunch box and toss in cloth napkins.

If you're going out to a restaurant, consider the eateries within walking distance of your office. Walking to lunch is a nice way to enjoy exercise and fresh air while eliminating auto travel. When co-workers select a restaurant farther away, suggest driving together to save on gas.

When ordering take-out meals, encourage the restaurants to avoid overpackaging. Tell them to leave out extra napkins, utensils, or other items you don't need. Some restaurants are switching from traditional petroleum-based plastic take-out containers to containers made from corn or other agricultural crops.

Excellent Packaging and Supply in California is among the suppliers. Its products include cutlery made from 80 percent potato or cornstarch and 20 percent soy or other vegetable oil.

Buying Power

Spending money on environmentally preferable products and services rewards suppliers and sends an economic message throughout the marketplace that consumers demand such items that are healthier, less wasteful, and nonpolluting.

For shoppers, browsing among the array of environmentally preferable products is relatively simple, especially when using the Internet. Various organizations promote green practices and provide directories listing businesses and products that meet specific standards.

Among them are the following:

◆ *Recycled-Content Product Directory* is an online listing of products made from recycled materials. The products are organized by category and include office supplies, flooring, paper, and packaging. The directory also includes organizations that provide ecological services. It is offered through the California Integrated Waste Management Board.

◆ *The National Green Pages* lists thousands of businesses with commitments to sustainable, socially just principles, including fair trade and cruelty-free products. The listing is produced by Co-Op America, a nonprofit organization established in 1982 that promotes the use of economic power to establish a sustainable and socially just society.

Co-Op America logo.

◆ Energy Star, www.energystar.gov, recognizes products and services that meet its standard of energy efficiency. Among the product categories are building materials, electronics, appliances, and office equipment. Energy Star is a joint program from the U.S. Environmental Protection Agency and the U.S. Department of Energy. In general, products that earn an Energy Star logo use about half as much energy as standard equipment. Some printers, for example, that earned the Energy Star rating reduce electricity use by more than 60 percent.

◆ Green Seal is a nonprofit environmental labeling organization based in Washington, D.C., that offers its endorsement, also known as the Green Seal of Approval, to products that meet its standards as environmentally preferable. For individual products, the Green Seal is accompanied by an explanation about why that product is environmentally preferable. The information includes significant environmental attributes of the product.

Hazard

Don't be misled by products with vague or overly general marketing messages. Here are some words of wisdom from the United States Federal Trade Commission:

"Claims that a product or service is 'environmentally friendly,' 'environmentally safe,' 'environmentally preferable,' or 'eco-safe' or labels that contain environmental seals—say, a picture of the globe with the words 'Earth Smart' around it—are unhelpful for two reasons. First, all products, packaging, and services have some environmental impact, although some may have less than others. Second, these phrases alone do not provide the specific information you need to compare products, packaging, or services on their environmental merits. Look for claims that give some substance to the claim—the additional information that explains why the product is environmentally friendly or has earned a special seal" (the Federal Trade Commission, www.ftc.gov/opa/1999/04/green.shtm).

Going Green

Energy Star–qualified light commercial HVAC equipment uses 7 to 10 percent less energy than standard equipment. These products can save your business approximately $3 to $4 per square foot over the life of the equipment. For example, a 12,000-square-foot building using an Energy Star–qualified HVAC product could save $36,000 to $48,000.

Some web-based buying guides focus on geographic regions:

◆ *The Northwest Green Directory* lists building products and services in the Pacific Northwest area, including Idaho, Washington, and Oregon.

◆ *The Environmentally Preferable Purchasing Guide* is published by the Solid Waste Management Coordinating Board in Minnesota for government and schools, but anyone concerned about making environmentally friendly purchases can apply its advice and information. It lists products based on various criteria including being less hazardous, conserves energy, and protects natural resources.

Set Up a Recycling Center

Make it easy for co-workers to feel good about doing the right thing for the planet by setting up bins for bottles, newspapers, and other recyclables in a handy location so workers are less tempted to toss these items in the garbage. For employees who use lots of paper, put individual paper recycling bins at each desk.

Ask the local recycling service which types of items they accept and how they want those items sorted. Label the bins accordingly.

Promote the recycling program. Provide information at staff meetings, through e-mail, and in bulletin board postings. Another tool to emphasize recycling is a customized poster. The Paper Industry Association Council offers a feature on its website that allows users to print out recycling posters customized for individual businesses. Log on to http://stats.paperrecycles.org/dynamicposter; type in the business name; and select the specific items from a list, including envelopes, cardboard, direct mail, magazines, and newspapers, that the firm wants employees to recycle. Set up the poster in the recycling area as a friendly reminder. To help get people in the recycling habit, you might start a contest to see who can contribute the most.

If the local recycling service doesn't offer pickups at the office, ask employees to take home their own bottles and other recyclable items and add them to their residential bins.

After an office recycling program is established, ask fellow workers for their input, according to a suggestion from the Paper Industry Association Council. Determine what they like and what they don't like; then implement their suggestions to enhance the program even further.

In addition to conventional recyclables, such as glass, plastic, paper, and aluminum cans, recycling services are available for other types of office waste, including old printer cartridges. Some businesses offer take-back programs for such items. "Each cartridge reclaimed conserves, on average, the equivalent of half a gallon of oil compared to manufacturing one from scratch," according to Office Depot, one of the businesses that accepts cartridges for recycling in their stores.

For food-related businesses, the Minnesota Office of Environmental Assistance recommends recycling leftover edible products by offering it to services that provide food to people or animals. Nonedible foods might be valuable to a composting service. In some areas, recycling services are available for grease and cooking oil.

Green Gamut

According to Xerox Corporation, remanufacturing printers and copiers involves rebuilding and upgrading returned products and parts to as-new appearance and performance. This practice kept 149 million pounds of waste from going to landfills in 2001. Energy savings from parts reuse totaled 500,000 megawatt hours—enough energy to light more than 380,000 U.S. homes for one year.

Other potential recyclables include desktops, laptops, printers, and other electronic equipment and related computer accessories, such as DVDs and disks. The equipment might be refurbished or dismantled to salvage usable parts. In some areas, old electronics are accepted in free drop-off programs run by the government or a nonprofit organization. Private services, such as GreenDisk, also offer recycling for so-called technotrash, including desktops, laptops, printers, CDs, and other computer-related waste. The electronics are sent to GreenDisk through the mail.

Check with your local municipal waste department to see whether it has a special electronic recycling program. Remember to remove hard drives from old computers or have a professional wipe clean the drives to avoid identity theft from discarded equipment.

Wealth of Info

With environmentally responsible standards a hot trend in the business world, various organizations and government agencies offer information and services aimed at helping firms outline and accomplish their eco-related goals:

◆ Green Power Partnership, sponsored by the U.S. EPA, supports renewable, less polluting energy sources, such as solar and wind power. The Partnership includes representatives from commercial, industrial, and public organizations that are entitled to technical assistance, information, and recognition for their use of green power.

Going Green

The Federal Trade Commission and the Environmental Protection Agency set up guidelines for environmental marketing statements in labels and advertising. These are available at the Consumer Response Center, 1-877-382-4357; by mail: 600 Pennsylvania Avenue, NW, Washington, DC 20580; and online at www.ftc.gov. Click on "Consumers" and then "Energy and Environment."

◆ WasteWise is a free voluntary program offered by the U.S. EPA that offers assistance forming, implementing, and measuring programs to reduce waste.

◆ The Green Building Initiative's Green Globes offers an online interactive tool to help project teams incorporate sustainability features into building projects.

◆ Co-Op America Business Network is a network of businesses screened for their commitment to socially and environmentally responsible business practices.

As you can see, it's easy, economical, and sometimes even fun to help your employers apply green office practices. And in the long run, by saving energy through recycling, reusing, and efficiency, you, your bosses, and your co-workers will be helping to reduce the carbon dioxide emissions related to your business. This in turn helps fight the effects of global warming.

The Least You Need to Know

◆ Simple activities, such as turning off lights, using less paper, recycling, and reporting leaky faucets, are valuable tools in the effort to boost green practices in the workplace.

◆ Enlist the support of managers and staff to boost the emphasis on environmentally responsible practices.

◆ When buying supplies, furniture, paints, and other items for the office, opt for those that are energy-efficient, preserve natural resources, promote healthy indoor air quality, and are recyclable or reusable.

◆ Enjoy the fact that many practices and techniques that are good for the environment also offer financial benefits for the business and health advantages for the workers.

Part 6

Living in the Emerald City

Cities are racing ahead in the run to create healthier, more responsible, and more desirable communities. Mayors across the country have signed on to reduce their cities' greenhouse gas emissions and waste products, and citizens are responding to the call to do the right thing to serve the best interests of all.

Power companies are refining their systems to utilize alternative fuels; city fleets are going hybrid and biodiesel. Chicago is carpeting its skyscrapers with green roofs, and many buildings are capitalizing on the sun with solar window films, roof panels, and passive and geothermal heating systems. Find out what your company is doing, and see how you can help!

Going Green in Our Communities

In This Chapter

◆ Going green: finally getting the green light across the nation

◆ Cities that have taken steps to reduce global warming even without federal mandates to do so

◆ Religious organizations getting involved in protecting the earth

◆ College students working to help bring their institutions into the twenty-first century

Although people resisted the truth about global warming in the United States for several years, suddenly in 2006 (thanks to Al Gore's *An Inconvenient Truth*) the tide began to change, and the public began to catch on to the fact that all the environmental concerns they had ignored in the past had become hot issues demanding attention.

In 2005, when the federal government chose to avoid taking a leadership position by failing to sign the Kyoto Protocol, a cooperative agreement with other nations to reduce global warming emissions, Mayor Greg Nickels of Seattle stepped forward and announced that his city would do its part to help his community meet the standards of the Kyoto agreement—lowering emission levels to 7 percent less than 1990 levels. Nickels invited other mayors to join him, and as of this writing 435 mayors have signed Nickel's U.S. Mayors Climate Protection Agreement, and the number continues to climb.

So don't despair when you learn that your nation isn't taking responsibility for the damage it's caused (the United States has 5 percent of the world's population yet produces 25 percent of greenhouse gases) and action to correct this dangerous situation. If your city hasn't joined the effort yet, perhaps you can help inform your city leaders to make the change.

The World Mayors Council on Climate Change planned a meeting to coincide with the Kyoto Protocol meeting in February 2007. Convened in 2005 by Mayor Yorikane Masumoto of Kyoto, Japan, the meeting attracted 350 mayors from 108 countries to develop plans for protecting citizens and communities from the effects of global warming. The Kyoto Protocol, an agreement formed between some participating nations in 2005, will expire in 2012, but this year's participants developed further plans which include a pledge to reduce greenhouse gases 30 percent by 2020 and 80 percent by 2050. The group calls on governments to reduce the use of fossil fuels and to promote renewable energy use, efficiency, and conservation.

Some Cities Are Leading the Way

The Sierra Club Cool Cities Guide provides stories about cities who've joined the movement of nearly 400 cities across the country who aren't waiting for slow federal initiative to curb global warming. These cities are implementing energy-saving technologies, implementing alternative energy resources, and cutting transportation emissions.

Going Green

Learn more about the U.S. Mayors Climate Protection Agreement and see if your mayor has signed: http://seattle.gov/mayor/climate.

The Green Guide, an online magazine that provides the latest in tips and news for those interested in environmental information, ranks cities annually for their green innovations, including fair labor policies, open and green space policies, energy consumption, transportation policies, and emissions.

Let's check out a few of the cities across the country that are going green and see what we can learn from them.

Seattle, Washington

Some of the changes underway in Seattle include an already achieved agreement with the power company to mitigate all power to zero-emission status using carbon offsets (see Chapter 10) and conservation methods. The city has undertaken a multimillion-dollar public transportation improvement program that includes a light rail system and is taking measures to encourage and increase pedestrian traffic and bicycling in the city. City fleets are increasing efficiency with biofuels, and the Seattle Police Department is transitioning to hybrid vehicles for its nonpursuit needs. The public utility company is helping residents conserve water with low-flow faucet conversions.

These are only a few of the measures being implemented in Seattle in an effort to reduce greenhouse gases and improve the quality of life for residents.

San Francisco, California

San Francisco has implemented a number of green innovations. Mayor Gavin Newsom has pledged to go beyond Kyoto Protocols with a goal of reducing greenhouse gas emissions by 20 percent less than 1990 levels by 2012. Newsom is aggressively challenging city residents to join the effort and has enlisted the help of the city power company, Pacific Gas and Electric (PG&E), in making it happen. A recent development is Newsom's proposed legislation to outlaw outdated fluorescent bulbs in commercial buildings, seeking to replace the long T-12 tube lights with slimmer, more efficient T-8 lights. The City Department of Environment estimates the change will save enough energy to power 1,200 homes and reduce CO_2 emissions by 16,500 tons, the equivalent of taking 3,000 cars off the road. PG&E offers incentive programs to help businesses make the transition to the more efficient lighting.

In 1999, San Francisco developed the first Green Building requirement for its city buildings in the nation. The city also offers incentives to builders to encourage green building in low-income neighborhoods to help improve quality of life and health for lower-income residents.

The city's strategic environmental plan for 2007–2009 states that through increased efficiency incentives it's already reduced energy consumption by 18 megawatts— enough to power 20,000 homes. Future plans include continuing reductions in energy usage as well as promoting renewable energy resources including solar power, tidal power, and wind power.

The city has committed to increasing pedestrian traffic, bicycling, and the use of mass transit as well as converting to cleaner fuel choices for its city fleet vehicles. Another leading innovation is the city's aggressive stance toward waste, which includes a commitment to reduce landfill use by 75 percent by 2010 and to reach a zero-waste standard by 2020. The city has a public composting program for food wastes, which converts scraps from restaurants into fertilizer, and a community pet waste program that provides biodegradable bags and community collection sites in public places for dog walkers. The collected waste is converted to methane gas and used as fuel, reducing waste sent to landfills.

San Francisco was also the first city in the nation to adopt the Precautionary Principal as part of its Toxics Reduction Program. City government offices are required to determine the safest solutions when making decisions about purchasing, building, and improving any other business, and the private sector and residents are encouraged to follow suit.

Green Gamut

In December 2006, San Francisco was the first city in the nation to pass a law banning the use of hormone-disrupting chemicals Bisphenol A and phthalates from children's toys and baby bottles. The American Chemistry Council and the California Chamber of Commerce sued the city for the proposed ban, saying that federal law overrides local laws, according to the Supremacy clause in the U.S. Constitution. This is another prime example of business and government fighting against the public's right to health and safety protection. The European Union passed a similar ordinance in 1999.

Other city policies address environmental justice and education programs to help move San Francisco into a healthier future.

Nearby Oakland and Berkeley are leaders in green government and businesses, too. Berkeley's fleet of public diesel vehicles, including fire trucks, runs on biodiesel fuel.

Austin, Texas

Austin has a reputation as a green city from way back. It has committed to source 20 percent of its energy needs from renewable resources by 2020 and has a stated goal of becoming the top solar manufacturing center in the nation. The city provides information resources and incentives to residents and builders to develop green buildings that protect the environment, improve air and water quality, conserve energy, and reduce waste. The city was ranked #2 Green City by *The Green Guide* in 2006.

Eugene, Oregon

In 2006, Eugene received *The Green Guide*'s #1 designation and for good reason. The small college town of about 140,000 residents produces 85 percent of its power with renewable resources—hydroelectric and wind power. It protects its 16 percent of green space for public enjoyment and owns more than 2,500 acres of protected wetlands. The city fleet includes biodiesel and hybrid vehicles, and the mayor has implemented a green business incentive program.

> **Green Gamut**
>
> Every gallon of gas burned creates 28 pounds of greenhouse gases, according to Oak Ridge National Laboratory, as reported by the *Sierra Club Magazine*.

Portland, Oregon

Portland has been following a sustainable guideline since 1994. More than 92,000 acres are protected green spaces and a thriving public transportation system serves 13 percent of the population, while another 11 percent carpool and 2 percent bike to work. The city recycles residential yard wastes and food scraps from businesses and draws 44 percent of its energy from hydropower. Portland was the first U.S. city to develop a plan to reduce its CO_2 emissions, and the city provides incentives to those who implement solar energy systems.

Huntsville, Alabama

Huntsville has dedicated one third of its land to green space with protected forests, preserves, gardens, and parks. More than 12,000 volunteers have helped clean up the city, and 13 percent of the city commutes by bus and trolley. The city is addressing water pollution with an innovative new industrial park which features roof catchment systems to filter all runoff into wetland filtering areas to protect the underground aquifer that provides the city water supply.

St. Paul, Minnesota

St. Paul has a well-established green building program and a commitment to provide green affordable housing for residents. The city protects one fourth of its green spaces, has already met its initial goal to reduce global warming, and has increased its commitment to reduce greenhouse gas emissions by 20 percent below 1988 levels by 2020. The city plans to develop a light-rail public transportation system and to generate 20 percent of its energy from renewable resources as part of the new goal. Residents benefit from property tax exemptions when implementing renewable energy systems in their homes.

Denver, Colorado

Denver has established a large city fleet of hybrid vehicles and is developing the country's largest light-rail transit system to serve an expected half-million commuters each day. The city has a five-year Greenprint plan that addresses greenhouse gas reduction, development of solar power systems, better waste management, water conservation, and quality protections. The city supports green building and green businesses.

Chicago, Illinois

Once known for its green-dyed river celebrating St. Patrick's Day, today Chicago is making a name for itself in the *green roof* department, a relatively new step in improving energy efficiency, regulating climate control, and bringing green spaces and gardens to urban environments previously known as asphalt and concrete jungles.

def•i•ni•tion

> **Green roofs** comprise an interesting architectural development which involves covering building tops with soil and planting sod and gardens. Green roofs provide a pleasant place to spend time, particularly in urban environments; process CO_2 in the atmosphere and produce oxygen; provide food through gardens; and help insulate buildings so they don't use as much energy to heat or cool. Chicago is leading the movement in the United States, with a city initiative from the Mayor's office to support the development of green roofs.

With a green-roofed City Hall, Chicago provides incentives to urban businesses of matching grants up to $100,000 to help implement green rooftops. The initiative has resulted in Chicago's claim to having more green roofs than any other city in the nation—over 200 buildings boast more than 2.5 million square feet of green roofs across town. Why develop green roofs? Green plants help process CO_2 into oxygen, mitigate greenhouse gases, and insulate buildings to help keep temperatures consistent with the earth's natural ground temperature, keeping buildings cooler in summer and warmer in winter.

New York City

New York City has been a focal demonstration point for many high-profile green buildings, including the Conde Nast building, which was the largest green office building in the world when it opened in 2000; the Hearst Tower, which won a LEED Gold award; and green residential projects, such as Solaire in Battery Park City.

Mayor Michael Bloomberg made an Earth Day 2007 promise to "create the first environmentally sustainable twenty-first-centry city." The city has been a leader in mass transit for decades and boasts hybrid buses and taxis. Also city developers demonstrated great foresight in setting aside the huge swath of Central Park, which provides much welcome greenery and wildlife in the midst of intense urbanity.

The city has switched all traffic signals to energy-efficient lighting, saving $6 million each year, and has replaced 200,000 refrigerators in public housing with more efficient models, cutting $7 million per year in energy costs.

The city of more than 8 million produces massive amounts of garbage—the city sends 26 million pounds of waste to the largest landfill in the nation, Fresh Kill on Staten Island. The city's water supply is drawn from the Hudson River ecosystem, where reservoirs near the river provide fresh water. The river itself is a hallmark demonstration of progress in environmental awareness. Polluted by many different industries and the country's largest *Superfund* site, several groups are working to resolve the issues and are making notable progress in cleaning up the messes left behind by unconscious growth. RiverKeeper, an organization represented by attorney Robert F. Kennedy Jr., manages the legal battles necessary to see that the Hudson River receives the attention required to provide for a fresh water supply. The sloop *Clearwater*, a sailboat project founded by singer and river resident Pete Seeger, sails the waterways providing education and cleanup activities to help raise awareness of and address water concerns. Sustainable Hudson Valley is a grass roots group that's bringing education about global warming to valley residents.

def•i•ni•tion

Superfund is the nickname for a federal program that was initiated to provide funds to clean up environmentally damaged sites. However, the program has become inactive in recent years since companies are no longer required to fund cleanups of problems they create. Without funds, the sites rely on voluntary compliance with environmental regulations, and often end up in endless legal battles instead of cleanup projects.

These challenges and the efforts to resolve them provide a glimpse of the future for the entire earth as we rocket toward waste and water issues everywhere.

There's also an international movement, the International Council for Local Environmental Initiatives (ICLEI), with 650 participating governments worldwide, and Cities for Climate Protection Campaign (CCP), both of which similarly engage local governments in environmental progress.

Reynolds, Indiana

Although they haven't signed the Mayors Climate Protection Agreement, Reynolds, Indiana, is another city that has taken it upon itself to show the nation that going green can be a reality. The town has trademarked the name BioTown, USA, for itself and has adopted the mission to completely meet the needs of all its residents using biodegradable renewable fuels.

Located in the corn belt of the Midwest, the town has focused a great deal of its energy interest on corn-based fuel, ethanol, and has installed several ethanol fueling stations for area residents. Biodiesel is another important element in Reynold's suite of solutions.

Another energy alternative being developed in Reynolds is biogas, generated from livestock and human waste, both treacherous environmental problems threatening our water supplies through contamination. All of these alternative technologies together are being developed and used to help the town of Reynolds achieve its bold goal to become self-sufficient.

States Are Taking Stands, Too

The state of California is well known as a leader in innovative and controversial arenas—sometimes laughed at by the rest of the nation as a state that's out there in space with ga-ga science (there's no coincidence that La-La Land is spelled L.A.). Yet in time, quite often it becomes clear that Californians can be prescient on important issues of health and wellness. Now, under the perhaps surprising leadership of the actor known as "the Terminator," Republican "Governator" Arnold Schwarzenegger, California is leading the nation in state-wide environmental initiatives.

This forward-thinking state was the first to pass legislation encouraging homeowners to produce their own solar power. The Million Solar Roofs bill, signed in August 2006, has a 10-year goal span and includes incentive programs and solar building standards.

California also led the way with legislation to reduce all industrial greenhouse gas emissions to 1990 levels by 2020.

California is among 35 states providing net-metering programs to residents using solar or other alternative means. Net metering allows them to earn an equitable retail price for selling excess energy back to the local power company—in many other states homeowners pay a premium for energy usage and yet are paid a minimum for power they provide back to the grid.

Californians welcomed the electric car when it was first introduced in the early 1990s, and the success of these vehicles prompted introduction of legislation to make 2 percent of all state vehicles emission free within 8 years. Alas, automakers reacted defensively to this initiative—even though it was inspired by General Motor's electric car—and responded by suing the state under a claim that only the federal government could mandate emission reductions. The Bush administration supported the claim, and California's attempt to bring emission-free electric cars to the low end of mainstream was derailed by our own federal government in conjunction with industry. Nonetheless, California continues to have the most stringent emission laws in the world.

Other states are jumping on the bandwagon, creating local and state-wide incentives for residents who implement efficient and renewable technologies in their homes and businesses. Local governments are finding power beyond federal control. A resource of ideas and reports from municipal governments can be found at SustainLane (www.sustainlane.us), a website to help advance knowledge and sustainability initiatives in government agencies.

Religion: Red or Green?

Conservative religions have sometimes aligned themselves with administrations that have not always had the environment as a priority. But finally, many religions began to break away from party lines, asking themselves, "What would Jesus do?" about these looming environmental issues. Finally, as reported by Bill Moyers on his TV special, *Is God Green?* religious leaders such as Tri Robinson, pastor of Vineyard Boise Church in Idaho, realized that protecting God's green Earth is part of the job.

Moyers sends us to the site www.ChristiansandClimate.org, where we can read "Climate Change: An Evangelical Call to Action," a statement prepared by the organization, which represents Christian Evangelical leaders of many faiths. The statement outlines four positions and urges action from the faith community to address them: "1) Human-induced climate change is real; 2) The consequences of climate change will be significant, and will hit the poor the hardest; 3) Christian moral convictions demand our response to the climate change problem; and 4) The need to act now is urgent. Governments, businesses, churches and individuals all have a role to play in addressing climate change—starting now." The statement ends thus: "In the name of Jesus Christ our Lord, we urge all who read this declaration to join us in this effort."

Reverend Richard Cizik is vice president for governmental affairs of the National Association of Evangelicals, representing more than 50 faiths in 45,000 churches. Cizik departs from the conservative stance on environmentalism to help advance concern for care of the earth—they call it Creation Care. He found himself in the hot seat among his colleagues, but he's held forth on his position and has seen many religious leaders come forward to recognize that caring for the earth is about caring for people and families.

"Heaven is God's throne and Earth is his footstool, according to the legend of Isaiah," Cizik told National Public Radio's *Fresh Air* anchor Terry Gross.

"The fate of the Earth may well depend on how Christians respond to global warming," Cizik told Moyers in his PBS television special, *Is God Green?*

College Students Do Their Part

Future generations depend on our strength of purpose to do the right thing today. But the kids aren't waiting on us to get motivated and get started.

Many universities have responded positively to the challenge, and changes have begun. More than 300 universities, high schools, and youth organizations have banded together to help their schools become more ecofriendly. Some, including Yale, Duke, and the University of Florida, have signed an international treaty called the Talloires Declaration, which is a 10-point commitment to develop ecofriendly practices and policies at the schools and to teach those to students. Some have joined a consortium called the Southern Alliance for Clean Energy, and have committed to try to get their schools to switch over to 100 percent clean energy.

Many innovations are taking place on college campuses, and new developments are constantly underway as students explore new technologies and business practices for more sustainable systems. The students are leading the way toward a clean, cool future.

Students are banding together across the country through several organizations to help bring their universities into the future by implementing energy-efficient technologies, organizing recycling programs, adopting hybrid fleets, and building green buildings on campus. More than 300 universities and organizations around the world have joined University Leaders for a Sustainable Future (www.ulsf.org) to ensure that universities incorporate environmental sustainability into their research, education, and operations.

The Southern Alliance for Clean Energy, a group of more than 30 youth organizations across the southeastern states, sponsors the Campus Climate Challenge: www.climateaction.net/. MTV has created ThinkMTV to work with viewers to inform and support environmental activities: www.mtv.come/thinkmtv/environment/.

A Changing Perspective

One factor that's really helping to move these green innovations forward is a changing perspective, a changing way of thinking about environmental issues. With science in our field of vision now, making it clear that global warming will have dire effects on our way of life and our health, people are realizing that global warming isn't a political issue and it isn't something to leave up to business or the profiteers. The time has come to put political differences aside and to put the health of our families and our neighbors above the desire for business profits. This issue is something that matters more than money, more than winning; and it matters to everyone, rich and poor, of every color, every religion, and every nationality. Everyone needs to work together to make the necessary changes, and that's what's happening in the communities listed earlier in this chapter and in many others all around the world. And the benefits of learning to put the well-being of others above sheer profit is surely bound to have far-reaching and long-lasting changes on our society and our future way of life—at least we can hope so.

Political leaders, such as Greg Nickels of Seattle, recognize that constituents want healthier lifestyles and a healthy future, and that's one way they appeal to voters to help bring about the changes necessary to curb global warming.

The Importance of an Informed Electorate

An informed electorate ensures responsible government and corporate actions. Voters set the pace of government, and it's important to choose candidates carefully when deciding who will get your vote. Attend rallies of candidates you're interested in so you can see them in person to better assess their character and to learn how they plan to represent you. Ask them straightforward questions about their energy policies. Find out how they feel about coal or nuclear power. Do they support renewable energy alternatives instead? Do they favor tax cuts for businesses and less liability for problems related to their products, or do they support environmental responsibility and the Precautionary Principle?

> **Going Green**
>
> In addition to hearing politicians' responses to these questions, check their voting records to see what actions they've actually taken on the issues that matter to you. The League of Conservation Voters (www.lcv.org) maintains a useful archive of voting records to help you ascertain your candidate's true positions on various issues.

Let your political candidates know that you want healthy change, ask them to support healthier environmental and energy choices, and select candidates who are making statements to that same effect. It is the harmony of all these various factions working together toward a common goal for change that is already helping to turn the tide toward a healthier, peaceful future.

The Least You Need to Know

◆ Many cities and communities are taking it upon themselves to move toward a healthier future.

◆ Conserving energy, developing renewable energy resources, reducing auto emissions through public transportation and use of hybrid vehicles, supporting green building and green businesses are just a few of the ways that cities are addressing global warming.

◆ Religious communities are joining the effort to protect the environment.

◆ College students are also helping to promote environmental education and changes in the academic communities.

◆ These groups are helping political leaders realize that government can take a positive role toward establishing changes to address global warming.

Chapter 20

Teaching Our Children Principles of Green Living

In This Chapter

- Fun ways to educate kids and get them involved
- Teaching our children about the food they eat
- Vacation experiences that teach kids about their environment
- Using the Internet to educate children about the world around them
- Earth-friendly organizations in our schools

I remember taking a favorite friend's child to a state park years ago. I was shocked by his racing along the trails, grabbing at trees and leaves as he passed by, giggling and yelling nearly at the top of his voice, drowning out, even silencing, the birdsong I normally heard on my solo hikes.

This same child begged for some fast food at lunch although he ate the tasty (and healthy) food before him. He tossed his paper napkin and cup to the side for someone else (Mom) to retrieve.

This was a child who had not yet learned about nature. It was a powerful example of how children might act if they are not taught to respect Mother

Earth and the resources she provides to make our lives truly wonderful. And of course, those children grow into adults who don't care or give nature and the environment a second thought as they pass through this world.

It was also a wake-up call. If we don't teach our children, they will not know that our resources are finite and should be cherished. This is a responsibility that parents, primary teachers in these situations, should take seriously.

But in our busy, fast-paced, overscheduled world, where for parents and kids alike recreation might just include a trip to the mall, teaching children about the environment and how to be good stewards of the environment is an increasingly difficult challenge.

Yet it is our job as parents—or just as friendly, concerned adults—to teach children about the world around us. Ideally we model the behaviors we hope they will carry with them and pass on to future generations. And of course, no matter how old your child is as you are reading these words, it's never too late to start.

Teaching Our Children About Food

Every day, when we sit down to meals, we get an opportunity to teach our children something about the world around us.

After years of not paying attention to the way our foods were grown or raised, we now have enough evidence that we can no longer ignore the fact that the fewer chemicals we use to raise our foods, the better off we will be.

While it's fantastic that big supermarkets, such as Whole Foods or Trader Joe's, have been leaders in the organic grocery store movement, the "trickle down" effect of these companies has been enormous.

While just 15 years ago I had to go out of my way to what many people considered "hippie" stores to find organic food, today, the smallest branch of the local chain offers me a nice variety of green choices and a new way to teach my youngest about what we buy and why we buy it.

By making shopping for groceries a family affair, you can talk to your children about what you choose and why you choose it. I let my kids make the list (which also teaches spelling skills) and add up the budget as we go along. Here are some great examples of easy-to-find (in local chains) products and what you might talk about with your children.

◆ *Milk.* The milk case is big these days, but send your child to find organic milk. Here's a chance to talk about drinking milk free from antibiotics and added growth hormones. Without going into something that might scare your child (early onset of puberty for girls, for example), you can talk about how using too many antibiotics in the world around us leads to germs that are harder and harder to fight.

◆ *Eggs.* Have your child find eggs from chickens raised without hormones or antibiotics. You can have the same discussion about the problems with those eggs as you do about milk. You might also want to take the time to point out the fact that these eggs cost more but that you know it's worth it because of the long-term benefits, which in turn can lead to a discussion about how what we do today will affect generations to come. These are big issues, but keep it small.

◆ *Cookies.* That's right. You get to indulge while going green, which is another topic worth mentioning to your children. Great food comes from great ingredients. If your child is old enough to read labels, have him grab a bag of organic sandwich cream cookies (for example, the cookies made by Newman's Own Organics) and a nonorganic sandwich cream cookie. Ask him to compare the ingredients listed on the labels. He'll be able to read the organic list pretty easily. The list of ingredients on nonorganic foods will give even the most well-read adult trouble. Hence the next lesson: the easier it is to say the ingredients, the more likely it is the product is better for you. And the reverse: if you can't pronounce an ingredient, you probably don't want to eat it.

Of course, these are just three small examples. The produce aisles are full of the same kinds of choices you can make and the same kinds of lessons you can teach. Another good one is to talk about what to eat in season. My daughter asks for watermelon year-round, which leads me to engage her in a conversation about eating food when it is affordable: when it's in season.

Take Your Kids to Farmers' Markets

Visiting a farmers' market makes a great field trip to take with your children, too. You can teach the same lessons about seasonality, and if you come across a gregarious farmer, he or she might be willing to talk about picking the food on the tables that very morning.

As parents, we should make every effort to connect the food we eat back to the food that farmers grow for us. If you are lucky enough to have any little bit of grass to call your own, one of the very best ways to teach about that connection is by having your child help you plan, plant, tend, and harvest your own backyard garden. If you refer to Chapter 12, which deals with organic gardening, you'll find plenty of ways and resources to tackle this as a hands-on project and an excellent way to encourage your kids to go green.

Teaching Kids About Bioethics

A bit more difficult to teach is our connection with animals. While many people opt to go green and become vegetarian, for plenty of people, eating organically includes choosing meat and poultry from organic sources, where the consumer can be confident the animals were cared for. This is referred to as *bioethics*.

Children don't need to be exposed to the atrocities of the big feedlot system. That can be an upsetting and gruesome picture. But we can teach children respect for the animals who give us sustenance.

def•i•ni•tion

Bioethics is the study of ethical issues raised by the developments in the life science technologies. This is a big word for something children worry about naturally. Encourage them to explore what they think about humane treatment of the animals that sustain us and why it is important for them to think about it.

Teaching children about the cows and chickens behind the hamburger and chicken strips is a tricky thing. I know children who became vegetarians overnight when they made that connection. It doesn't have to be that way—though that's not a bad thing.

The Niman Ranch story captures the respectful attitude. This company, long-known in the industry for its quality meats, raises grass and grain-fed animals (the cows don't eat meat-based feed). In the company's words, "We treat our cattle with dignity and respect. Our ranch managers do whatever is necessary to reduce the amount of stress in the animals' day-to-day lives."

It's common in our culture today for humans to be omnivores. But kids should know that it does matter where our food comes from and how it lived on this planet before it became food for our tables. This is kindness in its most basic form. It's easy to teach children about being kind to animals, farm animals included. But organic meats and poultry come from places where farmers care about the way their animals are raised. The same cannot be said for the meat from feedlots and chicken houses.

Going Green _____

Now might be the perfect time to look at just how disconnected our children are from the animals around us. Unfortunately the closest many children get to animals besides their own pets is to watch animals behind bars in the zoos. While zoos have come a long way in their approach to building habitats for the animals they keep, it's still not a natural existence for them.

You can help your children learn to love and respect the animals in their immediate community and perhaps help engender a love for these creatures we often take for granted. Perhaps a volunteer stint at the local animal shelter would be a good idea.

Around the House

Household chores and purchases offer similar "teachable moments." When you care for your lawn, explain why you don't use chemicals. Point out that your lawn may have more dandelions than your neighbors but that you can be comfortable knowing your children don't play in chemicals when they play in your yard. Teach your children the inherent beauty of all the plants you have in your yard—even the dandelions.

In fact, even the choices you make when you decorate your home or your child's room offer ways to introduce your child to the concept of living green.

"If we want these beautiful homes, they have to be breathable, livable, and of healthy construction," says interior designer Bernadette Upton of EcoDecor, a green design firm.

Upton teaches other interior designers, builders, and architects about the importance of choosing natural fibers and building materials for our homes.

JoAnn Munroe of Southeast Interior Design, Inc., won an award for her green approach to decorating a safe and beautiful nursery, which used real wood furniture, organic fabrics, and natural fibers (such as wool carpets, which don't have the toxic glue found in synthetic carpets).

Going Green _____

For more information on Healthy Baby Rooms, contact the American Lung Association of South Florida at 561-659-7644. Request their free booklet, *A Baby's Breath*, at www.lungfla.org.

Say It in Art

Art is a fun way to engage children while they are learning. At a young age, children have few inhibitions about the way they paint and draw and can find joy in each stroke of a paintbrush or in the original tunes with which they entertain us.

That joy wasn't lost on Lanny Smith, a.k.a. Earthman. Smith founded the Planet Earth Project band in 1992.

As Earthman, Smith dresses in a blue and green Earth costume, topped off with Blues Brothers' style shades and a sport coat. He sings the earth blues as he teaches children about the challenges facing the environment, one song at a time.

And what is Smith's approach? He tries to teach children about how valuable our Earth and her resources are as well as teach them about the little things they can do to fix some of the problems facing us. Smith figures if kids learn to be responsible, caring stewards of the environment at a young age, they will grow into responsible, caring stewards of the environment when they become CEOs and corporate decision makers. He even hopes the kids might pass some of the lessons they learn on to their voting-age parents.

Smith's songs include lessons about turning off the water, recycling, conserving resources, and explaining general knowledge about the earth's ecosystems.

"It's all about getting into the dialogue, educating yourself, then activating yourself," Smith says. "It's all linked into action."

Smith managed to get the show on the road starting in 1995 with a band of talented professional musicians. He made connections with educators and landed gigs performing at local events, museums, and schools.

The Earthman Project, as it is known, is finding itself a national audience, and although the warnings are dire, Smith would not persevere if he didn't also have his fair share of hope.

"Scientists agree, far and away, it's time to act," he says. "The environment is the bridge issue. It doesn't matter what your religion is or where you're from. We're all in the big ballpark, and we've got to deal with the big issues.

"We challenge people to lead, to do what we need to do to save our nation. Don't stop until we can send the poorest of the poor a solar panel to light up their hut that says, 'Made in U.S.A.' They'll love us. We can do it, but it's going to take commitment from the wealthiest and the government of this nation." Sing it, Earthman.

Other activities for kids can take place in your own backyard. Take your children into the yard to gather leaves, sticks, feathers, rocks, and so on. There are no limits to what children can decide are beautiful found objects. Encourage them to draw pictures of their treasures, to make collages, or to do charcoal or crayon rubbings of the treasures.

The same treasures can be great jumping-off points to start learning about the environment in our own backyards. Identify the bird a feather has come from, for example. Then find out what might threaten the bird's environment.

Art is what we make it for our children. Let them see the beauty of the world around them. That alone should be enough for them to want to save it.

Vacation Experiences That Will Change the Way Your Children View the World

Have you ever thought about combining your family vacation time with learning about the environment? It's a great way to teach everyone, young and old, about some of our precious resources.

One possibility is swimming with the dolphins—not in a manmade enclosure, but in the open waters of the Florida Keys. Captain Victoria Rose is a woman championing the movement toward respect for animals. Rose, who runs boat trips for people to swim with the dolphins, preps her passengers for *possible* (nothing is guaranteed!) encounters with the dolphins by noting that the less equipment the swimmers wear, the more likely they will be approached by the dolphins. She also encourages the swimmers to be open to what dolphins give to humans lucky enough to swim near them, noting "You get what you give."

Rose also makes it a point to educate her passengers, who range from children to adults, by giving them some lessons about how what we put on our land ends up in the sea.

Her respect extends to the spiritual aspects as well. She believes the dolphins can determine a person's spirit through their own radar. She also maintains that those who swim with the dolphins leave with lasting results from the encounter, which encourages the release of endorphins.

The possibilities for environmentally friendly vacation experiences abound. Choices range from hiking in local parks and forests, learning about your local environment, camping out and learning how to not leave any traces of your visit behind, to the more exotic option of spending time at an ecoresort.

At an ecoresort, guests stay in places away from general civilization, in quarters that are basic but comfortable. Ecoresorts strive to protect the surrounding environment while allowing environmentally conscious visitors in to enjoy that environment. The resorts are set in spectacular locations, such as the Caribbean Islands, but "far from the madding crowd." Visitors find electricity generated from solar power, water warmed by the sun, water collected from rainfall, and cooling breezes provided by nature alone.

Vacation memories are some of our longest-lasting memories. Give your family the gift of learning to respect the environment, of being truly away from the ravages of our crowded society, and of being able to enjoy each other's company without the distractions of our everyday world.

Both the Boy Scouts and the Girl Scouts offer long-lasting experiences that educate young people about the importance of our environment.

The Boy Scouts actively teach the "Leave no Trace" principle. It includes choosing campsites in order to minimize the effects of an overnight visit, for example, as well as teaching scouts about the long-term impact any destruction has on the environment.

> **Green Speak**
>
> "Appreciation for our natural environments and a knowledge of the interrelationships of nature bolster our respect and reverence toward the environment and nature."
>
> —Boy Scouts of America (www.scouting.org/boyscouts/resources/21-105/).

The Girl Scouts also instill environmental protections awareness. The Elliott Wildlife Values Project (EWVP), which started in 1977, takes girls to natural environments where they can have hands-on experiences that lead to "a lifelong commitment to the conservation of wildlife."

The Girl Scouts also offer an environmental health badge, which the scouts earn as they learn about ways a clean environment leads to cleaner health.

The Girl Scouts also have online games such as My Planet which teach players ways to protect the environment. Go to www.girlscouts.org/program/program_opportunities/environment/.

Internet-Savvy Kids

Even our youngest seem to be spending time in front of computers these days, so don't overlook fun sites for them to learn about the environment.

Rodale's www.KidsRegen.org seeks to teach children to make environmentally sound choices in their lives. Sponsored by Rodale, which publishes *Organic Gardening* (among many other titles), this site passes on the company's philosophy of "Healthy Soil, Healthy Food, Healthy People."

KidsRegen.org, which was started in 2001, is full of information written for young visitors. On this site kids can read about plants, find fun craft activities, learn all about the "celebrity" vegetable of the season (when I visited, the celebrity vegetable was the dynamic beet), find family-friendly recipes for the celebrity vegetable, find winter games (encouraging kids to get out and enjoy nature no matter the season), and even post questions or answer questions other kids have posed. The site engages visitors (young and old—I can vouch for that).

Another online, environmental magazine just for kids is EEK, Environmental Education for Kids, at http://www.dnr.state.wi.us/org/caer/ce/eek/, sponsored by the Wisconsin Department of Natural Resources.

Like Rodale's site, EEK encourages kids to learn about animals, nature, and the earth's ecosystem. The "Get a Job" link introduces children to people in different environmental/naturalist jobs through people profiles.

EarthForce for Kids engages kids as "active citizens to improve the environment" (www.earthforce.org).

The Natural Resource Defense Council provides info for kids at www.nrdc.org/greensquad/intro/intro_1.asp.

Kids For a Clean Environment, or Kids F.A.C.E., is at www.kidsface.org.

These are just a few sites of many, but they illustrate how teaching the kids can be done by engaging them, too. It's about encouraging their natural curiosity and letting them have some say in where they click through.

Getting Our Schools to Go Green

Our children spend about eight hours a day in the classroom. With cooperation from the schools, classrooms are great places to introduce children to the concept of protecting the environment, and with so many schools now encouraging community service hours, the two concepts can be taught together.

Sometimes teachers come to school prepared to discuss concepts of environmental conservation, which often blend right into lessons about biology and chemistry in the world at large.

But if this doesn't work, there are plenty of organizations already in action that can serve as examples of ways to educate the youth of America about environmental concerns.

One successful program is Earth Force (www.earthforce.org). This organization seeks to engage students by showing them how they can be participants in society with a voice in how we treat our environment now and in the future.

Earth Force started in 1994 when it recognized that the youth of America already had a desire to protect the environment and a mindset of giving back to the community.

Earth Force established programs that empowered young people to do something positive for the environment by teaching them how to focus on a project and plan a course of action to solve a problem.

A good example was a group of students in Pittsburgh, Pennsylvania, who decided they needed to educate the community about "nonpoint source pollution" getting into Pittsburgh's rivers through storm drains. A class from the Schiller Classical Academy inventoried the trash they removed from storm drains, mapped the drains, produced a radio piece about their project, passed out door hangers to get the word out about the project, and stenciled signs on the drains announcing "Dump No Waste. Drains to Rivers." The class hoped the stencils would remind people that the drains weren't trash bins but direct routes to the beautiful rivers around the city.

While Earth Force can't just come into a city on a moment's notice and set up shop (an endeavor which requires long-term plans and funds), they can and do pass on their knowledge and examples such as the one above to encourage others to take some action in their own communities.

> **Green Gamut**
>
> Remember when we talked about growing your own vegetables as a way to connect to the earth at the beginning of the chapter? If you are not lucky enough to have some of your own land, maybe this is the perfect way for you to volunteer your time at school. Propose establishing a garden, and recruit students to help you with it, start to finish. Approach the school with a plan as well as with reasons the project would benefit the students.

Earth Force logo.

(Courtesy Earth Force)

Other organizations strive to do similar work by educating the educators and providing lesson plans and projects for students to get involved in the world around them. Scouting programs provide great opportunities for kids to get to know their natural environment and learn to be better stewards of the earth.

Go Green Initiative is one such organization that starts with schools as a way to educate our population. They start with students specifically because schools produce a huge amount of waste that can be recycled.

According to the Go Green Initiative, "schools that model and teach principles of environmentally responsible behaviors to students will have a long-term impact. Teachers and parents are working every day to educate the next generation of business owners and government officials. We can equip them with the knowledge and skills they will need in the future to manage the complexities of the environmental impact inherent in all activities."

Teach them while they are young. Their future depends on it.

> **Green Speak**
>
> "Any genuine teaching will result, if successful, in someone's knowing how to bring about a better condition of things than existed earlier."
>
> —John Dewey, a pioneer of the American education system and developer of the Dewey Decimal System used worldwide to organize and catalog library collections

The Least You Need to Know

◆ Parents need to teach their children to be good stewards of the world around them.

◆ Use trips to the grocery store and farmers' markets to encourage your kids to think about the food they put into their bodies.

◆ Groups, such as Girl Scouts or Boy Scouts, even feature environmental protection badges, so encourage your own children to participate in some way to learn these world-friendly lessons.

◆ Take your kids on a vacation that will forever change the way they think about their environment.

◆ Internet sites such as www.KidsRegen.org can help kids to make sound environmental choices in their lives.

◆ You don't need to scare your kids into going green, but rather use positive techniques and teaching to show them the good they can do on this earth.

Chapter 21

The New Green Economy

In This Chapter

- ◆ Economic changes necessary to thrive in a post–fossil fuel world
- ◆ Making strides toward oil-free, emission-free, and waste-free production practices
- ◆ Fair Trade agreements—visible and fast-growing evidence of more socially and environmentally responsible business practices
- ◆ Emerging new jobs in the green economy

Although perhaps unintentional at the outset, oil spills, chemical factory explosions, polluted wastewater contaminating fresh water supplies, deforestation leaving barren and unsustainable communities behind, air polluted with carbon dioxide, and global warming are all trademarks of the twentieth-century economy.

But this is the new millennium, and it is time for a change. We often read or hear that changing the way things are done will be costly, and reading of industry lay-offs inspires great fears. But new jobs will replace the old, and the end result could be much better lives for many more people, rather than extreme luxury for a select crowd. Change will require synchronistic cooperation among government, business, and individual citizens. A few prescient thinkers have developed ideas about what our new sustainable economy could look like and how we can get there. So let's take a look.

The Outlook on Sustainability

The Worldwatch Institute describes itself as an independent research organization for an environmentally sustainable and socially just society. Each year, Worldwatch issues its *State of the World* report, which provides an overview of conditions and trends that bear observation and consideration when evaluating one's worldview. In its 2007 report, the institute notes, among many other salient points, that

- ◆ If $40 billion had been spent on preventing natural disasters in the 1990s, $280 billion in disaster-related losses would have been saved.

- ◆ Population in cities has quadrupled over the past 50 years.

- ◆ Sales of Fair Trade goods increased by 50 percent from 1997 to 2004.

- ◆ China is the world leader in the solar industry, employing about 250,000 workers.

Clearly, money could be better spent to help alleviate disasters caused by global warming, and the increasing populations in urban environments indicate that more people will be affected by disasters that occur in densely populated areas, where the natural environment has been displaced by asphalt and concrete. And yet the second pair of significant notes indicates that movement toward a healthier economy is underway—both Fair Trade and solar industries are growing.

Natural resources, such as oil, metal, and wood, are finite, and oil is in dwindling supply, so it's important that we now create new products that don't rely on these materials. We may all have to look at things in a different light and change the way we do things.

We must also factor in the environmental costs. In business today, that most often means calculating the cost of fines for polluting that occurs during the course of manufacturing or otherwise conducting business. But that's a long way from the real environmental cost that we should consider.

When a coal plant produces CO_2 emissions, what will it cost to clean that out of the air? What will it cost to repair the damage caused by the global warming which will result from the CO_2 emissions? Coal-fired power plants also emit particulate smog, which contributes to hundreds of thousands of respiratory illnesses and fatalities. How do we calculate that cost? What are lost lives worth?

The coal industry has partnered with the government to provide compensatory payment to the families of coal miners who die from black lung disease, and that is recognized as a cost of doing business, just as the miners recognize that sacrificing their lives is a possible cost of earning a living by mining to support their families. The government pays subsidies to the coal industry to help offset this expense and other expenses of doing business. Yet the coal companies don't have environmental destruction on their balance sheets to help recover the mountaintop landscapes and waterways in devastated mountain towns. That is an environmental cost that no one has factored into the equation, and we must consider this cost in a sustainable economy instead of leaving it behind for others to deal with.

> **Green Speak**
>
> "The same human ingenuity that created the climate problem is now urgently needed to solve it. By collectively rising to this challenge, and gathering the political will to move aggressively, we can avoid serious climate disruption and increase economic prosperity as well."
> —Christopher Flavin and Seth Dunn, Worldwatch Paper #138: *Rising Sun, Gathering Winds: Policies to Stabilize the Climate and Strengthen Economies*

The Eco-Economy

In 2001, Lester Brown, the visionary who founded the Worldwatch Institute and then later established The Earth Policy Institute as a means of putting into action the necessary changes made visible through the work of the Worldwatch Institute, wrote *Eco-Economy*. The book describes the huge deficits being caused by our industrial economy, including air and water pollution, soil damage that impairs food production, dwindling water supplies, desertification, and encroaching sea levels. Brown sets a plan for leaving the fossil fuel–based economy behind and cites active examples of sustainability already in practice, such as the growing wind and solar industries in Europe and Asia, steel recycling in the United States, and reforestation projects.

Another report, *Ecosystem Challenges and Business Implications*, prepared by the Earthwatch Institute, the World Conservation Union, the World Business Council for Sustainable Development, and the World Resources Institute, suggests that corporations lead the way in adapting to new economic values and practices as a means of coping with the necessary changes instead of allowing the changes to destroy their businesses.

Green Speak

"Business simply cannot function if ecosystems and the services they deliver like water, biodiversity, food, fiber, and climate regulation are degraded or out of balance. There must be a value attached to natural resources, and businesses need to start understanding this value."
—Björn Stigson, President, World Business Council for Sustainable Development, as reported by *Edie News*

The Union of Concerned Scientists reports that if the United States adopts a 10 percent renewable electricity standard, it would generate $5.7 billion in income to farmers and landowners from biomass energy and wind power leases; $3 billion in property tax revenues for local jurisdictions; and nearly 100,000 jobs by 2020.

If we follow the UCS recommendation to increase fuel efficiency to 40 mpg, we'd generate more than 160,000 jobs across the country in the next decade—40,000 in the auto industry alone.

Clearly, adopting a sustainable economy need not mean an end to jobs or prosperity.

Indeed, business is likely to play the primary role in initiating the necessary economic changes.

Businesses Leading the Way

Entrepreneur Paul Hawken wrote a pair of groundbreaking books, *Growing a Business* in 1987 and *The Ecology of Commerce* in 1993, which set new, more sustainable perspectives for business owners. Among many other divergent ideas, Hawken suggested that profit needn't be the only indicator of success. That, in fact, successful leaders could reach a point where enough money is enough and allow other values to reclaim levels of importance, such as quality lifestyles for workers and protecting the environment.

Green Speak

"Business is the only mechanism on the planet today powerful enough to produce the changes necessary to reverse global environmental and social degradation."
—Paul Hawken, co-founder of Smith and Hawken

Gary Erickson, who founded CLIF Bar when he wanted a better sports snack and created an ecologically and socially responsible company with 170 employees and revenues of $150 million, noted in an *INC. Magazine* cover story on green businesses (November 2006), "the core problem is that we in business don't tend to accept that at a certain point, enough profit is enough."

Yet spreading out the wealth among workers and spending more money to create a more sustainable and environmentally friendly product is the best investment for a healthy future. And as more businesses work these values of human and natural capital into their business plans, *closing the loop of sustainability*, we will be on the road toward that new green economy.

Amory Lovins and Hunter Lovins of The Rocky Mountain Institute, a nonprofit organization dedicated to helping businesses and entrepreneurs develop more sustainable policies and practices, paired with Paul Hawken to write a tome for business leaders with an eye toward the future, *Natural Capitalism* (Little Brown, 1999).

Learn more from these forward thinkers at: www.natcap.org, www.paulhawken.com, and www.rmi.org.

def•i•ni•tion

Closing the loop of sustainability means eliminating waste and pollution from the life cycle of products so that our resources are in continuous use, are not wasted, and do not create a burden on the environment through pollution.

Green Gamut

"These principles: redesigning industry on biological models with closed loops and zero waste; shifting from the sale of goods (for example, light bulbs) to the provision of services (illumination); and reinvesting in the natural capital that is the basis of future prosperity, are so profitable that firms adopting them can gain striking competitive advantage—as early adopters are already doing. These innovators are also discovering that by downsizing their unproductive tons, gallons, and kilowatt-hours, they can keep more people, who will foster the innovation that drives future improvement."

—*Natural Capitalism*, Amory Lovins, Hunter Lovins, Paul Hawken

Applying the Green for Greenbacks

Several businesses have already demonstrated financial success by following sustainable principles. LOHAS, a group that studies the market it calls Lifestyles of Health and Sustainability (www.lohas.com), estimates the value of the U.S. natural and organic markets at $230 billion.

Seventh Generation, one business that began green with products targeted at a small market of environmentally aware consumers offering bleach-free paper products and petroleum-free cleaning products, has now grown into a multimillion-dollar company with products in mainstream chain department and grocery stores. Following the healthy and socially responsible line has paid off for this company.

Interface is a company that is on a mission to become the world's most sustainable business, thanks to the leadership of Ray Anderson, who credits Hawken's book, *The Ecology of Commerce*, for sparking the epiphany to turn his very successful but traditionally oil- and waste-intensive textile business into a model of environmental responsibility. Although the company continues working toward the completely closed loop system, they are already making great strides in sustainable responsibility. *INC. Magazine* reports that Interface has saved $300 million by recycling waste materials into new products.

Anderson hopes that other business leaders and their customers will take note of his actions and take steps of their own in the same direction. "Jeff Immelt has doubled GE's commitment to clean technologies," he told *INC. Magazine*. "He's not doing it out of altruism alone. He's hearing his marketplace, just as we heard ours 12 years ago …. There are new fortunes to be made in the next Industrial Revolution."

Some of the most recognizable industry leaders are following sustainable principles. Wal-Mart, the biggest seller of organic milk and the world's biggest buyer of organic cotton, has committed to increase its fleet's fuel efficiency by 50 percent within the decade, reduce energy use by 30 percent, reduce greenhouse gas emissions by 20 percent, and reduce waste by 25 percent. Other leaders include BP Solar, a division born from a petroleum company which has become a leader in solar energy; Toyota, with its Prius, the world's top-selling car; and Whole Foods, the nation's fastest-growing grocery chain, which features only socially and environmentally responsible products and specializes in organic foods.

The Pew Center on Global Climate Change convened a group called Businesses Environmental Leadership Council (BELC), which includes 42 companies with a combined worth of $2.4 trillion. They include DuPont, Shell, Cinergy/Duke Energy, Whirlpool, and Alcoa.

Green Speak

"Climate change is an issue that will affect virtually all aspects of society. The consequences of these changes will be most severe for those who do nothing to prepare for them today. The companies that the Pew Center works with in the BELC and USCAP [U.S. Climate Action Partnership] recognize this, and their proactive stance on the issue is the only intelligent choice left in dealing with climate change."

—Truman Semans, Pew Center for Global Climate Change, posted at www.greenbiz.com/ship

What Is a Green Job?

Lester Brown, founder of the Earth Policy Institute, cites several job possibilities emerging in the new economy, including solar cell manufacturing and installation, wind turbine manufacturing and installations, fuel cell manufacturers and research scientists, forestry specialists, fish farmers, recycling engineers, geothermal geologists, and environmental architects.

There are growing opportunities for naturalists, organic farmers and gardeners, green builders, sustainable designers, green interior designers, waste management specialists, and those who can implement the changing technologies in many different fields, from pulp processors to cistern builders and solar technologists who calibrate and set up home energy production with onsite computers.

A few resources for searching for green jobs include

◆ www.SustainableBusiness.com/jobs: Jobs listed by industry and state provide details such as skill level required, salary range, and contact information for jobs as varied as sustainable program designer, to solar company president, water and waste managers, research scientists, writers, marketers, organizers and interns.

◆ www.ecobusinesslinks.com/environmental_jobs.htm: A web directory of all things green gives information and how-to's as well as where to find green products, supplies, hotels, jobs, and much more.

◆ www.greenjobs.com/public/index.aspx: This site for businesses provides updates on businesses, their leadership, and stock market activity.

◆ www.greenbiz.com/ship/: Turning the Ship Blog is a board where business members post articles and comments about making their businesses more sustainable.

As Ross Gelbspan, author of *The Heat is On* and an expert on global warming, predicted, this can and will be a time of burgeoning creativity, when engineers and inventors can tackle these newly identified needs with excitement and enthusiasm for creating a new world paradigm—a healthy planet and a healthy future for generations to come.

The Least You Need to Know

◆ The time has come for a new approach to business that includes an array of values in addition to profit, such as concern for workers and the environment.

◆ Government regulations and economic policies must help shape the transition.

◆ Many businesses are already making big changes that benefit their bottom lines as well as the earth and its inhabitants.

◆ Many resources help find new jobs that are evolving to replace those lost to obsolete industries.

Chapter 22

Investing in Progress: Socially Responsible Investment Opportunities

In This Chapter

- Putting your money into the changes you wish to see happen
- Mutual funds that help channel money toward social and environmental causes
- Investing directly in stocks of companies you wish to support
- Investing in your community or other communities through socially responsible banks or credit unions
- Spending your dollars on direct investments, such as environmental improvements to your home

So you've reached the point where you have money to invest, and you want to protect your funds and grow them to fund your future retirement. In this chapter, you'll learn how to invest in your future and in the future of the earth at the same time. It's a win/win for you and for the environment.

Keep in mind that this chapter provides a brief, but not comprehensive, overview of investment opportunities available to those interested in supporting environmentally and socially responsible businesses. Please don't consider my comments as endorsements or recommendations of any fund or stock mentioned. My personal small forays into the investment world have not been impressive! So carefully do your own thorough research, and consult with a financial adviser when making your own investments.

Investing Carefully

Your elder advisers may encourage you to invest in traditional "blue chip" stocks, but if you look closely, you may find that some of the biggest, oldest companies and most reliable stock performers are doing businesses in ways that don't meet green standards.

Many large companies exploit poor workers in poverty-stricken developing nations. Some intentionally locate their industrial plants in these countries because they can use more toxic chemicals in processing or produce more pollutant waste because of poor regulation. Some companies test their products on animals or kill animals to use their body parts or fluids in their products. Maybe they raise animals to sell as meat in tiny cages and feed them sawdust and drugs instead of real food. Perhaps they spend a considerable amount of customer revenue and shareholder funds on lobbyists who influence laws allowing them to emit more pollutants or resist regulation to remove dangerous ingredients from their product lists. Perhaps the company clear-cuts forests in the course of manufacturing. Maybe the company is involved in a major superfund cleanup action that consumes billions of shareholder dollars because of irresponsible practices in the past.

All of these scenarios are part of the business world today. How will you find out whether these happenings are part of the practices at a company you're interested in investing in? Not by checking the company's website, that's for sure!

Mutual Funds

Fortunately, there are several mutual fund companies whose focus is to examine company policies and practices before including them in their portfolios. Two of the oldest and most revered funds, Pax World Fund and Domini Social Fund, have close founding ties to religious institutions working for social and environmental change. Pax World Fund is the oldest socially responsible fund, started in 1971.

> **Green Speak** _____
>
> "Pax World Funds (PAXWX) portfolio managers seek companies that not only pro-
> duce goods and services that improve the quality of life but also behave as good
> corporate citizens, treating their employees and the environment well. Individual factors,
> such as involvement in weapons production, automatically exclude a company, while
> cumulative concerns from a mix of issues can also lead to exclusion."
> —www.Paxworld.com

Another of the industry leaders is the Domini Social Equity Fund, founded by Amy
Domini (DSEFX). Domini manages $1.6 billion in assets in individual and mutual
fund accounts. The firm considers two basic principles when making all investments:
the promotion of a society that values human dignity and the enrichment of our natural environment. Domini considers these goals as "crucial to a healthier, wealthier, and
more sustainable world."

> **Green Speak** _____
>
> "As a shareholder in the Domini Funds, you make a difference in the world.
> Engaging companies on global warming, sweatshop labor, and product safety.
> Revitalizing distressed communities. Bringing new voices to the table. Redefining corpo-
> rate America's bottom line. Invest for your future while helping to build a world of peace
> and justice."
> —Domini Social Investments

Founded in 1990, today Domini has a broad array of funds available, serving international communities as well as the United States. Returns on its investments appear to
be very impressive.

The Sierra Club has established a mutual fund called Sierra Club Mutual Funds
(SCFLX). Any participating companies must pass a strict set of criteria that includes

- ◆ Any agricultural companies that participate in genetic modification of plants and
  animals, house livestock in factory farms, or manage industrial fish farms must be
  excluded.

- ◆ All companies must have cruelty-free animal treatment policies and must not test
  products on animals unless required by law to do so.

- Companies must be accountable and transparent in business conduct.

- Companies must allow no predatory lending or taking advantage of uninformed consumers.

- Companies must practice responsible policies in regard to the use of fossil fuels and carbon emissions.

- Companies must exhibit fair and acceptable labor policies and practices.

- Companies must practice sustainable, responsible development and not contribute to urban sprawl or environmental degradation or pollution.

- Sierra Club mutual funds must not invest in military weaponry, nuclear power, or tobacco products.

- Companies must demonstrate reduction in toxic emissions and minimize environmental costs.

There is plenty of reason to think that companies who conduct business according to the old rules of profit above all may have a hard time staying in the black as a new green century dawns. And there is every reason to believe that companies who have taken a proactive stance toward thriving in an age of the green economy will make great strides.

It seems a good choice to invest in socially and environmentally responsible mutual funds managed by trusted financial firms. One would hope they're also screened to flag leadership flaws (greed and dishonesty) like those that felled Enron and many pension plans a few years ago.

The Green Century Balanced Fund (www.greencentury.com, GCBLX) uses the following criteria in determining its holdings:

◆ Demonstrate a commitment to preserving and enhancing the environment.

◆ Maintain clean, open environmental records.

◆ Actively contribute toward improving the environment.

◆ Be responsive to shareholder environmental advocacy.

◆ Be proactive, responsible, benign, and best in class in terms of industrial practices, and must not engage in tobacco or nuclear-related business.

Green Century also has an Equity Fund. As representative of its shareholders, Green Century presents environmental agendas to companies to help them develop more sustainable practices. Advocating with your dollars is perhaps the single most effective means of effecting change. Some of the companies Green Century invests in include Whole Foods, Johnson & Johnson, McGraw Hill, and Emerson Electric.

Parnassus Mutual Funds (PARNX), started in 1984, was called the best large-cap fund by *Financial Times* in 2005 (www.parnassus.com).

By 1999, Dow Jones had caught on to the financial attractiveness and viability of socially and environmentally responsible funds. The Dow Jones Sustainability Index (DJSI) was born (www.sustainability-indexes.com).

More than 200 funds have joined the "socially responsible" forum, so you have plenty to choose from today. To research your choices, you might begin at the Social Investment Forum: www.socialinvest.org.

Stock Investments

If you're feeling more risky, you may wish to invest directly in stock of companies pursuing environmental values.

A *New York Times* article recently touted one of the fastest-growing companies in China. As reported by Thomas Friedman, SunTech Power has made its founder, Shi Zhengrong, the seventh richest man in China. The firm makes photovoltaic solar panels and has grown aggressively because Shi Zhengrong knows that China has no choice but to move from fossil fuels to clean energy—the air and water in China are already badly polluted. Shi Zhengrong wants to make solar power available and affordable to mainstream buyers, not just the well-heeled. Since its founding in 1992,

SunTech Power (STP) has moved up to the fourth largest solar cell manufacturing firm in the world, following Sharp (SHCAF.PK), Kyocera Kyocera Corp (KYO), and BP (BP).

Here are just a handful of the many options available for you to consider:

Fuel Cell Energy, which manufactures fuel cell power plants for electricity generation (FCEL); Ballard Power Systems, which builds fuel cells (BLDP); PowerShares WilderHill Clean Energy Portfolio, an index fund of clean, renewable energy companies (PBW); Earth Biofuels, a biodiesel fuel producer (EBOF.OB); Sustainable Energy Technologies, which makes power inverters for wind, solar, and fuel cell power sources (STG.V); Gaiam, a natural lifestyle media company (GAIA); Whole Foods Market, natural foods retailer (WFMI); Appliance Recycling Centers of America, which prevents usable appliances from hitting the landfills through recycling and reselling (ARCI); Interface Flooring, a leader in the sustainable carpet industry (IFSIA); Energy Developments, which generates power from renewable resources such as methane from landfills (ENE.AX); Ocean Power Technologies, generating energy from ocean waves (OPT.L); SunPower, which develops solar power systems (SPWR); and Vestas Wind Systems, developer of wind power systems (VWS.CO).

You can find many more green stocks listed at www.sustainablebusiness.com/stocks/, or consider investing in their newsletter, *The Progressive Investor*, for stock updates. Do your own research or consult with a financial adviser to determine which is the best place for your investment.

Socially Responsible Financial Institutions

Some banks focus on socially responsible investing or consider nonprofit credit unions—they'll invest in your community or other like-minded community efforts.

Helping to protect natural resources, such as forests, and to promote ecotourism, responsible farming, and recycling are all advances in the fight against global warming.

If you're interested in these or in helping communities develop by underwriting housing projects; or helping to finance home loans, small business activities, or infrastructure projects like renewable power development or water purification systems, Co-Op America provides a comprehensive information resource: Community Investing Center, www.communityinvest.org.

Co-Op America also provides a guide for responsible investing, the *Financial Planning Handbook*, available free with membership or for $11.95 online at www.coopamerica.org/pubs/fph/.

Personal Investments

Instead of sending your money away from home to help others, consider investing in environmentally wise improvements for your own home and business for immediate savings on energy expense or water expense as well as concrete reduction in greenhouse gases or other pollutants.

Let's take a look at what kinds of innovations you might consider and how much you can save.

Buy a Wind Turbine

You can build your own or buy a wind turbine to generate your own energy if you have adequate space (half an acre is recommended) and sufficient wind (8 mph average minimum). There are many resources for building or buying a turbine. Check The American Wind Energy Association (AWEA): www.awea.org/faq/wwt_smallwind.html.

AWEA says that a typical residential installation will cost around $40,000 and last up to 20 years, reducing energy bills by 50 to 90 percent. At that rate, it will take 5 to 15 years to pay for itself in utility cost savings, after which the electricity produced is free and the equipment is virtually maintenance free.

The Skystream 3.7 windpower turbine is available for home and small businesses. At a cost of $10,000 and guaranteed for 5 years, the Skystream generates 400 kilowatt hours a month with winds of 12 mph, which could save 20 to 90 percent on utility bills, according to the company.

So you should save money with a wind turbine, and even more important, since wind power is pollution free, you'll be saving more than 6,000 pounds of greenhouse gases each year. You'll also be creating your own offset program. For more information, visit www.skystreamenergy.com.

Go Solar

While solar water heaters and electricity-producing photovoltaic systems can be very expensive compared to traditional water heaters and electric utility bills, the costs of these systems continues to come down, thanks to both new technologies and increasing demand. And even though the costs are high at the time of installation, the systems will pay for themselves after years of low or no utility bills, and then they'll produce free energy or heat for the duration of their lifetimes.

You can find a calculator to help estimate your costs for going solar (full system, water heater, or pool heater) at www.findsolar.com. It will factor in rebates and incentives available to you based on your city and state, and it will estimate your long-term cost savings. For my small house, the estimated cost was $40,000, and it would pay for itself in about 25 years, saving 187 tons of CO_2 in the meantime.

When I used the calculator for a solar water heater, I learned that rebates and incentives actually cut the cost in half (from $3,500 to $1,700), and it estimated that I would break even in less than a year. After that, it's money saved each month.

Buy a Hybrid Car

Swapping your compact car for a second generation (2006 or newer) Honda Civic Hybrid will double your mileage and cut your gas cost, oil usage, and emissions in half. The car cost $21,000 new, comparable to other traditional compact vehicles. At press time a federal tax credit is available for fuel-efficient vehicles such as the Honda Civic Hybrid credit of $2,100, further reducing the cost of your investment. These tax credits are limited though, and are set to expire after a certain number of vehicles have been sold, so when you're making a purchase, check with your car dealer or accountant to confirm that a credit is available. Also inquire about state incentives and discounts.

Put Your Money Where It Will Make a Difference

Whether you choose to create a retirement fund based on renewable energy or invest in a portfolio of green stocks in a developing community or in green improvements for your own home or business, we hope your investment will be money well spent. These are just a few ways that you can put your money where it will make a difference in helping to move our world further away from global warming and toward a healthier future.

 Hazard _____

Again, please do your own thorough research, and consult with a financial adviser when making your own investments.

The Least You Need to Know

◆ The surest way to increase the development and deployment of renewable energies, high efficiency technology, and sustainable businesses is to invest in them.

◆ You can invest in a mutual fund, individual stocks, or buy the products that you wish to support.

◆ Many resources are available to help you make decisions about investments in this fast-growing sector.

◆ Please don't take my word for it—invest time in your own research before investing money in anything!

Appendix A

Green Glossary

anaerobic   Oxygen-free.

bioethics   The study of ethical issues raised by developments in the life science technologies. Encourage children to explore what they think about humane treatment of the animals that sustain us and why it is important for them to think about it.

biofuels or biomass fuels   Fuels derived from sustainable biodegradable resources including wood, plant material, and grains, such as soy, which is converted to oil and used as biodiesel oil.

bisphenol A   A chemical commonly used as a preservative in the lining of food cans that has been linked to chromosomal damage and cancers in scientific testing.

brominated fire retardants   Used in many materials including sleepwear and mattresses. But research has found that some flame retardants are carcinogenic and others are endocrine disrupters. These chemicals migrate from the clothing and furniture they're applied to and leach into water from landfills and the air through incineration, spreading their contamination into the food chain.

carbon footprint   An estimate of how much carbon is produced in support of your life and activities, determinable using online calculators (www. climatecrisis.net/takeaction/carboncalculator/) that measure your travel time and energy usage to provide an idea of your carbon dioxide output.

The resulting figure is used to buy carbon offsets, or to engage in other activities, such as planting trees, to balance the CO_2 production with CO_2 elimination to arrive at a carbon neutral status.

carbon neutral   A term that implies that a person or company has theoretically reduced carbon emissions to zero by offset CO_2 production using energy credits and carbon offsets. This is only theoretical, however, and is an inferior alternative to reducing CO_2 output directly.

carbon offsets   Credits earned for activities that help to balance out CO_2 usage such as planting trees.

carbon sequestration   An as-yet unproven theory that carbon dioxide emissions can be captured and buried underground instead of being released into the atmosphere. Skeptics believe that the idea is a solution proposed by industry to try to keep coal-fired power plants in operation rather than encourage the development of clean, renewable energies.

CDC   The Centers for Disease Control, a national health research and information resource agency.

cellulosic   Refers to the source material, specifically to plant matter, such as wood chips, stalks, grasses, and leaves, rather than grains that are also food.

compost   A mixture of organic matter (leaves, grass, vegetable and fruit scraps) that soaks into a nutrient-rich soil. By building a compost pile, you can recycle yard waste into rich soil for your garden, flower beds, and yard. Find instructions at www.organicgardening.com.

CSA program   Community Supported Agriculture, a program that connects local customers directly with local farmers to provide fresh local produce each week. Farmers organize together and offer whatever items they have in abundance; the resulting bounty is divided into shares for each CSA customer, who pays a flat rate each week with the understanding that they'll get a variety of items each week, determined by the farmers.

daylighting   The use of windows and skylights to bring sunlight indoors.

ecohomes   A trendy catch term applied to sustainable design in home building.

ecolodge   An authentic lodging set in its natural environment that allows visitors to experience the local setting and community as it really is, rather than in an artificial "comfort-based" environment. Ecolodges offer the opportunity to meet members of the local community, sample their cuisine, and explore their territory and their culture.

ecoresort   A blend of the environmental experience available at an ecolodge but combined with the comforts of luxury travel, including high-style cuisine, wifi, and high-end accommodations.

EIDS   Emerging Infectious Diseases, often caused by changing weather patterns such as by global warming, which creates hospitable environments for infestations and sometimes killing off natural predators. Influenza viruses, mosquito-borne illnesses spreading around the world, malaria, and other epidemics are examples of these.

embodied energy   Refers to the energy that goes into manufacture and transportation of a commodity during its productive life.

endocrine disrupting compounds   Endocrine or hormone disrupting chemicals which interfere with the development and processes of bodily hormonal systems. These EDCs are prevalent in industrial pollution and plastics, including many persistent organic pollutants, PCBs, and phthalates.

endocrinologist   A doctor who studies hormones in the human body.

fuel cell   Technology is hydrogen-based alternative fuel that is promising in development but is not yet commercially available.

genetically modified   Refers to the changing of the genetic material of a living organism. You may also read "genetically engineered." Typical examples of GM products include seeds changed in order to resist harm from a pesticide (so surrounding weeds are killed, but the plant survives).

geothermal   Simply means heat from the ground.

global warming   A rapid increase in the temperature of the earth's surface, water, and atmosphere, which is causing changes in most natural systems, such as seasons and life cycles of plants and animals, with far-reaching effects and impact.

gray water   Water that has been used and can be reused for other purposes rather than being immediately disposed of. For example, laundry rinse water can be used again for outdoor cleaning, car washing, or watering the lawn.

green hotel   A green hotel is not as environmentally sensitive as an ecoresort or ecolodge, but its owners have addressed some environmental concerns—they may use ecofriendly cleaning products, launder on intermittent days, and recycle whenever possible.

green roof   An interesting architectural development which involved covering building tops with soil and planting sod and gardens. Green roofs provide a pleasant place to spend time, particularly in urban environments; they process CO_2 in the atmosphere and produce oxygen, provide food through gardens, and help insulate buildings so they don't use as much energy to heat or cool. Chicago is leading the green roof movement in the United States, with a city initiative from the Mayor's office to support their development.

green tags   Another name for renewable energy credits.

greenhouse effect   The greenhouse gases carbon dioxide, methane, and others form a sort of ceiling over the earth, holding warmth in our atmosphere and reflecting the heat back on the surface of the earth, increasing the heating of the planet—global warming.

grid   The power supply network that connects homes and buildings to a municipal power source.

hemp and kenaf   Both are fast-growing and easily cultivated fibrous plants which are excellent resources for paper and fabric making.

hormone disruptor   Many chemicals are now being recognized as hormone disruptors as they mimic estrogen in the body and cause related hormonal changes. Amphibians in the wild have been identified as changing from male to female, and several studies indicate that male births are declining, probably as a result of this influx of estrogen and hormone-disrupting chemicals into our environment.

hybrid cars   Cars specially made to run on both gasoline and electricity, getting more miles to the gallon and conserving fuel.

IPM   Integrated Pest Management. This method of pest control includes planting to suit the environment, encouraging beneficial insects (such as praying mantises), watering correctly, using organic fertilizer correctly, and using physical means to control pests, whether it means plucking beetles from leaves or covering delicate plantings with row cover (lightweight fabric) to protect them from insects.

LED lights   Light emitting diodes have emerged in recent years as the next best bulb since compact fluorescents. The bulbs have a low glow intensified and directed by a tiny mirror—so light goes only where it's needed instead of flooding the area and adding to light pollution. Although the cost is much higher than an incandescent bulb (estimated at $34.95 vs. .67 by manufacturer C.Crane), they use much less electricity and last for many years. C.Crane says one LED light will outlast 60,000 incandescent bulbs and will save $353.25 per bulb (www.ccrane.com)!

LEED   The U.S. Green Building Council's Leadership in Energy and Environmental Design (LEED) program applies points for each ecosensitive feature, based on how much energy a building consumes, what impact it makes on the local environment, how well it conserves natural resources, and whether it provides educational information to buyers and residents.

light rail   Term that refers to electric transit cars that are similar to trolleys.

light rapid transit   Term that refers to buses with minimal stops along dedicated traffic lanes to provide faster, more efficient service to passengers.

manure lagoon   A pit where waste product from livestock farms is deposited for slow composting or storage to prevent release into local waterways.

mercury   A toxic heavy metal commonly found in waterways around the world and in many fish and shellfish. A neurotoxin, mercury can damage brain and other cells in fetuses and young children and may cause birth defects; warnings are issued advising children, pregnant women, and women of childbearing age to limit their consumption of fish and to consult local and federal guidelines to learn which fish are the safest to eat.

nanotechnology   The study of microscopic subatomic particles called nanoparticles, their uses and safety.

organic   Food, fabric, or other plant-based commodity which is grown and produced without the use of synthetic chemicals or processes.

passive solar   Refers to capitalizing on the warmth of the sun's rays without further devices. Allowing sunlight to stream through windows, falling on materials such as concrete, which holds the sun's warmth for long periods of time, is a good way to reduce the need for additional heat sources, cutting expense and energy use.

persistent organic pollutant (POP)   Chemicals which don't dissipate in the environment or in the body and may accumulate, causing increased levels of exposure over time. Some POPS also are carried genetically from one generation to the next and may cause genetic damage and disease.

petrochemical   Petroleum-based synthetic chemical.

photovoltaic cells (PVs)   Solar energy collectors that can be placed on rooftops and in yards. New technology even includes photovoltaic shingles and window film that makes solar heat easier and more cost effective for homeowners.

phthalates   Chemicals used in many plastics to soften them. They have become the most abundant man-made substance in the environment and turn up in the blood and urine of most children and adults. Some phthalates are known carcinogens.

polychlorinated biphenyls (PCBs)   Synthetic chemical compounds found in plastics. They have not been made in the U.S. since 1977; however, many materials containing PCBs are still in use, such as electronic equipment and some plastics. PCBs remain in the environment for an extended time, and have been linked to health problems including liver cancer and developmental difficulties in children.

precautionary principle   A standard adopted in Europe and proposed for international use whereby manufacturers will not use a substance of questionable health or environmental effects until its safety has been proven.

radiant foil barrier   A thin metallic material much like aluminum foil that can be applied under the roof to block up to 90 percent of radiant heat from entering or leaving the interior and make a significant difference in energy usage.

rBGH   Recombinant Bovine Growth Hormone, a synthetic chemical injected into dairy cows to increase milk production. The additive has been banned in Canada and Europe but is approved for use by the U.S. FDA. Organic milk does not contain rBGH.

renewable   A resource that can be replenished as it is used.

renewable energy credits (RECs)   Credits earned for generating green power. One REC usually is equivalent to one megawatt of renewable energy. RECs can be bought, sold, and traded on the market, or consumers can purchase RECs from their utility company to promote the use of renewable energy.

renewables   A term that refers to renewable energy resources such as solar, wind, geothermal, hydro, and biofuel power.

saltwater intrusion   Refers to the natural process whereby saltwater will encroach on dried-up fresh water reservoirs, replacing the empty wells, aquifers, creeks, etc. that once flowed with fresh water with saltwater.

sink   Something that absorbs greenhouse gases naturally, helping to maintain a healthy atmospheric balance on earth. Forests serve as a natural sink for CO_2 because trees process the CO_2 into oxygen through photosynthesis; however, our diminishing forests mean less natural neutralization of atmospheric CO_2.

solar tubes   Cylinders usually about 8 to 12 inches in diameter that bring sunlight into interior rooms. The tube is capped with a dome on the roof, which allows light into the chamber, which is lined with reflective paint or material to enhance the light as it comes down into the room. The tubes are simple to install, even in existing homes, and are relatively free of leaks and problems often experienced with traditional skylights.

superbug   A bacteria that has developed resistance to antibiotic treatment, usually due to overexposure to the antibiotic because of their use in livestock production and other food applications.

Superfund   The nickname for a federal program that was initiated to provide funds to clean up environmentally damaged sites. However, the program has become inactive in recent years since companies are no longer required to fund clean-ups of problems they create. Without funds, the sites rely on voluntary compliance with environmental regulations, and often end up in endless legal battles instead of clean-up projects.

sustainability   The ability to meet our needs without compromising the ability of future generations to meet theirs.

tundra   The cold, normally frozen soil surrounding the ice caps.

USDA   United States Department of Agriculture.

U.S. EPA   United States Environmental Protection Agency.

U.S. FDA   United States Food and Drug Administration.

volatile organic compounds (VOCs)   Toxic substances in gases emitted from many caustic chemicals, paints, adhesives, formaldehyde, and common building materials. If you must use VOC-containing products, keep the area well-ventilated.

B

Resource Guide for Going Green

In this resource guide I've collected references to websites and organizations mentioned throughout the book in case you want to learn more about a particular topic. For easy reference I've organized them according to the sections in which they appeared.

Part 1: Our Earth: The Big Picture

Public Media Discussing Peak Oil and Climate Issues
640 Broadway
Vancouver, BC V5z 1G4
globalpublicmedia.com/peakoil

U.S. Department of Energy
www.eia.doe.gov

The Rocky Mountain Institute
1739 Snowmass Rd.
Snowmass, CO 81654
www.rmi.org

U.S. PIRG Federation
44 Winter St., 4th Floor
Boston, MA 02108
www.uspirg.org

Intergovernmental Panel on Climate Change
www.ipcc.ch

Union of Concerned Scientists
2 Brattle Square
Cambridge, MA 02238
www.ucsusa.org

Projects of the Union of Concerned Scientists
www.climatechoices.org
www.NortheastClimateImpacts.org

Re-energize America
Natural Resources Defense Council
www.reenergizeamerica.org

Zero Waste America
217 S Jessup St.
Philadelphia, PA 19107
www.zerowasteamerica.org/Landfills.htm

Bill Moyer's TV special: *Is God Green?* carbon calculator, and more
www.pbs.org/moyers/moyersonamerica/green/index.html

Evangelical Climate Initiative
www.christiansandclimate.org

The Center for Media & Democracy
www.sourcewatch.org

Green Cross International
160a route de Florissant
1231 Conches
Geneva, Switzerland
www.greencrossinternational.net

Science and Environmental Health Network—Pushing the Precautionary Principle
PMB 282
217 Welch Ave. #101
Ames, IA 50014
www.sehn.org/precaution.html

Geothermal Resources Council
PO Box 1350
Davis, CA 95617
www.geothermal.org/index.html

Pellet Stoves
www.hometips.com

The Hadley Report on Climate Change
Met Office
Fitzroy Rd.
Exeter, Devon EX1 3PB UK
www.metoffice.com/research/hadleycentre/pubs/brochures/2005/climate_greenhouse.pdf

U.S. Environmental Protection Agency
www.epa.gov/greenpower/locator/index.htm

Energy Start, U.S. EPA
1-800-STAR-YES
www.energystar.gov/

Southern Energy Network, a project of the Southern Alliance for Clean Energy
2199 L St. NW
Washington, D.C. 20037
202-778-6133
www.climateaction.net/

University Leaders for a Sustainable Future
www.ulsf.org

Campus Climate Challenge
616 P St. NW
Washington, D.C. 20036
www.climatechallenge.org

Youth Energy/Climate Blog
www.itsgettinghotinhere.org

American Wind
1-877-810-8670
www.renewablechoice.com/index.php?option=com_content&task=view&id=81

The Center for Resource Solutions
PO Box 29512
San Francisco, CA 94129
415-561-2100
www.green-e.org

Sustainable Water Resources Roundtable
Reston, VA 20192
703-860-1038
www.water.usgs.gov/wicp/acwi/swrr

WorldWatch Institute
1776 Massachusetts Ave. NW
Washington, D.C. 20036
202-452-1999
www.worldwatch.org

National Renewable Energy Laboratory
www.nrel.gov

Part 2: Going Green at Home

U.S. Green Building Council
Leadership in Energy and Environmental Design (LEED)
1800 Massachusetts Ave. NW #300
Washington, D.C. 20036
202-828-7422
www.usgbc.org

Planetary Solutions
PO Box 1049
Boulder, CO 80306
303-441-6228
www.planetearth.com

Solar Village in Longmont (a green-built community)
2795 Pearl St. #200
Longmont, CO
303-247-9400
www.solarvillagelife.com

William Hutchins, architect and designer of ecofriendly homes
www.heliconworks.com.

BP Solar
1-866-BP-Solar

Florida Solar Energy Center
321-638-1000

EPA on solar shingles and how photovoltaics work
www.nrel.gov/learning/re_photovoltaics.html

Fannie Mae
Energy Efficient Mortgage
www.hud.gov/offices/hsg/sfh/eem/eemhome.cfm

American Solar Energy Society
2400 Central Ave. #A
Boulder, CO 80301
303-443-3130
www.ases.org

Online Mall of Solar Products
www.solardirect.com

Clivus Multrum: composting toilets
15 Union St.
Lawrence, MA 01840
1-800-4-CLIVUS
www.clivusmultrum.com

U.S. Dept. of Energy
Energy Efficiency and Renewable Energy Consumer's Guide
www.eere.energy.gov/consumer/

Energy Star
www.energystar.gov/index.cfm?c=products.pr_tax_credits#6

U.S. Department of Energy and U.S. Environmental Protection Agency
Phone: 1-888 STAR-YES, 1-888-782-7937
www.energystar.gov

Energy Star lightbulbs
Top Bulb Inc.
5204 Indianapolis Blvd.
C Chicago, IN 46312
1-866-867-2852
www.Topbulb.com

U.S. Dept. of Energy
Radiant Barrier Fact Sheet on the World Wide Web at URL
www.ornl.gov/roofs+walls/radiant/rb_02.html

Real Goods
GAIAM, INC.
360 Interlochen Blvd.
Broomfield, CO 80021
www.realgoods.com

Florida Solar Energy Center (FSEC)
University of Central Florida
www.fsec.ucf.edu

American Wind Energy Association
1101 14th St. NW, 12th Floor
Washington, D.C. 20005
202-383-2500
www.awea.org

Ron Jones
Green Builder
PO Box 196
Montpelier, VT 05601
1-877-847-3368
www.thegreenbuilder.com
www.greenbuildermag.com
www.greenbuilder.com/sourcebook/PassiveSol.html#Define

Jersey Devil Design Build Team
www.jerseydevildesignbuild.com/index.htm

Database of State Incentives for Renewables and Efficiency
www.dsireusa.org

BP Solar
www.bpSolar.com

A blog moderated by real scientists publishing peer-reviewed work in this field
www.realclimate.org

National Association of Home Builders
1201 15th Street, NW
Washington, D.C. 20005
1-800-368-5242
202-266-8254
WWW.NAHB.org
A PDF graphic of green home features is available on NAHB's website: www.nahb.
org/greeninnovation.

Buy or Sell a Green Home
PO Box 30085
Santa Barbara, CA 98130
805-898-0079
www.greenhomesforsale.com

Reusable Bags
916 W Illinois St. #6E
Chicago, IL 60610
773-912-1562
www.reusablebags.com

Zero Waste Alliance
121 SW Salmon St. #210
Portland, OR 97204
503-279-9382
www.zerowaste.org

Free Cycle Network
PO Box 294
Tucson, AZ 85702
www.freecycle.org

Freeware Windows Disk Cleaning Software
www.shareware.com

Active Kill Disk Hard Drive Eraser
www.killdisk.com/eraser.htm

Macintosh Disk Cleaning Software
ShredIt
PO Box 96010
Richmond, BC V7A 5J4 Canada
www.mireth.com/pub/sxme.html

SuperScrubber
Jiiva Inc.
PO Box 130
Manhattan Beach, CA 90267
www.superscrubber.com

Green Everything for Your Home
1-877-82-6400
www.greenhome.com

Part 3: Green Living on the Road

Reduce fuel usage and emissions
www.fueleconomytips.com

MPG Research—discussions on saving fuel and dramatically reducing emissions
www.mpgresearch.com

National Bio Diesel Board
3337a Emerald Lane
Jefferson City, MO 65110
1-800-841-5844
www.biodiesel.org

Willie Nelson's Biodiesel
3001 Knox St.
Dallas, TX 75205
www.wnbiodiesel.com

Flexcar
www.flexcar.com
1-877-FLEXCAR

Zipcar
www.zipcar.com
1-866-4ZIPCAR

Chicago Climate Exchange
190 S LaSalle St.
Chicago, IL 60603
www.chicagoclimatex.com

Terrapass
405 El Camino Real #234
Menlo Park, CA 94025
1-877-879-8026
www.terrapass.com

*Native*Energy
823 Ferry Rd.
Charlotte, VT 05445
www.nativeenergy.com

Climate Trust
65 SW Yamhill St. #400
Portland, OR 97204
www.climatetrust.com

CarbonCounter.org
www.carbonneutral.com/calculators/flightcalculatorshop.asp

Nature Airlines
1-800-235-9292
www.natureair.com

Part 4: Green Living in Your Daily Life

A climate-friendly diet
www.eatkind.net/inconvenient.htm

EarthSave Canada
The Aquarian
16 Victoria Row
Winnepeg, Manitoba R2M 1Y2 Canada
www.aquarianonline.com/Eco

"A New Global Warming Strategy: How Environmentalists are Overlooking Vegetarianism as the Most Effective Tool Against Climate Change in Our Lifetimes," by Noam Mohr
Earth Save
PO Box 96
New York, NY 10108
1-800-362-3648
earthsave.org/globalwarming.htm

"Green Guide's Fish Picks" list
www.ewg.org/issues/mercury/20031209/calculator.php
www.ewg.org/reports/brainfood/sidebar.html

www.cfsan.fda.gov
1-800-SAFEFOOD

Organic Trade Association
PO Box 547
Greenfield, MA 04302
www.ota.com

Organic Consumers Association
www.organicconsumers.org

Fair Trade Action
1612 "K" St. NW #600
Washington, D.C. 20006
1-800-584-7336
www.fairtradeaction.org

Equal Exchange
500 United Dr.
W Bridgeport, MA 02379
774-776-7400
www.equalexchange.com

Environmental Working Group (studies of chemicals in the body)
Body Burden
1436 "U" St. NW #100
Washington, D.C. 20009
202-667-6932
www.ewg.org/reports/bodyburden/
www.safecosmetics.org
www.ewg.org/reports/skindeep2

Center for Health, Environment, and Justice
703-237-2249
www.chej.org

Environmental Defense
www.environmentaldefense.org

Children's Health Environmental Coalition
www.checnet.org

Natural Resources Defense Council
40 W 20 St.
New York, NY 10011
www.nrdc.org

Children's Health Environmental Coalition
12300 Wilshire Blvd. #410
Los Angeles, CA 90025
310-820-2030
www.checnet.org

Natural Lawn Care
PO Box 531
Parksville, BC V9p 2G6 Canada
www.eartheasy.com/grow_lawn_care.htm

Safer Pest Control Project
25 E. Washington, Suite 1515
Chicago, IL 60602-1849
312-641-5575
info@spcpweb.org

Environmental Defense
317 Adelaide St. W #710
Toronto, Ontario, MSV 1P9 Canada
www.environmentaldefence.ca/toxicnation/resources/glossary.htm#1

National Institutes of Health Household Products Database
U.S. Library of Medicine
Specialized Information Services
8600 Rockville Pike
Bethesda, MD 20894
hpd.nlm.nih.gov/index.htm

Make Your Own Non-Toxic Cleaning Kit
CARE2.com, Inc.
275 Shoreline Dr. #150
Redwood City, CA 94065
www.care2.com/channels/solutions/home/344

American Lung Association
61 Broadway, 6th Floor
New York, NY 10006
1-800-LUNGUSA
www.lungusa.org/asthma/asthma_children_index.html

The Web Goddess
8603 Haapala Rd.
Babbitt, MN 55706
1-800-481-1390
healthycleaning.com/whycleanhealthy.html

Physicians For Social Responsibility
1875 Connecticut Ave. NW, Suite 1012
Washington, D.C. 20009
202-667-0426
www.psr.org/site/PageServer?pagename=Toxics_main

Greenpeace International
702 "H" St. NW, Suite 300
Washington, D.C. 20001
1-800-326-0959
www.greenpeace.org/international/news/eu-reach-chemical-law-vote131206

HealthyLiving Foundation
11406 172 PL. N
Jupiter, FL 33478
561-743-5840
www.healthylivingfoundation.org

Edible Nature
4653 Carmel Mountain Rd., Suite 308 #201
San Diego, CA 92130
703-637-9377
www.ediblenature.com/index.asp

U.S. Environmental Protection Agency
Ariel Rios Building
1200 Pennsylvania Ave. NW
Washington, D.C. 20460
www.epa.gov/iaq/voc.html

CARE2: information on green cleaning
www.care2.com/channels/solutions/home/118

Lavera Skin Care North America
12015 115 Ave. NE #E110
Kirland, WA 98034
1-877-528-3727
www.Lavera.com

Dr. Hauschka Skin Care
59 North St.
Hatfield, MA 01088
1-800-247-9907
www.drhauschka.com/about/our-ingredients

Ecco Bella Botanicals
50 Church St. #108
Montclair, NJ 07042
www.eccobella.com

Dr. Bronner's Magic Soaps
PO Box 28
Escondido, CA 92033
1-877-786-3649
www.drbronner.com/index.html

The Body Shop International
1-800 BODYSHOP
www.thebodyshop.com/bodyshop/index.jsp

Peacekeeper Cosmetics
50 Lexington Ave. #22G
New York, NY 10010
1-866-732-2336
www.iamapeacekeeper.com

Burt's Bees
PO Box 13489
Durham, NC 27209
1-866-422-8787
www.burtsbees.com

Aubrey Organics
449 N Manhattan Ave.
Tampa, FL 33614
1-800-287-7394
www.aubrey-organics.com

BDIH, an association in Germany that certifies natural and organic cosmetics, pharmaceuticals and food products:
www.kontrollierte-naturkosmetik.de/gesamt_en.htm

Environmental Working Group
www.ewg.org/reports/skindeep2/index.php

Check for your nanoparticles in favorite products
www.ewg.org/issues/cosmetics/20061010/table2.php

The Environmental Health Association of Nova Scotia
PO Box 31323
Halifax, Nova Scotia, B3K 5Y5 Canada
www.lesstoxicguide.ca/index.asp?fetch=personal

Friends of the Earth
177 Massachusetts Ave. NW #600
Washington, D.C. 20036
1-877-843-8687
www.foe.org/camps/comm/nanotech/nanocosmetics.pdf

Campaign for Safe Cosmetics
info@safecosmetics.org
www.safecosmetics.org

Ecomall.com
www.ecomall.com/greenshopping/nthouseholdproducts.htm

The Carpet America Recovery Effort (CARE)
www.carpetrecovery.org.

Ray Anderson's textile and carpet company, Interface, Inc.
www.interfacesustainability.com

Milliken & Company
PO Box 2956
LaGrange, GA 30341
1-800-528-8453
www.millikencarpet.com/sustainability

HealthyLiving Interiors
561-743-1412
www.healthylivinginteriors.com

Expanko Inc. (cork flooring manufacturer)
1129 W Lincoln Hwy.
Coatesville, PA 19320
1-800-345-602
www.Expanko.com

TriCycle Inc.
1-800-808-4809
www.tricycleinc.com

EcoDecor
561-845-5433
www.ecodecor.com

Part 5: Going Green at Work

The U.S. Department of Energy High Performance Buildings
www.eere.energy.gov/buildings/highperformance

American Institute of Architects' Top Ten Green Projects
1735 New York Ave. NW
Washington, D.C. 20006-5292
1-800-242-3837
www.aiatopten.org

The Green Building Initiative
2104 SE Morrison
Portland, OR 97214
1-877-424-4241
www.thegbi.org/gbi

U.S. Environmental Protection Agency
Ariel Rios Building
1200 Pennsylvania Ave. NW
Washington, D.C. 20460
202-272-0167
www.epa.gov

EPA WasteWise
www.epa.gov/wastewise

EPA Green Power Partnership
www.epa.gov/greenpower

The Bay Area Green Business Program
www.greenbiz.ca.gov

California's Waste Reduction Awards Program
PO Box 4025
Sacramento, CA 95812-4025
916-341-6604
www.ciwmb.ca.gov/WRAP

Sustainable Oregon
Natural Capital Center
721 NW Ninth Ave., Suite 200
Portland, OR 97209
503-467-0769
www.sustainableoregon.net

The Sustainable Business Institute
18598 Aspesi Ave.
Saratoga, CA 95070
408-370-5783
www.sustainablebusiness.org

Greenbiz Leaders
www.greenbizleaders.com

The Green Restaurant Association
89 South St., Suite LL02
Boston, MA 02111
858-452-7378
www.dinegreen.com

Recycline
681 Main St.
Waltham, MA 02451
1-888-354-7296
www.recycline.com

Hanger Network
1-877-646-2422 or 212-500-5960
www.hangernetwork.com

New Belgium Brewing Company
500 Linden
Fort Collins, CO 80524
1-888-622-4044
www.newbelgium.com

Aurora Glass
St. Vincent de Paul Society
2345 W. Broadway
Eugene, OR 97402
541-681-3260 or 1-888-291-9311
www.auroraglass.org

Affordable Internet Services Online
25655 Louisa Lane
Romoland, CA 92585
1-800-781-9004
www.aiso.net

Whole Foods Market
550 Bowie St.
Austin, TX 78703-4677
512-477-4455
www.wholefoods.com

ThinkHost
971-234-9568
www.thinkhost.com

Hewlett-Packard
3000 Hanover St.
Palo Alto, CA 94304
650-857-1501
www.hewlettpackard.com

Hotlips Pizza
Portland, OR
503-224-2069
www.hotlipspizza.com

Stonyfield Farm
Ten Burton Drive
Londonderry, NH 03053
1-800-776-2697
www.stonyfield.com

Elixir
16th and Guerro
San Francisco, CA
415-552-1633
www.elixirsf.com

Starbucks Coffee Company
www.starbucks.com

Inkworks Press
2827 Seventh St.
Berkeley, CA 94710
510-845-7111
www.inkworkspress.com

Nomad Café
6500 Shattuck Ave.
Oakland, CA 94609
510-595-5344
www.nomadcafe.net

Nike
1-800-806-6453
www.nike.com

Forever Resorts
7501 E McCormick Parkway
Scottsdale, AZ 85258
480-998-7199
www.foreverresorts.com

The Grand Targhee Resort
3300 E. Ski Hill Road
Alta, WY 83414
307-353-2300 and 1-800-827-4433
www.grandtarghee.com

Hyperion Solutions Corporation
5450 Great America Parkway
Santa Clara, CA 95054
1-800-286-8000
www.hyperion.com

Eco-Wise
110 West Elizabeth
Austin, TX 78704
512-326-4474
www.eco-wise.com

Natural Built Home
4020 Minnehaha Ave.
Minneapolis, MN 55406
612-605-7999
www.naturalbuilthome.com

Pedro's Planet
St. Louis, MO 63146 and Denver, CO 80207
1-800-853-9218
www.pedrosplanet.com

Baltix Sustainable Furniture
2160 Daniels St.
Long Lake, MN 55356
763-210-0155
www.baltix.com

The Environmentally Preferable Purchasing Guide
Solid Waste Management Coordinating Board
411 Selby Ave.
St. Paul, MN 55102
651-222-7227
www.greenguardian.com/EPPG/

EPA Green Power Partnership
www.epa.gov/greenpower

Green Seal
1001 Connecticut Ave. NW #827
Washington D.C. 20036
202-872-6400
www.greenseal.org

Co-op America Business Network
1612 "K" St. NW #600
Washington, D.C. 20006
1-800-584-7336
www.coopamerica.org/greenbusiness/network.cfm

American Evergreen Foundation
1-888-872-4733
www.usagreen.org

The Northwest Green Directory
www.nwgreedirectory.com

The Green Building Initiative's Green Globes
2104 SE Morrison
Portland, OR 97214
1-877-424-4241
www.thegbi.org/greenglobes

National Green Pages (directory of green businesses from Co-Op America)
1612 K St. NW, Suite 600
Washington, D.C. 20006
1-800-584-7336
www.greenpages.org

New Leaf Paper Company
www.newleafpaper.com

GreenLine Paper Company
631 S Pine St.
York, PA 17403
1-800-641-1117
www.greenlinepaper.com

Sustainable Group
844 NW 49th St.
Seattle, WA 98109
206-706-0966
www.sustainablegroup.net

GreenDisk
1-800-305-3475
www.greendisk.com

Green Seal of Approval
1001 Connecticut Ave. NW #827
Washington, D.C. 20036
202-872-6400
www.greenseal.org,

Join the "Do Not Mail" list by writing to:
Mail Preference Service
Direct Marketing Association
PO Box 643
Carmel, NY 10512
dmaconsumers.org/cgi/offmailinglist

Part 6: Living in the Emerald City

Earth Policy Institute
www.earth-policy.org

Economic Policy Institute
Communications Department
Phone: 202-775-8810
After hours: 202-533-2587 or 301-537-0172
Email: news@epi.org
Web: www.epi.org/newsroom
www.sharedprosperity.org/overview.html

Lifestyles of Health and Sustainability or LOHAS
www.lohas.com
www.SustainableBusiness.com/jobs
www.ecobusinesslinks.com/environmental_jobs.htm
www.greenjobs.com/public/index.aspx
www.greenbiz.com/ship/

Chemical Glossary
http://www.seventhgeneration.com/household_hazards/glossary.php?tid=13

Earth Resource
1706 B Newport Blvd.
Costa Mesa, CA 92627
949-645-5163
www.earthresrouce.org

Ecology America Inc.
www.ecomall.com

Co-Op America
1612 "K" St. NW #600
Washington, D.C. 20006
1-800-584-7336
www.coopamerica.org

Green Century Capital Mgmt.
114 State St. #200
Boston, MA 02109
1-800-93-GREEN
www.greencentury.com

Social Investment Forum
www.socialinvest.org

Sierra Club Mutual Funds
http://sierraclubfunds.com

Dow Jones Sustainability Indexes
www.sustainability-index.com

Domini Social Investments: Socially Responsible Mutual Funds
1-800-762-6814
www.domini.com

Pax World Funds
1-800-767-1729
www.paxworld.com

Parnassus Investments
www.parnassus.com

For Further Reading (and Viewing)

Here are a few more informative and interesting resources about going green, including some books from my library, some movies, and some additional websites.

Books

Brown, Lester R. *Eco-Economy: Building an Economy for the Earth*. New York: Norton, 2001.

Colborn, Theo, Diane Dumanoski, and John Peterson Myers. *Our Stolen Future*. New York: Dutton/Penguin Books, 1996.
www.ourstolenfuture.org

Editors of *E/The Environmental Magazine*. *Green Living: The E Magazine Handbook for Living Lightly on the Earth*. New York: Plume, 2005.
28 Knight St.
Norwalk, CT 06851
203-854-5550
www.emagazine.com

Fagin, Dan, Marianne Lavelle, and the Center for Public Intergrity. *Toxic Deception: How the Chemical Industry Manipulates Science, Bends the Law, and Endangers Your Health*. Secaucus, NJ: Carol Publishing Group, 1996.

Gelbspan, Ross. *Boiling Point: How Politicians, Big Oil and Coal, Journalists and Activists are Fueling the Climate Crisis—And What We Can Do to Avert Disaster*. New York: Basic Books, 2004.
www.heatisonline.org

Gore, Al. *An Inconvenient Truth: The Planetary Emergency of Global Warming and What We Can Do About It*. Emmaus, PA: Rodale Books, 2006.

Hartmann, Thom. *The Last Hours of Ancient Sunlight*. New York: Three Rivers Press, 2004.

Hawkins, Paul, L. Hunter Lovins, and Amory Lovins. *Natural Capitalism*. New York: Little Brown, 1999.
www.natcap.org/sitepages/pid5.php

Lovins, Amory. *Oil End Game*. Snowmass, CO: Rocky Mountain Institute, 2004.
www.oilendgame.com

McDonough, William, and Michael Braungart. *Cradle to Cradle*. New York: North Point Press, 2002.

Newman, Nell, with Joseph D'Agnese. *The Newman's Own Organics Guide to a Good Life*. New York: Villard, 2003.

Steingraber, Sandra. *Living Downstream: A Scientist's Personal Investigation of Cancer and the Environment*. New York: Vintage Books/Random House, 1997.

Trask, Crissy. *It's Easy Being Green*. Salt Lake City, UT: Gibbs Smith, 2006.

Films

Kilowatt Ours
The film details the problems associated with coal, helps viewers become more efficient, and shows many renewable energy success stories.
Jeff Barrie, Producer/Director
Southern Energy Conservation Initiative
PO Box 60322
Nashville, TN 37206
615-438-5060
www.kilowattours.org

An Inconvenient Truth: The Movie
www.climatecrisis.net

Websites

Grist Magazine
www.Grist.org

Planet Ark News
www.planetark.org

E/The Environmental Magazine
www.emagazine.com

The Green Guide
www.greenguide.com

Audubon Magazine
www.audubonmagazine.org

Sierra Magazine
www.sierraclub.org

Natural Home Magazine
www.naturalhomemagazine.com

Green Light Magazine
www.greenlightmag.com

Metropolis Magazine
www.metropolismag.com

Ode Magazine
www.odemagazine.com

Ecofriendly information and resources
www.idealbite.com

Ecoproducts
www.alternativeconsumer.com

Rachel's News, helping you protect nature, human health, and democracy since 1986
www.rachel.org/bulletin/

John Robbins, author of several books detailing the food industry with guidelines for healthier diets
www.foodrevolution.org

Index

H

thermal chimneys, 56
thermostats, 58
ThinkHost, 200
ThinkMTV, 237
threats
  water quality, 19
    agricultural contamination, 20-21
    degrading water pipes, 23
    industrial contamination, 20
    nonpoint source pollution, 21
    pharmaceutical contamination, 21, 22
    wastewater, 22-23
tile floors, 177
tile roofs, 55
toilet leaks, 216
toilets, 70-71
totally chlorine free (TCF), 79
Toyota
  Camry Hybrid, 103
  Highlander Hybrid, 105
  Prius, 103
train carbon offsetting, 119
travel
  eco vacations, 119-122
  off-setting
    light rail, 117
    light rapid transit, 118
    planes, 115-117
    trains, 119
tree-free paper
  fibers, 216
  suppliers website, 79
trees, 64
Tricycle Inc., 176
The Twin Cities Green Guide, 213

U

University Leaders for a Sustainable Future, 237

unplugging small appliances, 61
U.S./Canada Shared Port of Entry, 192
U.S.
  Department of Energy R-values website, 57
  Green Building Council, 186
  Mayors Climate Protection Agreement, 228
  Postal Service Alabama District, 204
USDA Certified Organic label, 127

V

vacations
  ecofriendly, 119-122
  teaching children green principles through, 245-246
valerian, 138
Vallejo Insurance Associates, 204
vegan diets, 135-136
vegetable gardens, 152-153
vehicles
  air pollution, 91
  alternative fuels, 95
    biodiesel, 96-98
    compressed natural gas, 99
    ethanol, 95-96
  biodiesel/clean diesel, 106-107
  businesses promoting efficient transportation, 207-208
  flex fuel, 107
  fuel efficiency, 92-93
    biking/walking, 94
    carpooling, 94
    combining trips, 94
    consumer demand, 91-92
  hybrids, 90, 102-103
    buying, 266
    consumer demand, 91-92

    conversion kits, 106
    costs, 102
    Ford Escape Hybrid, 105
    Honda Insight/Civic/Civic GX, 103-104
    Lexus RX 400h, 105
    Mercury Mariner Hybrid, 105
    Nissan Altima Hybrid, 104
    plug-in, 105-106
    tax incentives/credits, 102
    Toyota Camry Hybrid, 103
    Toyota Highlander Hybrid, 105
    Toyota Prius, 103
  hydrogen fuel cell, 107-109
  oil consumption, 89-90
  reducing single-vehicle transportation, 200
Vermont Law School Oaks Hall, 191-192
vinegar as cleaning agent, 171
Virgin Atlantic Airlines, 116
Virgin Earth Challenge, 116
voter impact on environmental issues, 238

W

Wal-Mart, 256
walking, 94
Walser's, 204
waste management, 76
  aluminum, 82-83, 205
  athletic footwear, 204
  businesses
    recycling programs, 201-202
    reducing waste, 204-207
  carpet, 176
  composting, 204
  converting waste to fuel, 85-86
  electronics, 84

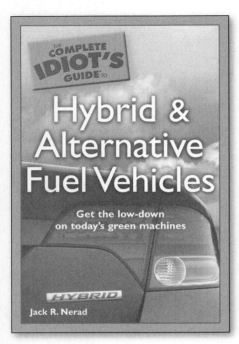
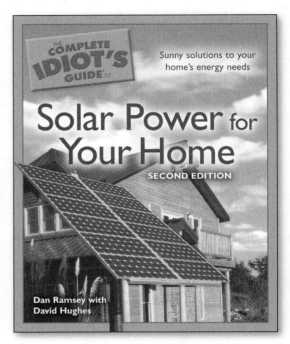